Savings Behavior:
Theory, International Evidence
and Policy Implications

Previous titles in this series:

Savings Behavior
Theory, International Evidence and Policy Implications

Edited by
Erkki Koskela
and
Jouko Paunio

Blackwell Publishers

Copyright © Scandinavian Journal of Economics 1992

ISBN 0-631-18266-7

First published 1992

Blackwell Publishers
108 Cowley Road, Oxford OX4 1JF, UK
and
238 Main Street,
Suite 501,
Cambridge, MA 02142, USA

Library of Congress Cataloguing in Publication Data applied for

British Library Cataloguing in Publication Data
Savings Behavior: Theory,
International Evidence and
Policy Implications (Scandinavian
Journal of Economics series).
 I. Koskela, Erkki II.
 Paunio, Jouko III. Series 332.

 ISBN 0-631-18266-7

Typeset by Unicus Graphics Ltd, Horsham
Printed in Great Britain by Page Bros, Norwich

Contents

Proceedings of a conference on
SAVINGS BEHAVIOR: THEORY, INTERNATIONAL EVIDENCE AND
POLICY IMPLICATIONS
Espoo/Helsinki, May 1991

Savings Behavior: Theory, International Evidence and Policy Implications

Editors' Introduction

Erkki Koskela and Jouko Paunio

University of Helsinki, Finland

I. Background

Savings behavior has traditionally occupied the center stage in many areas of macroeconomic research. Recently, problems and issues related to savings have assumed added importance. Some stylized facts, particularly the fairly general decline in household saving rates in the 1980s, their large differences across countries and variations in the sectoral breakdown of savings among countries, seems to call for an explanation.

The idea behind this conference was that new insights could be gained by combining theoretical analyses with empirical analyses and with comparisons of country experiences. It was believed that the explanatory power of theories of savings could be improved by taking into account housing conditions, developments in financial markets and demographic changes. Measurement issues and the need for a long time perspective were also emphasized. How, for example, should the downward movement in saving rates in the 1980s be perceived from a long-run viewpoint?

This volume contains the proceedings of a conference devoted to these issues, held in Espoo, Finland, in May 1991.[1]

II. Description and Measurement of Saving Ratios

Two papers focused on describing and measuring saving ratios. The study by **Jeffrey Shafer, Jorgen Elmeskov** and **Warren Tease** examines the broad trends in savings in the OECD area over the past thirty years. Using data on gross savings derived from national accounts, the authors pay special attention to numerous adjustments that have been proposed to bring national accounts data closer in line with theoretical concepts. These

---

[1] The conference was arranged under the auspices of the Finnish Savings Banks Research Foundation. The members of the program committee were Professors Erkki Koskela, Jouko Paunio, Lawrence Summers and Alexander Swoboda.

adjustments include valuation, reclassification and coverage effects of various kinds. The authors report the following "stylized facts" based on their review of savings: (i) there are considerable differences in average gross national saving ratios across OECD countries; (ii) despite these differences, broad movements in saving have been remarkably similar across countries, i.e., most countries experienced lower saving rates, on average, in the 1980s than in the 1960s or 1970s; (iii) changes in government saving account for much of the variation in national saving over time, with little tendency for private saving to offset these changes; (iv) the share of private saving in GNP has been relatively stable; and (v) household saving generally increased sharply in the 1970s before falling during the 1980s.

In his comment, **Edmond Malinvaud** suggests that using net figures might change the picture. It is also pointed out that changes in relative prices of assets, e.g. due to financial market liberalization, might have played an important role in explaining household savings behavior. While the paper gives some references to this aspect, no data are presented.

In his article, **Angus Maddison** provides long time series of gross saving rates in 11 countries, which account for nearly half of world savings. In most cases the data sample covers more than one hundred years. Maddison confirms the finding about the general decline in saving rates during the past decade, but he also demonstrates that from a historical perspective, saving rates of the 1950s and 1960s were exceptionally high. This suggests that the recent decline in saving rates can well be interpreted as a reversion towards the longer-term average rather than a deviation from postwar normality. Another important finding by Maddison is that U.S. long-run experience has not conformed to the norm for other countries; the gross national saving rate seems to be roughly constant in the U.S. — as Kuznets suggested more than forty years ago — whereas saving rates have been on an upward trend for most other countries included in the data sample. The atypicality of U.S. experience is interesting in the sense that it may have had a decisive impact on the development of theories of saving after Keynes' General Theory. Both the Life Cycle Hypothesis (LCH) and the Permanent Income Hypothesis (PIH) came to reject Keynes' theory that savings rise with income, because there was no upward trend in the U.S. savings estimates developed by Kuznets.

III. Cross-Country Differences

Differences in the levels of saving rates across countries were mentioned as one stylized fact. The traditional LCH suggests that the growth rate is a key determinant of cross-country differences in saving rates; see Modigliani (1986). The papers by **Luigi Guiso, Tullio Jappelli** and

Daniele Terlizzese and by **Erkki Koskela** and **Matti Virén** indicate that the LCH goes some way towards explaining both cross-country differences in saving rates and their movement over time. The decline in the growth rate helps to explain the fall in private saving in Italy as well as the fall in household saving in the Nordic countries.

But this basic insight of the LCH is far from representative of the overall picture. Private and household savings behavior may be influenced significantly by the ability to borrow and share risk via capital markets. If capital market imperfections vary across countries, then they may help to explain international differences in saving rates. Guiso, Jappelli and Terlizzese present evidence on credit and insurance market imperfections in Italy, where the saving rate is "high", while Koskela and Virén demonstrate that the size of consumer credit markets in Nordic countries, where the saving rate is "low", exceeds the OECD average. The excess sensitivity tests provided in the two papers reinforce these findings; in Italy aggregate consumption seems to track predictable changes in disposable income much more closely than in the Nordic countries. These studies also hint at, but do not explore in depth, the potential impact of government transfer and insurance schemes on saving. As **Marco Pagano** suggests in his comment, further research in this direction might prove fruitful.

Despite differences in levels of saving rates, their movements over time have been similar. In some countries the household saving rate fell in the 1980s. Such shifts in saving rates did not receive very much attention at the conference. Koskela and Virén, however, provide some evidence which suggests that in the Nordic countries, rising real housing prices and housing wealth — associated with financial market liberalization — have contributed to the decline in household saving ratios.

The earnings profile appears to rise steeply with age in most countries, especially those with rapid growth such as Italy and Japan. Thus, because of the consumption smoothing principle, young people would be expected to dissave. However, in the paper by **Albert Ando, Luigi Guiso, Daniele Terlizzese** and **Daniel Dorsainvil**, it is shown that microdata for Japan and Italy do not conform to this prediction provided by the LCH. In these countries households save and accumulate net wealth throughout their working lives, even when they are quite young and their current income is lower than their future income.

The authors pose the question as to why these young people do not dissave. While this finding may be explained by the presence of liquidity constraints and/or myopia, the authors offer a new explanation, based on the potential role of "social status". If, in the future, not only an individual's income will be higher than his current income, but his "social status" will also be higher, and if higher social status increases the marginal utility of consumption at all consumption levels, then these individuals will consume less of their current income than those who experience the same rise in future income without any change in their social status. To the extent that the young are more likely to experience future rises in their social status, this hypothesis may explain the absence of dissaving by young people. This explanation, according to which current savings can be interpreted as a choice of flexibility, is clearly interesting. The weakness in the liquidity constraint and myopia explanations of saving by young consumers are also noted. The authors test whether expected future income significantly influences current consumption in addition to current income. They find no significant (significant) effect for households in the age group 25–29 (30–34). But, as pointed out by **T. N. Srinivasan**, in his comment, it is difficult to test their hypothesis directly without a workable definition of social status and a data set which connects changes in income with changes in social status.

The paper by **Angus Deaton** takes the model of liquidity constraints under income uncertainty as its starting point; see Deaton (1991). He also considers the case where some borrowing is allowed in limited amounts and at high rates of interest. The fact that borrowing may be unavailable when needed the most is a reason to save, and the model implies that the dynamics of consumption and income — in contrast with the LCH — are such as to detach consumption from income in the short run, but not in the long run. Moreover, Deaton's buffer model suggests that in a cross-section, dissaving is likely to be common.

In the second part of his paper, Deaton uses his models as a guide for data exploration in the cases of Ghana, Côte d'Ivoire and Thailand. Data on borrowing and lending in Ghana and Côte d'Ivoire suggest that credit markets play some role in consumption smoothing. The age-consumption profiles of Thailand, which is a fast-growing country, and Côte d'Ivoire, which is a slow-growing country, indicate that, contrary to the implication of the LCH, the profile is tipped more towards the young in Côte d'Ivoire than in Thailand; see also Carroll and Summers (1989) for similar evidence from 15 OECD countries over the period 1960–85. If liquidity constraints are a problem for many households, assets, particularly liquid assets, should play a role in guaranteeing future consumption. The data on Côte d'Ivoire do not, however, fully conform to this view. The main conclusion of the paper is that households in LDCs "look ahead at least some way when deciding how much to consume and save, but they do not support the full permanent income hypothesis, nor any simple modification based on the way liquidity constraints might work".

In his discussion, while appreciating Deaton's work in this area, **Costas Meghir** pointed to some theoretical and empirical issues that should be part of the forthcoming research agenda. These include the specification and source of risk and the measurement of assets and activities that households may be involved in for the purpose of insurance and/or consumption smoothing.

IV. Demographic and Generational Issues

Demographic and generational aspects were analyzed in two papers. **Alan Auerbach** and **Laurence Kotlikoff** report simulation exercises on the potential consequences of the ageing of the U.S. population for national saving rates and discuss some related policy issues. The simulations are carried out using a model for studying the general equilibrium effects of demographic transition. As expected, the base-case simulation predicts a gradual decline in the national saving rate. Even with a declining saving rate, capital deepening is predicted, thereby implying a strongly reduced rate of growth in the supply of labor. Capital deepening is expected to have generational redistribution effects since the return to capital will decline, while the return to labor will increase over time. The authors consider their simulation results by comparing general equilibrium and partial equilibrium simulation models. They point out the potential impact of the demographic transition on the structure of wealth held by the population. They discuss the potential effects of the demographic transition on the government budget, also considering the growing political power of the elderly.

The comment by **David Weil** focuses on various aspects of the model construction used and, in particular, on the "correctness" of the theory of saving applied in the analysis.

Alan Auerbach, Jagadeesh Gokhale and **Laurence Kotlikoff** develop an accounting framework for analyzing governments' generational policies. Generational accounts aim at measuring what existing and future generations will, or will not, pay in net terms to the government. Using generational accounting to determine the impact of alternative policies in the U.S., the authors' analysis indicates that the fiscal deficit is a totally unreliable measure of the stance of fiscal policy. From the point of view of the theme of this conference, it is worth noting that in their illustration of U.S. generational accounts, the authors find that fiscal policies which redistribute across generations may have a considerable impact on national savings. Their paper suggests that U.S. generations born after 1989 will contribute a significantly higher (20 per cent higher) share of their lifetime incomes in net payments to U.S. governments than the 1989 generation.

In his comment, **John Muellbauer** points to a number of important issues, such as intergenerational equality, key intergenerational transfers and inclusion of the generational effects of public consumption and investment, which are all worthy of further research, possibly extended to applications to other countries.

V. Broad Aspects

Two papers take a broader view of savings behavior than the rest of the contributions to the conference. **Robert Barro** adopts a world perspective and focuses on determination of the world real interest rate measured by short-term expected real interest rates. The paper is an elaboration of an earlier study by Barro and Sala-i-Martin (1990). This new version of the study attempts to explain the world interest rate by a model in which this rate is determined by the condition that world aggregate investment demand is equal to the world aggregate of desired national saving. Empirically, the world is represented by the aggregates for ten industrialized countries treated as a closed economy with a single capital market.

The results suggest that there is a major world component in the development of real interest rates for the industrial countries. the world interest rate is influenced, in particular, by events on world stock and oil markets and less so by world monetary and fiscal policies. As told by Barro, savings behavior seems to take a backseat in the study. His estimation of the aggregate saving function suggests that the saving rate relates especially to the expected real interest rate and to an oil variable interpreted as reflecting temporary deviations of current from permanent income. A higher real rate of interest induces an increase in the saving rate, while a temporary increase in current income, as interpreted in the paper, has a positive influence on the saving rate.

In his comment, **Nicola Rossi** casts some doubts on the extreme simplicity of the theoretical model, which suppresses many important features of economic development. On the other hand, it is admitted that this simple model does a surprisingly good job in tracking complicated phenomena. Barro's approach bypasses the capital market imperfections which, in some papers presented at the conference, were found to be an important element in explaining differences in levels of savings across countries. Instead he keeps the world interest rate as a maintained, untested hypothesis.

While the study by Barro adopts a cosmopolitan viewpoint, **Hans Genberg** and **Alexander Swoboda** approach matters from the standpoint of a single country. The main aim of their survey is to make a case for regarding the current account problem in terms of the saving–investment relationship. The authors also examine alternative approaches to current account issues, and conclude that a general equilibrium framework is generally necessary, although a partial approach may be appropriate in particular circumstances. They review the recent theoretical literature, which emphasizes intertemporal optimization considerations in analyzing current account developments. By introducing this approach into policy analysis, a "new" view of current account imbalances emerges. According to this view, the current account need not be a policy concern at all under certain fairly general assumptions. The authors conclude their survey by noting that while most of the recent theoretical work on current account problems has incorporated the intertemporal optimizing approach, the same cannot yet be said of empirical analysis.

In his comment, **Thorvaldur Gylfason** agreed with the general usefulness of looking at current account determination in terms of the saving-investment relationship. However, he emphasized that it does not justify neglect of the important interaction of saving and investment with several other variables which jointly influence the current account determination of the balance of payments.

References

Barro, R. J. & Sala-i-Martin, X.: World real rates. In O. J. Blanchard & S. Fisher (eds.), *NBER Macroeconomics Annual 1990*, MIT Press, Cambridge MA, 15–59, 1990.

Carroll, C. & Summers, L. H.: Consumption growth parallels income growth: Some new evidence. NBER WP No. 3090, 1989.

Deaton, A.: Saving and liquidity constraints. *Econometrica 59*, 1221–1248, 1991.

Modigliani, F.: Life cycle, individual thrift, and the wealth of nations. *American Economic Review 76*, 297–313, 1986.

Saving Trends and Measurement Issues[*]

Jeffrey R. Shafer, Jorgen Elmeskov and Warren Tease

Economics and Statistics Department, OECD, Paris, France

Abstract

A review of broad trends in saving over the last thirty years results in a number of stylized facts. After considering measurement issues, the overall picture that emerges from the data is summarized in terms of three main questions: (i) how should saving be measured? (ii) do we understanding saving? and (iii) should a decline in saving be a matter of policy concern?

I. Introduction

Saving has recently emerged as a prominent policy issue in the OECD countries. Concern about saving has been augmented by the possible implications of low saving rates in the 1980s for the rate of capital formation and, in some countries, for the size of current account deficits. Persistently high real interest rates have been taken as an indicator that profitable investment is being constrained more than in the past by the flow of saving. More recently, the adequacy of saving flows globally has also become an issue because of a potential increase in investment demand in central and eastern Europe, rising investment in infrastructure in the Asian NIEs, the reappearance of certain developing countries as capital importers and, in a slightly longer perspective, population aging in OECD countries.

Broad trends in saving in the past thirty years are examined in Section II. A number of measurement issues are considered in Section III. In particular, since saving is the difference between income and consumption, problems of measuring them are reflected in saving. Section IV brings

*This paper is an abbreviated version of Elmeskov *et al.* (1991). It draws on several previous papers concerned with saving and, as such, represents the work of a number of our colleagues. In particular, thanks are due to Derek Blades, Andrew Dean and Peter Höller, who provided helpful comments on an earlier draft. Efficient statistical assistance was provided by Anick Bouchouchi-Lotrous and Martine Levasseur. High quality typing was done by Sheena Bohan, Lyn Louichaoui, Terri Meehan and Pat Tuveri. The responsibility for all remaining errors rests with the authors. The views expressed are theirs and not necessarily those of the OECD nor the governments of its member countries.

together the overall picture that emerges from the data, taking into account the uncertainties and distortions arising from measurement problems.

II. Broad Trends

Gross saving rates for the world economy were lower in the 1980s than earlier; see Figure 1.[1] There are signs in the data that the downward trend of world saving may have been reversed — a recovery has occurred in the OECD countries and in most non-OECD regions. However, the behavior of saving, and also of investment, in the non-OECD region has varied considerably among country groupings; see Tease *et al.* (1991).

Gross national saving ratios have differed substantially across OECD countries. In high-saving Japan, saving is around 30 per cent of GNP and in Denmark, the saving rate is about 15 per cent. Countries with higher saving rates have also had higher investment rates, and conversely for low-saving countries. There has been little tendency for the dispersion in saving and investment rates across countries to decline over time.

Despite substantial differences in the level of saving rates, broad movements in saving have been remarkably similar across countries. Most countries experienced lower saving rates, on average, in the 1980s than in the 1960s or 1970s; see Table 1 and Figure 1. For the OECD region as a whole, the ratio of gross national saving to GNP was, on average, around 3 percentage points below that of the 1960s and 1970s. Despite recent recovery in the saving ratio, it remains below the levels of the two previous decades.

Government Saving[2]

The most widespread, and in most countries the largest, decline in saving from the 1960s to the 1980s occurred in the government sector; see Table 1 and Figure 2. During the 1960s, government saving made a positive contribution to aggregate saving in many OECD countries. In many cases, government saving was in excess of 5 per cent of GNP. During the 1970s, government saving fell. It declined more than capital outlays of the government sector, so that large fiscal deficits emerged in a number of countries. The growing weight of debt interest payment in expenditures contributed further to government deficits. Government saving fell again in the early-to mid-1980s, so that many governments became dissavers. However, the

---

[1] The data used here and in the charts relate to gross national saving and investment relative to GNP for the OECD, and GDP elsewhere.

[2] Components of saving are measured here as ratios to GNP, not sectoral income, which is not a straightforward concept given the dual role of households as owners of private business and as taxpayers who provide the resources of governments.

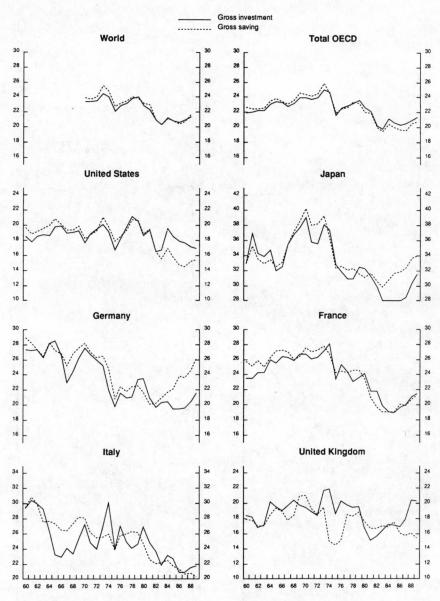

Source: World Bank and OECD, National Accounts.

Fig. 1. Investment and saving ratios (percentage of GNP).

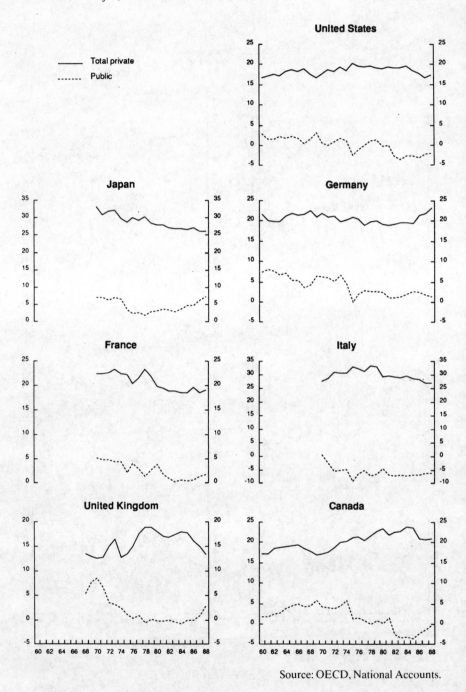

Source: OECD, National Accounts.

Fig. 2. Government and private saving ratios (percentage of GNP).

Table 1. *Saving (gross saving as a ratio of GNP)*

	1960s	1970s	1980s	Change between 1980s and 1960s	1970s
United States					
National	19.7	19.4	16.3	− 3.4	− 3.1
Public	2.0	0.4	− 2.1	− 4.1	− 2.5
Private	17.7	19.1	18.5	0.8	− 0.6
Household	9.2	10.7	9.5	0.3	− 1.2
Corporate	8.5	8.4	9.0	0.5	0.6
Japan					
National	34.5	35.3	31.6	− 2.9	− 3.7
Public	6.2	4.8	4.6	− 1.6	− 0.2
Private	28.3	30.4	26.7	− 1.6	− 3.7
Household	13.3	17.9	15.6	2.3	− 2.3
Corporate	15.0	12.6	11.2	− 3.8	− 1.4
Germany					
National	27.3	24.3	22.5	− 4.8	− 1.8
Public	6.2	3.9	2.0	− 4.2	− 1.9
Private	21.1	20.4	20.5	− 0.6	0.1
Household	6.9	8.7	7.8	0.9	− 0.9
Corporate	14.2	11.8	12.7	− 1.5	0.9
France					
National	26.2	25.8	20.4	− 5.8	− 5.4
Public	−	3.6	1.3	−	− 2.3
Private	−	22.2	19.0	−	− 3.2
Household	−	13.6	10.3	−	− 3.3
Corporate	−	8.6	8.4	−	− 0.2
United Kingdom					
National	18.4	17.9	16.6	− 1.8	− 1.3
Public	3.6	2.6	0.1	− 3.5	− 2.5
Private	14.8	15.3	16.6	1.8	1.3
Household	5.4	6.1	6.0	0.6	− 0.1
Corporate	9.4	9.2	10.4	1.0	1.2
Italy					
National	28.1	25.9	21.9	− 6.2	− 4.0
Public	2.1	− 5.6	− 6.7	− 8.7	− 1.1
Private	26.0	31.2	28.3	2.2	− 2.9
Household	−	24.5	21.1	−	− 3.4
Corporate	−	6.6	7.5	−	0.9
Canada					
National	21.9	22.9	20.7	− 1.2	− 2.2
Public	3.6	2.7	− 1.6	− 5.2	− 4.3
Private	18.2	20.1	22.3	4.1	2.2
Household	7.8	10.4	12.3	4.5	− 1.9
Corporate	10.5	9.7	9.9	− 0.6	0.2

Source: OECD National Accounts.

main factor behind the recovery of saving ratios over the past few years has been a turnaround in government saving.

Private Saving

The extent to which government saving affects national saving depends on the response of the private sector. If consumers anticipate the future implications of current government deficits and investment, lower government saving may be offset by additional private saving. However, the data in Figure 2 do not suggest such a close offsetting relationship between private and public saving.[3]

Indeed, rates of private sector saving have been relatively stable over time; see Table 1 and Figure 3. In many countries, the average ratio of gross private saving to GNP in the 1980s differed only slightly from the averages for the 1960s. However, private saving ratios declined in a number of countries during the latter half of the 1980s. In most cases this decline was concentrated in the household sector.

Household Saving Rates

In general, household saving increased sharply in the 1970s, but fell during the 1980s. A number of factors may have contributed to these swings, including the economic uncertainty and inflation of the 1970s, followed by disinflation and economic recovery in the 1980s. Financial market liberalization may have contributed to the decline in household saving in some countries during the 1980s. Tax systems in some countries distorted incentives in favor of borrowing, thereby providing additional impetus to a build-up of household debt once constraints were relaxed. As additional demand pushed up asset prices (and consquently wealth), households were able to borrow still more, which further induced them to save less. This process may have run its course. The rise in asset prices has ceased, or is even being reversed, so that both the incentive to borrow in order to buy assets such as housing and the value of current asset holdings as collateral have diminished. Income growth has also slowed considerably, especially in countries where household debt accumulation has been important, thus limiting the capacity of individuals to carry higher debt burdens. There are also indications that, after a period of laxity, the lending criteria of financial intermediaries may have tightened as pressure has arisen on borrowers' capacity to service debts. These factors help to explain why the decline in household saving has reversed in some countries.

---

[3] The more formal empirical evidence on this point yields mixed results, but does not support a one-for-one offset of private saving by public saving; see, for example, Nicoletti (1988).

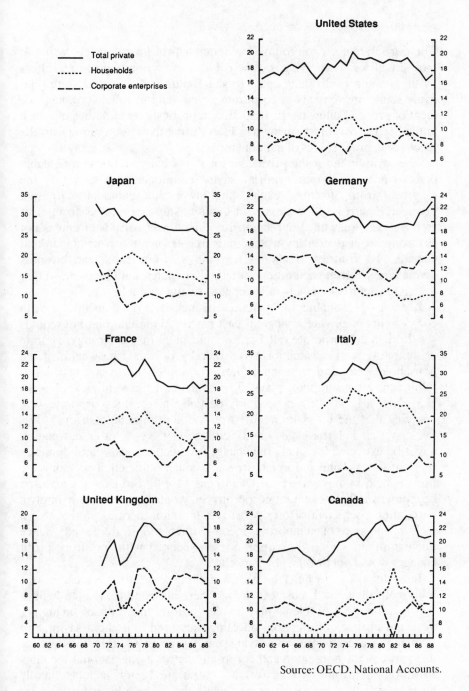

Source: OECD, National Accounts.

Fig. 3. Household and corporate saving ratios (percentage of GNP).

Corporate Saving

The corporate sector accounts for about half of gross private saving in most countries. This saving is closely linked to corporate profits; it differs by the amount of dividends paid to shareholders. As dividends are relatively stable, movements in corporate saving tend to follow the development of profits. Following the reduction in profit shares and rates of return in the 1970s, corporate saving has risen during the 1980s, along with the recovery in profit shares of national income.

The saving rate for the private sector as a whole has been more stable than its household and corporate saving components, as shown by the relatively strong offsetting relationship between household and corporate saving in Figure 3. In some cases, this relationship seems to be strongest at high frequencies, while the relationship over longer periods of time is not as strong, as evidenced by trends in aggregate private saving (Japan and Canada). By contrast, medium-term swings in household and business saving largely offset each other in the United States and Germany, so that the aggregate private saving ratio remains relatively stable.

It seems reasonable to attribute the negative relationship between components of private saving, at least partly, to the fact that households see through the corporate veil. For example, in periods of strong corporate profitability, market valuations rise, thereby boosting the wealth of the household sector and reducing the need for households to save in order to fulfill future consumption plans. The evidence from various studies on U.S. data suggests that households partially pierce the corporate veil, implying that the offset between corporate and household saving is less than one; cf. Poterba (1987) and Schultze (1988). A lower correlation might be expected for small, financially open economies, where domestic residents hold claims in foreign firms and much of the equity of domestic firms is held by foreigners; see Dean *et al.* (1990). But even for a closed economy, a fully transparent corporate veil would not necessarily imply a correlation coefficient of one. Most consumption theories predict that a high proportion of temporary income fluctuations are saved; hence fluctuations in saving by corporations associated with transitory profit changes would not be offset by households.

In addition to this behavioral explanation for negative correlations of household saving with business saving, there are good reasons to believe that measurement problems play a role. Sectoral measures of saving are distorted in times of inflation, boosting measured household saving and reducing measured corporate saving (see below). In addition, the dividing line between the household and corporate sectors in the national accounts is somewhat arbitrary because the corporate sector includes family businesses if they are incorporated, while the household sector includes unincorporated enterprises that may be distinct entities; cf. Edey and Britten-Jones (1990).

Before turning to conceptual measurement issues, a word of caution may be warranted concerning the broad patterns in the System of National Accounts (SNA) data. Saving at the national and sectoral levels is defined in the SNA as current receipts less current disbursements. Saving is therefore a residual and will be affected by errors in the measurement of either receipts or disbursements; cf. Blades (1983). Hence, little significance should be attached to small differences (of 2 to 3 percentage points of GNP) in saving measures over time or across countries.

III. Adjusting National Saving and Its Sectoral Distribution

Gross saving data from national accounts do not correspond very closely to concepts of saving that appear in economic theory. Numerous adjustments have been suggested to bring measured saving closer to theoretical concepts.

Three kinds of adjustments to traditionally measured national-accounts concepts are distinguished below. First, changes in real asset values may call for adjustments to income as measured in national accounts. Second, the classification of economic activities is problematic in a number of respects. Some issues have implications primarily for the definition of income, with investment or consumption affected accordingly. Others pertain to the allocation of output and income to investment and saving as opposed to current consumption. Third, a number of activities are not covered by national accounts even though they generate income and welfare or affect future income and welfare.

Valuation Effects

Valuation effects arise when changes in prices of assets relative to consumption goods alter the real value of wealth. An economic unit which owns an asset with an increasing relative price can consume all of current income in a given period and still be better off at the end of the period than at the beginning. Thus, income in the Hicksian sense is higher than current income as conventionally measured when the relative prices of assets are rising.

Inflation. In the case of inflation, there is a change in the relative price of (unindexed) financial assets in terms of a basket of goods. Financial asset holders regard part of the nominal interest earned on financial assets as compensation for the loss in the real value of their assets. In the national accounts, nominal interest payments are included fully as a component of current income, but the erosion of the real value of financial assets and gains on debt is not accounted for. Consequently, the current income of financial asset holders will exceed Hicksian income (and conversely for debtors).

For a country with a limited net foreign debt position, an adjustment for inflation will not affect the aggregate saving ratio, but it will affect the sectoral composition of saving. Specifically, in many countries the private sector is a net holder of government financial liabilities. In this case, traditional measures will overstate private sector income and saving, while understating government income and saving. To illustrate the potential size of these effects, estimates of private saving, adjusted for inflation-induced gains and losses on net holdings of government debt, have been calculated for a number of countries; see Figure 4.

In each case, inflation adjustment alters the level of the private saving ratio (in some cases substantially) and in some countries the trend in private saving is also changed. The effects are largest in those countries (e.g. the United Kingdom, Italy and Belgium) that have had both large stocks of government debt and large changes in inflation. In some cases, the adjusted saving series was up to 10 percentage points of GDP below the traditionally measured series. In most cases, however, adjustment does not alter the picture to any large extent. In some countries (Japan and western Germany) where the government switched from being a net creditor to a net debtor in about the mid to late 1970s, the main effect of the adjustment is a slight accentuation of the decline in the private saving ratios.

Similar mismeasurement associated with inflation may occur in the allocation of income and saving between the household and corporate sectors. In a number of countries, adjustment between the household and business sectors would alter the sectoral picture given by national accounts data by more than adjustments between the government and private sectors, since enterprise sectors are often much larger net debtors than governments. In addition, any inflation (or exchange-rate) component in the return on the net position of the private sector *vis-à-vis* the foreign sector leads to distortions of private and total saving.

Other Valuation Effects. Among other explanations offered for the decline of household saving in many countries during the 1980s is increased wealth arising from capital gains on shares and fixed property. The argument is that households realized that Hicksian income exceeded current income, and consequently reduced saving out of current income. To the extent rising share prices reflect corporate saving, this is just another way of stating that households see through the corporate veil.

Capital gains on fixed property (and capital gains on shares other than those related to corporate saving) do not represent saving with a counter-

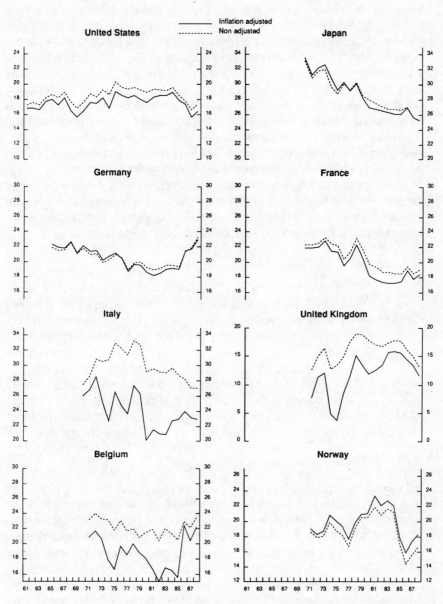

Source: OECD, National Accounts and Secretariat estimates.

Fig. 4. Gross private saving ratios (percentage of GNP).

part in the accumulation of investment goods or foreign assets. They may nevertheless reflect expectations of higher future real income flows owing to improved terms of trade or higher productivity (this seems more realistic for equity prices than for housing). Such gains would allow higher consumption (that is, they represent income in the Hicksian sense) and they are therefore likely to affect household saving in much the same way as corporate saving. Other reasons for asset price changes would suggest a smaller effect on household savings. For example, changes in the rate at which future returns are discounted affect prices of assets without altering the future stream of consumption that can be maintained. Also, higher housing prices which reflect higher implicit rental costs of housing leave households with no scope to increase consumption of other goods, except by consuming less housing. Hence the household sector as a whole may not feel much better off from such capital gains.[4] In addition, capital gains on equity and fixed property suffer a high risk of being reversed, except when there is a secularly increasing scarcity of desirable land for housing.

Reclassification effects

In setting up a system of national accounts, choices have to be made regarding the classification of various activities. For example, what output should be classified as investment and consumption, respectively? This choice is not always clear; education expenditure and household purchases of durable consumer goods are important grey areas. Another choice arises in deciding which activities result in final output and income, and which activities contribute to production and income as intermediate inputs. A prime example is the classification of research and development (R&D) expenditure, which is mostly treated as an intermediate input rather than a final output that adds to the stock of intangible capital.

Reclassifications between Output Components

Education is regarded as consumption in the SNA, but it is clear that education contains an aspect of investment in human capital with an economic return. The importance of this aspect may be regarded as strongest in education which qualifies for specific occupations, whereas broader types of education, such as primary education, aim at least partly

---

[4] This point was stressed by Harris and Steindel (1991), whose research also showed that stock-market based estimates of corporate assets were poor at explaining future output. However, it may be noted that this may not be a relevant test in some cases. If, for example, a country experiences a terms-of-trade gain, which leads to higher stock-market values in the affected sectors, the value of output or income will be higher as long as the gain is sustained. Thus, it would make sense to include such a gain in income even though no physical investment is undertaken or no foreign assets are acquired.

Table 2. *Gross national saving rates and measurement adjustments (per cent of GNP or adjusted GNP)*

	1960s	1970s	1980s	Change between 1980s and 1960s (including adjustment)	1970s
United States					
National saving rate	19.7	19.4	16.3	− 3.4	− 3.1
Adjustment for:					
Higher education expenditure (1)	—	1.3	1.2	—	− 3.2
Total education expenditure (2)	—	5.1	4.6	—	− 3.6
Durable consumer goods (3)	5.2	5.3	5.5	− 3.0	− 2.9
Business sector R&D (4)	1.6	1.3	1.6	− 3.4	− 2.8
Total R&D (5)	2.5	2.0	2.4	− 3.5	− 2.8
Depreciation (6)	− 8.9	− 10.3	− 12.6	− 7.1	− 5.4
Japan					
National saving rate	34.5	35.3	31.6	− 2.9	− 3.7
Adjustment for:					
Higher education expenditure (1)	—	0.5	0.6	—	− 3.6
Total education expenditure (2)	—	4.6	4.9	—	− 3.4
Durable consumer goods (3)	—	2.1	2.3	—	− 3.5
Business sector R&D (4)	0.6	0.7	1.2	− 2.3	− 3.2
Total R&D (5)	1.3	1.5	2.1	− 2.1	− 3.2
Depreciation (6)	− 9.4	− 8.7	− 10.8	− 4.3	− 4.8
Germany					
National saving rate	27.3	24.3	22.5	− 4.8	− 1.8
Adjustment for:					
Higher education expenditure (1)	—	0.7	0.7	—	− 1.8
Total education expenditure (2)	—	4.6	4.3	—	− 2.1
Durable consumer goods (3)	—	—	—	—	—
Business sector R&D (4)	0.7	1.0	1.5	− 4.0	− 1.3
Total R&D (5)	1.4	1.8	2.2	− 4.0	− 1.4
Depreciation (6)	− 7.4	− 9.4	− 10.9	− 8.3	− 3.6
France					
National saving rate	26.2	25.8	20.4	− 5.8	− 5.4
Adjustment for:					
Higher education expenditure (1)	—	0.7	0.6	—	− 5.5
Total education expenditure (2)	—	5.2	5.5	—	− 5.1
Durable consumer goods (3)	—	3.5	3.8	—	− 5.1
Business sector R&D (4)	0.7	0.8	1.0	− 5.5	− 5.2
Total R&D (5)	1.6	1.5	1.8	− 5.6	− 5.1
Depreciation (6)	− 7.0	− 8.8	− 11.9	− 10.7	− 8.5
United Kingdom					
National saving rate	18.4	17.9	16.6	− 1.8	− 1.3
Adjustment for:					
Higher education expenditure (1)	—	1.3	1.2	—	− 1.4
Total education expenditure (2)	—	5.8	5.2	—	− 1.9
Durable consumer goods (3)	4.2	4.5	4.7	− 1.3	− 1.1
Business sector R&D (4)	1.1	1.0	1.2	− 1.7	− 1.1
Total R&D (5)	1.9	1.8	2.0	− 1.7	− 1.0
Depreciation (6)	− 7.5	− 9.6	− 11.2	− 5.5	− 2.9

Table 2 — *Continued*

	1960s	1970s	1980s	Change between 1980s and 1960s (including adjustment)	1970s
Italy					
National saving rate	28.1	25.9	21.9	− 6.2	− 4.0
Adjustment for:					
Higher education expenditure (1)	—	0.5	0.6	—	− 3.9
Total education expenditure (2)	—	4.3	4.8	—	− 3.5
Durable consumer goods (3)	—	—	—	—	—
Business sector R&D (4)	0.3	0.4	0.8	− 5.7	− 3.6
Total R&D (5)	0.6	0.4	1.2	− 5.6	− 3.2
Depreciation (6)	− 8.3	− 9.7	− 11.3	− 9.2	− 5.6
Canada					
National saving rate	21.9	22.9	20.7	− 1.2	− 2.2
Adjustment for:					
Higher education expenditure (1)	—	2.2	1.1	—	− 3.3
Total education expenditure (2)	—	7.8	7.4	—	− 2.6
Durable consumer goods (3)	6.2	6.2	6.3	− 1.2	− 2.1
Business sector R&D (4)	0.3	0.3	0.6	− 0.9	− 1.9
Total R&D (5)	1.1	1.0	1.2	− 1.1	− 2.0
Depreciation (6)	− 10.6	− 9.8	− 11.2	− 1.8	− 3.6

(1) Public expenditure on higher education as a percent of GDP.
(2) Total public expenditure on education as a percent of GDP.
(3) Change in national saving rate as a result of adding consumer spending on durable goods to both the numerator and demoninator.
(4) Change in national saving rate as a result of adding business-sector R&D to both the numerator and demoninator.
(5) Change in national saving rate as a result of adding total R&D expenditure to the numerator and business R&D to the demoninator.
(6) Change in national saving rate as a result of deducting depreciation in both the numerator and demoninator.

Note: Adjustments have been made taking averages of available observations. Thus, for some countries and some adjustments, decennial averages are based on a limited number of observations.

to fulfill some wider social goals. Unfortunately, available statistics do not allow educational expenditure with a strong investment aspect to be clearly distinguished from the other types.

Table 2 shows adjustments to the gross national saving ratio for public expenditure on higher education and education in general, respectively.[5] The first might be seen as having a strong investment aspect, whereas total education expenditure comprises both consumption and investment

---

[5] The exclusion of private expenditure on education, which is an important component for some countries, calls for caution in attaching importance to differences across countries.

aspects.[6] Typically, the adjustment for public expenditure on higher education adds between 1/2 and 2 percentage points to the national saving ratio
but does not change the trend of saving significantly. Treating total public
expenditure on eduction as gross saving gives rise to much more significant
upward adjustments of saving ratios, often exceeding 5 percentage points.

A much wider issue, which rightly belongs under the heading of
"coverage effects" below, is whether public expenditure on education is an
appropriate measure of the investment in human capital. First, it evaluates
investment on a cost basis, with no market test of value. The change in
discounted future value of lifetime income of the population would be a
more appropriate measure. Second, even with these cost measures, the
opportunity costs of not working while engaged as a student or trainee — a
significant portion of the cost of post-secondary education — are ignored.

Purchases of consumer durables are treated differently in the system of
accounts depending on the purchaser. If a firm purchases a durable good
in order to sell its services to consumers, the transaction is regarded as a
business investment. Consumers who buy a durable in order to enjoy its
services are recorded as consuming the full amount of the purchase in the
period in which it takes place. It is not clear why a purchase of a consumer
durable should be considered less of an investment when it is made by a
household than when it is made by a firm.

Adjusted gross national saving ratios are presented in Table 2, where
household purchases of consumer durables are treated as investment. Two
simplifying assumptions have been made in order to facilitate the adjustment — in both cases concerning the adjustment to income to take into
account the services flowing from the stock of consumer durables.
Depreciation of the assets is, in each year, assumed to equal the new
purchases of consumer durables, corresponding to an assumption of a
constant stock of consumer durables, and the net return on durables is
assumed to be zero.[7] These approximations are rough and ready, but they
affect only the denominator of the saving rate and, as such, they introduce
relatively little bias. In most countries the adjustment adds about 4–5
percentage points to the gross national saving ratio. The effect is somewhat
larger in Canada and relatively small for Japan.

What one makes of this adjustment depends on the purpose at hand. If
it is to evaluate theories of saving behavior over the relatively short run,

---

[6] It should be noted that due to widely differing educational systems across countries, the
classification of education as higher or otherwise may also be uncertain.

[7] It may be argued that due to taxation on services from durables, when sold by firms,
consumers receive an incentive to boost their stock of durables to a point where the
undistorted return is relatively low compared with e.g. the real rate of interest. This
tendency is strengthened by taxation (and consequent tax deductibility) of interest flows.

the distinction between spending on services and goods for immediate consumption and spending on durable goods is crucial (although in this time perspective, the crude assumptions used to construct the adjusted data may lead to some numerical inaccuracies). The distinction is of only limited importance when looking at household behavior over the medium-to-long term, when depreciation and scrapping follow expenditures on durable goods, thus leaving additions to durable stocks very small relative to gross expenditures. If the concern is with flows of funds available for business investment, whether consumers spend on durables or non-durables is of no consequence.

Reclassifications between Input and Output

In the present version of SNA, *research and development* (R&D) undertaken in the public sector is treated as consumption while business R&D is treated as an intermediate input and not counted directly in final output. The result is that current business expenditures on R&D are treated as a cost of production. To the extent output prices are raised correspondingly, R&D contributes to GDP and indirectly adds to consumption or investment depending on whether it is undertaken in the consumption or investment goods sectors. However, current R&D expenditure that is not reflected in output prices is not counted in either GDP or saving. At the same time, creating facilities for undertaking R&D, i.e., building the necessary infrastructure, is treated as investment.

It is unsatisfactory both to regard business R&D as an intermediate input because it has little impact on final production in the current period, and because the decision to undertake R&D in many cases resembles a decision to undertake a traditional investment. The practice of recording public sector R&D as public consumption may be more defensible since it has not been subject to the same kind of investment calculus as business R&D (much of it is pure research).

Table 2 shows adjustments of gross national saving rates for business-sector and total-economy R&D expenditure, respectively. Adding business R&D expenditure to both national saving and GNP is based on the implicit assumption that output prices are not adjusted to take into account the current costs of R&D. The adjustment only slightly increases the saving ratio over the last three decades — most notably in the U.S., Germany, Japan and the U.K. The trend of the saving ratio is modified slightly, since business R&D has been rising relative to GNP in virtually all countries. Adjusting gross saving for total-economy rather than just business R&D raises saving ratios somewhat further.

Depreciation is one of several considerations that suggest, in contrast to the adjustments considered so far, much lower saving rates. A net income and net saving measure is called for by the Hicksian definition of income. A switching from considering gross to net saving amounts to reclassifying part of investment as intermediate input. Saving and income are reduced accordingly. Unfortunately, measurement problems are very large in connection with depreciation; they affect comparisons across countries, trends and levels.

The depreciation adjustments in Table 2 give rise to two conclusions: net saving ratios are significantly smaller than gross ratios and they have fallen more than gross ratios over the last decade. The relative increase in depreciation over time is related to a shift in the composition of investment towards components with shorter service lives.

The adjustments to gross saving rates discussed above would also affect investment and, thus, depreciation and net saving rates. However, the related depreciation would modify the various adjustments to very different extents. Consumer durables, which generally have relatively short service lives, are near one end of the spectrum. The other extreme may be adjustment to take investment in education into account. A substantial part of investment in education may not be depreciated before the persons in question withdraw from the labor market.

Coverage Effects

Many areas of economic activity are not recorded in national accounts. With a few exceptions, SNA records activities that involve exchanges in a market — either factor markets or output markets or both. However, many unrecorded activities also have effects on material well-being, which may be compared to those arising from goods and services sold on a market.

Household production and underground economic activities are not counted in the standard national accounts. The size of saving out of household production is unclear, but household work may considerably affect the estimate of income and, thus, the demoninator of the saving ratio. For the United States, estimates of the value of household work have been in the range 25–50 per cent of GDP; cf. Murphy (1982). The underground economy comprises many different activities that by their nature are unregistered. Estimates of the magnitudes involved have varied considerably for individual countries, depending on the methods used, as well as across countries; cf. Frey and Weck-Hanneman (1984). In consequence, it is difficult to say how these activities affect saving ratios.

The depletion of natural resources and environmental degradation should, in principle, be considered in assessing saving, but it is not reflected in the usual saving measures. Natural resources are in many ways comparable to a capital stock and have been treated as such in the literature and in much of the policy debate on sustainable development in the wake of the Brundtland report; see e.g. Solow (1986) and Nicolaisen *et al.* (1991). Given this view, the Hicksian income concept, which insists on unchanged real net worth, will be affected by changes in the stocks of natural-resource or environmental capital.[8]

The theoretically appropriate corrections of net national income, and thus net saving, have been derived from the Hamiltonian expression and first-order conditions commonly used in intertemporal maximisation; see Hartwick (1990). In the case of nonrenewable natural resources used in production, net income as normally defined should be reduced by the rents on the reduction in the stocks of these resources. This is the price less the marginal cost of extraction (assuming that the price properly reflects its marginal contribution to output). Making such an adjustment will lower NNP and net saving measures for a country which is depleting its resource stocks.

Renewable natural resources are important in a number of countries. The rule analogous to that for nonrenewable resources for adjusting standard income and saving concepts for changes in such stocks is to value them at the rent component of their value. However, rents on natural resources have been notoriously volatile, and behavior in response to changes in natural-resource availability is likely to share some of the characteristics of behavior in response to valuation changes in stock markets discussed above.

Among the many difficulties in correcting saving and income measures for environmental degradation is the inappropriate or nonexistent pricing of environmental "services". While natural resources generally fetch a market price that represents their scarcity value, this is not the case for environmental goods — for which property rights are not well defined. Consequently, while it would clearly be appropriate to adjust national saving for changes in environmental stocks, doing so is problematic. It is not just a matter of valuing changes in stocks — if traditional income and saving concepts were adjusted to take into account degradation of the environmental capital stock, however valued, the flows of environmental services would also have to be added into the income flow for consistency. Such adjustments would lead to lower measures of saving ratios so long as the value of the environmental capital stock were declining, since the services from the stock, as with any services, are not storable and cannot have a higher value than the stock.

IV. Conclusions

A number of stylized facts emerge from the foregoing review of saving:

---

[8] This discussion ignores the distinction between income and welfare.

— Average saving ratios differ substantially among OECD countries.
— Broad trends in saving are similar across OECD countries, suggesting that common factors are at work.
— Swings in saving of the government sector account for a great deal of the variation in total saving over time, with little tendency for private saving to offset these swings.
— Private saving has been relatively stable as a share of GNP, with changes in household and business saving tending to cancel one another.
— For some countries where household access to credit improved, a tendency for household saving to be especially weak can be discerned in the 1980s, at least until late in the decade.

Although subject to very large errors and implemented only selectively, consideration of various adjustments suggests the following:

— Most adjustments to gross saving would boost national saving ratios. Some make a large difference in relative sectoral contributions to saving with little or no effect at the national level. But deducting depreciation (which is provided by the SNA, but measured quite poorly), and depletion of both resource and environmental stocks (which is not now measured) would give net saving ratios that are much lower than the SNA gross ratios, even if other adjustments were made generously.
— It is difficult to draw any conclusion about saving trends, taking adjustments into account, because the errors involved are large in relation to the observable trends, and some adjustments have offsetting effects. Nevertheless, the general picture of the 1980s as a period of weak saving in the OECD area, at least until the last years of the decade, seems relatively robust.

How should saving be measured? The range of possible measures of saving clouds the overall picture. There are two problems. One is that adjustments of saving measures to obtain closer correspondence with theoretical concepts come at a cost of introducing new sources of measurement error. The second problem is that the most useful measure depends on the purpose at hand. For the specific purpose, for example, of documenting the future cost of natural resource depletion or degradation, it is useful to extend measures of saving and capital to include them. But they are not of much significance for short run macroeconomic analysis.

An effort to develop an inclusive measure of saving, including all activities which make provisions for the future, may not be worthwhile. The conceptual ambiguities and measurement problems have been illustrated here. Such efforts also detract attention from more direct evidence of how well a society is providing for the future. After all, if saving is found to have been undermeasured in the past, this does little or nothing to change the picture of the evolution of consumption possibilities. For a given flow of goods and services production, it simply means that the social return to saving and the productivity of capital, more inclusively defined, have been lower than suggested by traditional measures.

Do we understand saving? The picture of saving sketched here provides some glimpses of patterns that pose challenges for theory. In particular, large differences in saving across countries are poorly explained. Indeed, high saving in some high growth countries (for example, Japan, Korea and Taiwan) is not easily accounted for, and very low saving in some other more slowly growing countries with aging populations (most notably, the United States) is only a little easier to understand in terms of standard theories. This makes saving, or perhaps more generally, the decision-making of individuals where intertemporal choices and uncertainty are involved, a particularly interesting area for research.

Should a decline in saving be a matter of policy concern? The evidence on saving behavior argues against resolving this question by appealing to an *a priori* presumption that saving is suboptimal only to the extent that households face identifiable distortions in their saving decisions. This evidence does not, however, directly support the view that there is too little saving rather than too much. It is doubtful that even a detailed and more formal analysis of data could resolve this issue objectively; in the end, subjective judgements are likely to be unavoidable.

If the conclusion is that saving ought to be higher, the stylized facts developed here suggest that policy efforts should concentrate on public finances. For one thing, this is where the decline in saving was concentrated. For another, more saving in the public sector is not likely, on the basis of the informal review of the data presented here, to be fully or even largely offset by private behavior.

References

Blades, D.: Alternative measures of saving. *OECD Occasional Studies*, June 1983.

Dean, A.: World saving since 1960: Trends in saving and its global allocation. 2nd annual Villa Mondragone Conference on World Saving: Prosperity and Growth, Rome, 1990.

Dean, A., Durand, M., Fallon, J. & Höller, P.: Saving trends and behaviour in OECD countries. *OECD Economic Studies*, No. 14, 1990.

Edey, M. & Britten-Jones, M.: Saving and investment. In S. Grenville (ed.), *The Australian Macro-economy in the 1980s*, Research Department, Reserve Bank of Australia, June 1990.

Elmeskov, J., Shafer, J. R. & Tease, W.: Saving trends and measurement issues. *OECD Economics and Statistics Department* WP105, 1991.

Frey, B. S. & Weck-Hanneman, H.: The hidden economy as an "unobserved" variable. *European Economic Review 26*, 1984.

Harris, E. S. & Steindel, C.: The decline in U.S. saving and its implications for economic growth. *Federal Reserve Bank of New York Bulletin*, 1991.

Hartwick, J. M.: Natural resources, national accounting and economic depreciation. *Journal of Public Economics 43*, 1990.

Murphy, M.: Comparative estimates of the value of household work in the United States for 1976. *Review of Income and Wealth*, 1982.

Nicolaisen, J., Dean, A. & Höller, P.: Economics and the environment: A survey of issues and policy options. *OECD Economic Studies*, No. 16, 1991.

Nicoletti, G.: A cross-country analysis of private connsumption, inflation and the "debt neutrality hypothesis." *OECD Economic Studies*, No. 11, 1988.

Poterba, J.: Tax policy and corporate saving. *Brookings Papers on Economic Activity 2*, 1987.

Schultze, C. L.: Setting long-run deficit reduction targets: The economics and politics of budget decisions. Meeting of the National Academy of Social Insurance, Washington, Dec. 1988.

Solow, R. M.: On the intergenerational allocation of natural resources. *Scandinavian Journal of Economics 88* (1), 1986.

Tease, W., Dean, A., Elmeskov, J. & Höller, P.: Real interest rate trends: The influence of saving, investment and other factors. *OECD Economic Studies*, No. 17, 1991.

Comment on J. Shafer, J. Elmeskov and W. Tease, "Saving Trends and Measurement Issues"

Edmond Malinvaud

Collège de France, Paris, France

This is an excellent paper for opening our conference on saving behavior. It gives many data on the relevant facts; it summarizes them clearly, at the proper level of generality; when discussing problems of measurement, it concentrates on the adequacy of the current statistical concepts for economic analysis and it tells what alternative measures would imply; it relates the main facts to the explanations given to them by economists nowadays. As a discussant I should, however, point to whatever does not fully satisfy me. I shall try to do so from three different viewpoints: description of the facts, measurement of the facts, explanation of the facts.

From the first viewpoint the main lacuna of the paper is the lack of data on assets. It is indeed difficult to understand savings, their evolution and their international disparities without considering wealth. Of course, we do not have the same convenient data base as the one, given for flows, by national accounts. This is regrettable. After four decades of developing these accounts, progress seems to have stopped in the process that would have led to the regular production of internationally consistent wealth estimates for the main economic sectors. I wonder whether this is not due to the fact that statisticians believe wealth accounts ought to reach the same degree or complexity and quality as flow accounts, and then the task remains beyond the means available for statistics. If so, economists ought to press for the production of estimates at benchmark dates, for instance the first day of every decade.

So far as I know, changes in wealth positions were important during the period under review. Data exist for public debts, they show that levels and trends were quite different in different countries and different subperiods. What about business debts, which may be very significant determinants of business saving and investment? What about the exact increase in household debts, which was induced by financial liberalization? What about gross household wealth, which seems to have grown considerably in some countries, as a consequence of often very fast increases in the relative price of assets? The paper makes occasional reference to these aspects, but gives no figures.

A more minor comment is that the paper downplays the significance of net, against gross, figures and of the sectoral breakdown such as between households and corporations. The main argument in both cases is poor statistical accuracy. I agree that there may be some problems with the accuracy and international comparability of depreciation estimates, or of sectoral breakdown. But in the first place the inaccuracies are not as large as the paper hints; second, the present situation may result in part from a misperception of statistical priorities, itself generated by the fact that for instance net figures were seldom used; third, considering only gross figures or only the aggregate of private saving may lead to erroneous assessments. An extreme case appears if it is stated that corporate saving provides about half of private saving: while true for gross saving, the sentence is quite wrong for net saving. On the other hand it is well mentioned in the paper that net saving ratios have fallen more than gross ratios over the last decades. Later on, I shall have to stress the significance of the sectoral breakdown for the inflation-adjusted saving ratios.

As regards questions of measurement, the authors consider a number of alternative saving concepts. They rightly point out in their conclusion that substituting any one of these concepts for the one presently used raises questions. Does it really make sense for understanding or monitoring developments over the short to medium run? They immediately add that the most useful measure depends on the purpose at hand.

For the problems to be discussed at this conference, the various refinements they consider should be examined separately, one after the other. Taking them in reverse order, I would say that the coverage effects (household production, natural resources and environmental degradation) mainly concern the performance of the economy and have very little to do, if anything, with the behavior and policies that we shall discuss.

Among the various "reclassification effects", attention should, in my view, focus here only on depreciation and on research and development. Treating expenditure on this last item as current input, as is currently done in national accounts, is particularly inadequate. The paper contains a good discussion of this point. Table 2 also gives some adjusted figures; unfortunately they concern the national saving ratio and not the business saving ratio, which I consider to be much more relevant here. But using Tables 1 and 2 together, we can see that corporate saving as a share of GNP decreased in Germany for instance, between the 1960s and the 1980s by 1.5 per cent as usually measured, but by only 0.7 per cent if business R&D is taken into account in (gross) income and saving.

The most interesting part for this conference, however, should be the discussion of valuation effects. The treatment of expected and irreversible capital gains and losses in present national accounts is particularly inappropriate when we use the data to study behavior. I understand the difficulties of statisticians who have no information on what was expected and is perceived as irreversible; but economists should at least compute adjusted figures. This applies, particularly but not only, to figures corrected for the effect of general inflation. Figure 4 in the paper plots some such adjusted figures, unfortunately not the most interesting ones. It shows well the varying importance of the correction to be made to the aggregate private saving ratio. But still more interesting would have been figures showing the adjustments in the household saving ratio and in the corporate saving ratio, with large changes in adjustment when inflation accelerates (which favors business) or decelerates (which favors households). It was, of course, impossible for the authors themselves to compute the adjustments since they did not have the required wealth and debt data; but quoting and reproducing a few figures computed by others would have been instructive.

In many places the paper goes beyond a simple presentation of facts and discussion of measurement issues. This is a good thing, since it makes a bridge with the questions considered in the other papers discussed here. It may be appropriate to point to some interesting statements.

This conference is devoted to "saving behavior", which should be clearly distinguished from investment behavior. There may be a problem in this respect when we look at the national saving ratios that the paper exhibits. There is no problem for those who think that interest rates adapt, so as to put investment in line with saving, which moreover is interest inelastic; but there is a problem for those who think that output adapts so as to put saving in line with investment. The problem is, however, somewhat mitigated because the correlation between investment and saving within countries has declined. Is it just an accidental and insignificant change in a partly spurious correlation or is it due to the liberalization of international capital flows?

Some have argued that national saving rather than household saving reflected household behavior, because individuals rationally perceive the long-run consequences of government deficits and similarly see through the corporate veil. The paper contains a number of references to this thesis, giving it some partial credit, but suggesting that it does not fit the facts. The arguments are then of two kinds: simple minded or relying on econometric references. As an example of the first kind, the observation is made that "private saving has been relatively stable as a share of GNP, with changes in household and business saving tending to cancel one another". Such a simple correlation is not very convincing because many other factors may have changed household saving or corporate saving. On the other hand, the econometric references are to quite recent articles that only specialists might know about. Having attention drawn to them is particularly welcome.

It is recognized that financial liberalization has relaxed liquidity constraints and is therefore responsible for a decline in the household saving ratio. The good point was made in an earlier version of the paper that the direct impact of the change should be distinguished from its long-term effect, which will occur when the lifetime consumption profile of everyone will have adapted to the new situation. This long-term effect will, of course, be smaller than the impact effect and could even conceivably have a reverse sign.

A Long-Run Perspective on Saving

Angus Maddison *

University of Groningen, The Netherlands

Abstract

Historical estimates of long-run gross savings rates are provided for 11 countries, which represent about 48 per cent of world product in real terms and close to half of world savings. Even though savings rates declined over the past decade in nine of the 11 countries, present rates are usually well above their prewar levels. Factors which influence savings rates are also examined.

I. Introduction

Recent comparative surveys of savings behaviour have focused on a rather narrow time period; see Dean *et al.* (1990) and Agherli *et al.* (1990). This affects the validity of their general finding that savings rates in the 1980s have been at historic lows.

This paper provides longer term evidence on gross savings rates in 11 countries (Australia 1870–1988, Canada 1870–1988, France 1820–1913 and 1950–88, Germany 1870–1913, 1925–39 and 1950–88, Korea 1911–38 and 1953–88, India 1870–1988, Japan 1885–1988, Netherlands 1921–39 and 1950–88, Taiwan 1903–38 and 1951–88, U.K. 1870–1988 and U.S.A. 1870–1988). My coverage of the historical evidence is not exhaustive (more countries could be included, and for some of those included it may be possible to go further back).[1] Nevertheless the 11 countries in this paper represent about 48 per cent of world

*I am grateful to Nanno Mulder for help in preparing the graphs and statistical appendix. The original version of this paper contained a statistical appendix of 50 pages with detailed figures and sources underlying the diagrams and tables. This is available from the author.

[1] Kuznets (1961b) provides a comparative survey of long term investment and savings experience. He covers 12 countries (Argentina, Australia, Canada, Denmark, Germany, Italy, Japan, Norway, South Africa, Sweden, U.K. and U.S.A.). In Maddison (1964, pp. 234–42), I presented long term investment ratios for some countries not included in this paper (Denmark, Italy, Norway and Sweden) and discussed some of the problems of comparability and measurement in more detail.

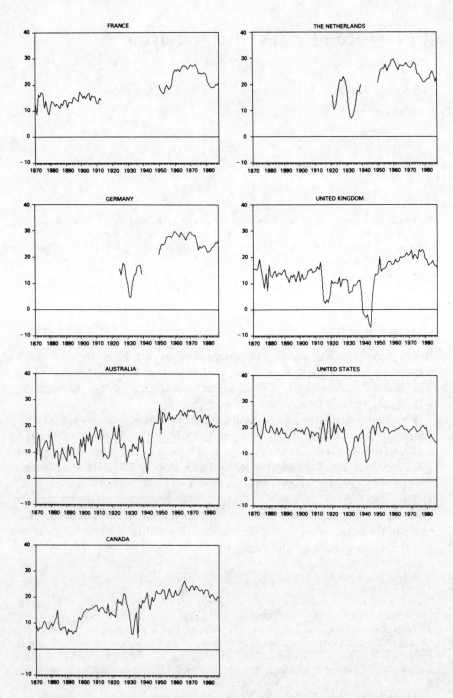

Fig. 1. Gross national saving as percentage of GDP at current prices.

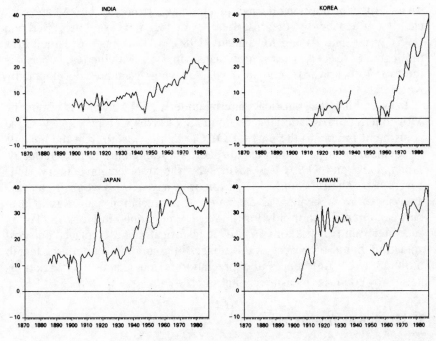

Fig. 1 — Continued

product in real terms and probably about half of world savings. They are also countries which are or have been important in the international flow of capital.

The historical evidence on savings is best summarised in Figure 1, which presents the record for the 11 countries in comparable form. The decline in savings rates over the past decade is clearly confirmed in nine of the 11 countries. The only exceptions are Korea and Taiwan. However, in most countries, the savings rates of the 1950s and 1960s were very high in terms of historical experience. Even at their present reduced level, savings rates in most of the countries are usually well above their prewar levels. It would therefore be just as feasible to conceive of recent savings patterns as a reversion towards longer term "norms" after an unusually prolonged postwar boom, as it is to consider them as an aberration from postwar normality.

It is also clear from inspection of Figure 1 that U.S. long run experience has not conformed to the norm for the other countries. In most of the other cases, it is possible to discern an upward trend in the long term savings rate, whereas this is not the case in the U.S.A. The atypicality of U.S. experience is important because a good deal of the theorising about saving (or consumption) behaviour emanated from the U.S.A. and was clearly influenced by the historical evidence. For example, Friedman (1957, pp. 3 and 4) and Modigliani (1986, p. 298) have explained how they came to reject Keynes' notion that savings rise with income — because there was no upward trend in the U.S. savings estimates developed by Kuznets.

In assembling the statistical material underlying the graphs, I kept in line with contemporary national accounting (SNA) conventions. However, one adjustment I made to the postwar OECD figures was to treat the balance of payments item "net transfers abroad" (substantial in France, Germany, Japan, U.K. and U.S.A.) as savings by the transferring country. This conforms to the procedure I used for prewar years. I have restricted the analysis to gross savings, as estimates of depreciation vary a good deal between countries, not only for the reason mentioned in Horioka (1990), i.e., intercountry variations in use of historical versus replacement cost valuation, but also because of differences in assumptions about the length of life of assets, differences in depreciation formulae and other variations in the way countries measure capital stock.

II. Domestic Investment

Figure 2 shows the behaviour of domestic investment. It is interesting to compare the contours of these diagrams with those in Figure 1 on total savings. In general the two sets of contours are not too different, except for the U.K., where pre-1913 investment was significantly lower than savings, so that its long run domestic investment trend is more clearly upwards than is the case for savings. For Canada, the contour for long term investment is significantly different from that for long term saving. There are also important differences for Taiwan where domestic investment rates have dropped considerably in recent years, but savings have continued to be very high.

III. Investment Abroad

Figure 3 presents the record for investment abroad. Suprisingly, Taiwan has proportionately had the biggest investment abroad, both in recent years and in the colonial period (when its experience was very different from that of the other Japanese colony, Korea). Over the long haul, Australia has been the most consistent foreign borrower, though not on as large a scale as pre-1913 Canada. Of the European countries, the U.K. appears as the biggest pre-1913 foreign investor (though its lending proportion may have been below that of the Netherlands in that period). In the postwar period the Netherlands and Germany have been lenders on a

Table 1a. *Total gross savings as a ratio of GDP at current market prices*

	1870–89	1890–1913	1914–38	1939–49	1950–73	1974–87	1950–9	1960–73	1974–80	1981–87
Australia	11.2a	13.0a	12.4	13.8	24.4	22.0	23.5	25.1	23.5	20.7
Canada	9.1b	12.2b	14.4b	19.3	22.5	21.5	21.4	23.4	22.7	20.4
France	12.8	14.7	n.a.	n.a.	23.5	22.3	18.8	26.8	24.9	20.0
Germany	n.a.	n.a.	12.9c	n.a.	27.5	24.0	25.9	28.6	24.1	24.0
India	n.a.	5.8d	7.4	6.7	12.8	20.2	10.8	14.3	20.7	17.3
Japan	12.4e	12.3e	16.7e	23.3e	32.8	32.9	28.1	36.1	33.0	32.8
Korea	n.a.	n.a.	4.3f	n.a.	8.1g	27.9	4.0h	10.1	24.3	31.0
Netherlands	n.a.	n.a.	15.2i	n.a.	26.8	22.9	25.8	27.4	23.2	22.7
Taiwan	n.a.	9.6j	25.5k	n.a.	19.9	33.2	14.7	23.2	31.9	34.5
U.K.	13.9	13.6	8.3	1.6	17.9	19.2	15.7	19.5	20.9	17.5
U.S.A.	19.1	18.3	17.0	15.2	19.7	18.0	19.7	19.7	19.7	16.7

(a) Excludes inventories; (b) 1870–1926 excludes inventories; (c) 1925–38; (d) 1900–13; (e) 1885–1940 excludes inventories and first entry is for 1885–9; (f) excludes part of inventories; (g) 1953–73; (h) 1953–9; (i) 1921–38; (j) 1903–13 and excludes part of inventories; (k) excludes part of inventories.
Source: Appendix, Table 2.

Table 1b. *Gross fixed domestic investment as a ratio of GDP at current market prices*

	1870–89	1890–1913	1914–38	1939–49	1950–73	1974–87	1950–9	1960–73	1974–80	1981–87
Australia	16.5	13.4	15.0	11.9	25.0	24.3	24.3	25.4	24.0	24.6
Canada	16.0	19.4	15.2	12.9	22.4	22.3	22.3	22.4	23.6	21.2
France	12.8	13.9	16.1a	n.a.	21.2	21.7	17.5	23.8	23.5	20.2
Germany	n.a.	n.a.	12.9b	n.a.	23.2	20.6	20.8	24.9	21.1	20.2
India	4.5c	5.6c	7.0	7.8	12.5	17.7	10.2	14.2	17.2	19.2
Japan	12.6d	14.4	16.2	18.6	28.3	30.4	22.3	32.6	31.7	29.2
Korea	n.a.	4.9e	7.0	n.a.	15.9f	28.9	9.8g	18.9	29.4	28.6
Netherlands	n.a.	n.a.	17.5h	n.a.	23.8	20.2	22.3	25.0	21.0	19.4
Taiwan	n.a.	8.7i	15.6	n.a.	17.0j	24.6	13.0k	19.5	28.3	21.8
U.K.	8.4	8.5	7.8	6.5	16.3	17.7	14.1	17.9	18.8	16.5
U.S.A.	16.3	15.9	14.2	13.1	18.0	18.0	18.4	17.8	18.4	17.7

(a) 1922–38; (b) 1925–38; (c) in separating fixed investment from inventories it was assumed for 1870–99 that inventories averaged 0.6 per cent of GDP; (d) 1885–9; (e) 1911–13; (f) 1953–73; (g) 1953–9; (h) 1921–38; (i) 1903–13; (j) 1951–73; (k) 1951–9.
Source: Appendix, Table 2.

Table 1c. *Net investment in inventories as a ratio of GDP at current market prices*

	1870–89	1890–1913	1914–38	1939–49	1950–73	1974–87	1950–9	1960–73	1974–80	1981–87
Australia	n.a.	1.7	0.8	1.2	1.2	0.5	1.2	1.1	0.7	0.2
Canada	n.a.	n.a.	0.3	1.0	1.3	0.5	1.5	1.1	1.1	0.0
France	0.0	0.2	n.a.	n.a.	1.9	0.5	1.9	1.9	1.1	0.1
Germany	n.a.	n.a.	0.1h	n.a.	1.9	0.4	1.9	1.6	0.8	0.0
India	0.6	0.6	0.4	0.2	1.9	3.4a	2.5	1.9	3.5	3.3b
Japan	n.a.	n.a.	n.a.	7.7	3.8	0.6	1.8	2.7	0.9	0.4
Korea	n.a.	n.a.	n.a.	n.a.	1.9c	1.1	5.2	1.4	1.6	0.7
Netherlands	n.a.	n.a.	−2.7e	n.a.	1.8	0.2	2.8d	1.5	0.7	−0.4
Taiwan	n.a.	n.a.	n.a.	n.a.	3.1f	2.1	2.7g	3.4	3.7	0.8
U.K.	0.9	0.6	−0.2	0.4	0.9	0.3	0.9	1.0	0.4	0.2
U.S.A.	3.5	1.9	0.9	0.9	0.9	0.6	1.0	0.9	0.6	0.5

(a) 1974–87; (b) 1981–7; (c) 1953–73; (d) 1953–9; (e) 1921–38; (f) 1951–73; (g) 1951–9; (h) 1925–38.
Source: Appendix, Table 2.

Table 1d. *Net investment abroad as a ratio of GDP at current market prices*

	1870–89	1890–1913	1914–38	1939–49	1950–73	1974–87	1950–9	1960–73	1974–80	1981–87
Australia	−5.4	−1.5	−3.5	0.7	−1.7	−2.8	−2.0	−1.5	−1.3	−4.2
Canada	−6.9	−7.1	−0.9	5.4	−1.1	−1.3	−2.5	−0.2	−1.9	−0.7
France	−0.1	0.6	n.a.	n.a.	0.4	−0.2	−0.6	1.1	0.3	−0.3
Germany	1.7	1.5	−0.1a	n.a.	2.4	3.1	2.7	2.1	2.3	3.8
India	n.a.	0.2	0.0	−1.3	−1.5	−0.9	−1.3	−1.8	0.0	−1.9
Japan	−0.3	−2.1	0.5	−1.9	0.7	1.8	0.7	0.7	0.4	3.1
Korea	n.a.	n.a.	−2.7	n.a.	−9.7b	−2.2	−8.7c	−10.2	−6.6	1.7
Netherlands	n.a.	n.a.	0.4d	n.a.	1.2	2.7	1.5	0.9	1.4	3.7
Taiwan	n.a.	0.9e	9.9	n.a.	−0.2f	6.4	−1.0g	0.3	−0.1	11.8
U.K.	4.5	4.6	0.7	−5.3	0.6	0.9	0.7	0.6	1.7	0.3
U.S.A.	−0.7	0.5	2.0	1.3	0.8	−0.6	0.4	1.0	0.7	−1.6

(a) 1925–38; (b) 1953–73; (c) 1953–9; (d) 1921–38; (e) 1903–13; (f) 1951–73; (g) 1951–9.
Source: Appendix, Table 2. Negative sign means negative investment (borrowing).

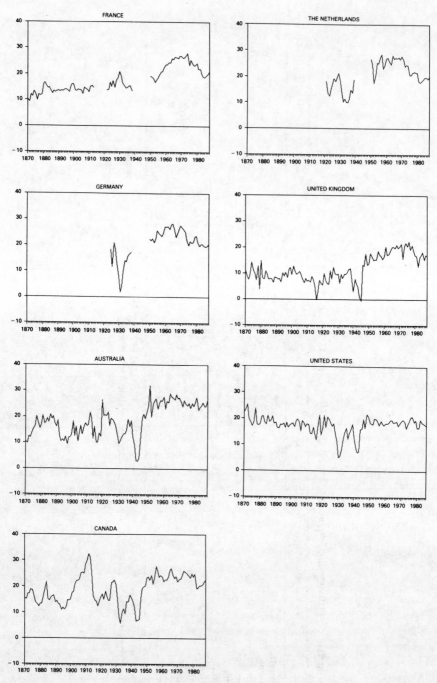

Fig. 2. Gross domestic investment as percentage of GDP at current prices.

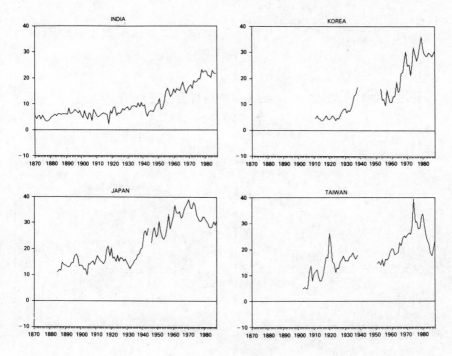

Fig. 2 — Continued

larger scale than the U.K., whose investment abroad has been modest by historical standards. France has also been relatively modest in its postwar lending abroad. The U.S.A. has been the most consistent in lending abroad in the twentieth century and its recent borrowing abroad is clearly an unusual break with precedent.

IV. Absolute Importance of Savers

All the graphs are in proportionate terms, showing total savings and uses of savings in relation to GDP in the country concerned. However, the importance of individual countries in the international market for savings depends not only on their savings rate but also on the absolute size of the country, its propensity to invest abroad, and the extent to which its exchange rate deviates from purchasing power parity. This is illustrated in Table 2, which shows the situation in 1988.

Thus it can be seen that Japan had the biggest savings in 1988 — $974 billion compared with $700 billion in the U.S.A., in spite of the fact that the real GDP of Japan was only 40 per cent of that of the U.S.A. Japan's

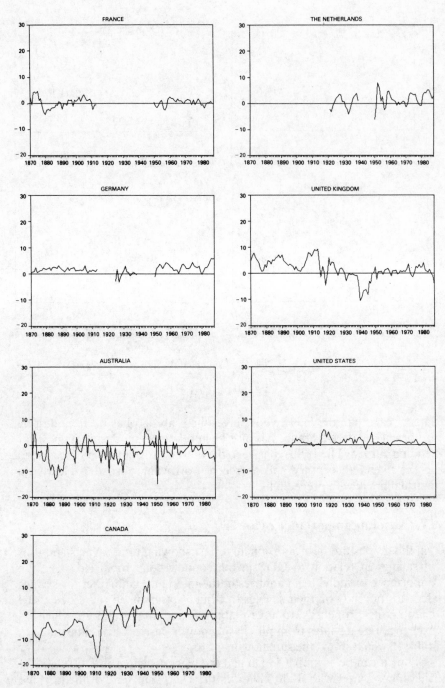

Fig. 3. Net investment abroad as percentage of GDP at current prices.

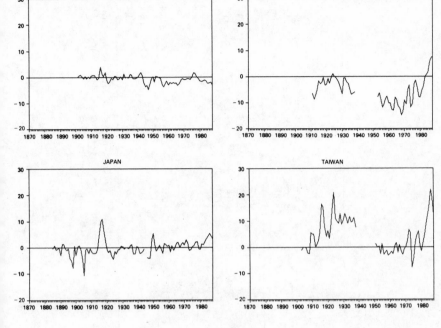

Fig. 3 — Continued

savings were high relative to the U.S.A. because it had one of the highest savings rates (34.2 per cent of GDP), whereas the U.S.A. had the lowest in our group (at 14.6 per cent of GDP). Japan also had the biggest deviation between its exchange rate and the purchasing power of its currency. In real terms, converting GDP at national prices with purchasing power parities supplied by Eurostat, its GDP was only 40 per cent of that in the U.S.A., but in money terms, with conversion at the exchange rate, it was 59 per cent of that in the U.S.A. The comparison between India and Japan is even more strongly affected by use of PPP rather than an exchange rate converter. In money terms Japanese GDP was 10 times that of India, but in real terms it was only twice as high.

As Japanese investment abroad was 3.2 per cent of GDP in 1988 whereas U.S. investment was negative — at − 28 per cent — the contrast in the position of the two countries was most striking in this respect: the U.S.A. being the biggest borrower ($132 billion) and Japan being the biggest investor ($92 billion).

Thus there are serious problems of aggregation if one wants to estimate savings trends for our eleven countries combined.

Table 2. Comparative levels of real GDP, money GDP and savings in 1988

	1988 GDP at U.S. Relative Prices $ Billion	1988 GDP Converted at Exchange Rate $ Billion	1988 Price Level Relative to U.S.A.	1988 Savings as Per Cent of GDP	1988 Savings $ Billion	1988 Investment Abroad as Per Cent of GDP	1988 Investment Abroad $ Billion
Australia	236.6	247.0	1.13	20.1	49.7	− 6.7	− 16.6
Canada	482.1	486.0	1.10	19.7	95.5	− 2.7	− 13.3
France	816.7	955.7	1.27	20.9	199.4	− 0.1	− 1.2
Germany	906.5	1,201.8	1.44	26.4	316.7	5.8	69.9
Netherlands	197.3	227.4	1.25	22.9	52.0	2.8	6.4
U.K.	815.5	833.8	1.11	15.8	131.6	− 4.2	− 35.3
U.S.A.	4,809.1	4,809.1	1.00	14.6	699.9	− 2.8	− 132.4
India	899.4	281.1	0.34	21.0	59.0	− 3.0	− 8.4
Japan	1,926.3	2,848.9	1.61	34.2	973.5	3.2	91.6
Korea	286.3	174.9	0.66	38.3	67.0	7.7	13.5
Taiwan	146.5	123.3	0.91	35.3	43.5	12.0	14.8

Source: First column represents GDP in national currencies converted by Eurostat ICP V PPPs at US relative prices, adjusted to 1988 basis; Indian, Korean and Taiwanese GDP converted by ICP IV PPPs updated to 1988. Second column from OECD sources. Column 3 is equal to column 2 divided by column 1. Columns 5 and 7 converted at exchange rate. Savings rates derived from Appendix, Table 2.

V. Factors Influencing Savings Rates

The main purpose of this paper is to provide estimates of savings rates over the long run for a significant sample of countries, and I cannot hope to make much of a contribution to diagnosing reasons for variation in such a complex phenomenon. However, it is worth looking at long term changes in some characteristics which savings theorists have considered to be important.

Most analysts of saving behaviour are concerned with identifying the motivations of various categories of savers — individuals, corporations or governments and their interaction (e.g. the impact of obligatory social security systems or fiscal deficits on private thrift). By contrast, the statistical evidence I present here concentrates on the uses of savings — for residential and non-residential fixed investment, for inventories, and for foreign investment — magnitudes which help illuminate business cycle or secular growth experience rather than intertemporal optimisation of individuals. As current saving and investment flows are equal at the aggregate level, there are obvious benefits from confrontation of the source of savings and use of savings approaches.

Tables 3 and 4 show absolute levels and growth of per capita real income in comparable units for the eleven sample countries. There has been very substantial long run growth in real income per head in all of these countries except India. This growth was generally fastest in the 1950–73 period and has slowed down appreciably since then, except in India, Korea and Taiwan. There is a general positive relationship between the faster postwar growth in output per head and the acceleration in savings rates, and a similar positive relation in the post 1973 slowdown. The U.S.A., which has the smallest postwar acceleration in per capita

Table 3. *GDP per capita in 1985 dollars at U.S. prices*

	1870	1913	1950	1973	1989
Australia	3,123	4,523	5,931	10,331	13,584
Canada	1,347	3,560	6,113	11,866	17,576
France	1,571	2,734	4,149	10,323	13,837
Germany	1,300	2,606	3,339	10,110	13,989
Netherlands	2,064	3,178	4,706	10,267	12,737
U.K.	2,610	4,024	5,651	10,063	13,468
U.S.A.	2,247	4,854	8,611	14,103	18,317
India	470	536	482	689	1,065
Japan	618	1,114	1,563	9,237	15,101
Korea	n.a.	819	757	2,404	6,503
Taiwan	n.a.	608	706	2,803	7,252

Source: Maddison (1991).

Table 4. *Rate of growth of GDP per capita (annual average compound growth rate)*

	1870–1913	1913–50	1950–73	1973–89
Australia	0.9	0.7	2.5	1.7
Canada	2.3	1.5	2.9	2.5
France	1.3	1.1	4.1	1.8
Germany	1.6	0.7	4.9	2.0
Netherlands	1.0	1.1	3.5	1.4
U.K.	1.0	0.8	2.5	1.8
U.S.A.	2.0	1.6	2.2	1.6
Average	1.4	1.1	4.0	1.8
India	0.3	− 0.3	1.6	2.8
Japan	1.4	0.9	8.0	3.1
Korea	n.a.	− 0.2	5.2	6.4
Taiwan	n.a.	0.4	6.2	6.1
Average	n.a.	0.2	5.3	4.6

Source: Derived from Table 3.

growth, was also the country with least change in its long run savings habits.

Contemporary rates of saving are, if anything, negatively related to per capita income levels, as the richest country, the U.S.A., has the lowest saving level and the highest levels are in two relatively low income countries — Korea and Taiwan. Even a very low income country like India has a higher savings ratio than the U.S.A. When we match the real income evidence of Table 3 with the savings ratios of Table 1, it appears that the savings ratio is more responsive to investment opportunity than to income.

When there are realistic opportunities for economic catch-up — produced by accelerated international diffusion of technology, increased absorptive capacity due to improvements in human capital, effective pro-growth policies, better international cooperation, or liberation from a colonial yoke — then the improvement in prospective returns seem to induce a rise in savings and investment in follower countries (whatever their level of income). The lead country — the U.S.A. — did not have this experience; hence, its savings behaved differently.

As follower countries aproach the leader more closely (the European and Japanese case), their opportunities for catch-up fade and this may help explain the fall in savings ratios since 1973. The lower-income Asian countries (India, Korea and Taiwan) are not yet in this situation (though the causes of the recent sharp fall in Taiwanese domestic investment rates are worth closer scrutiny).

The fall in savings rates in OECD countries since 1973 has been greater than would be warranted by the erosion of special opportunities for catch-

Table 5. *Changes in demographic structure, 1870–1987*

	Percentage of population aged 65 and over					Percentage of population 0–14				
	1870	1910	1950	1973	1987	1870	1910	1950	1973	1987
Australia	1.8	4.0	8.1	8.5	10.7	42.3	35.2	26.6	28.2	22.6
Canada	3.7	4.7	7.4	8.3	10.9	41.6	33.1	29.7	28.0	21.2
France	7.4	8.4	11.4	13.2	13.5	27.1	25.8	22.7	24.4	20.6
Germany	4.6	4.9	(9.2)	13.9	15.1	34.0	33.9	(23.5)	22.4	14.9
Netherlands	5.5	6.1	7.7	10.5	12.4	33.6	34.5	29.3	26.4	18.6
U.K.	5.0	5.3	10.7	13.6	15.5	36.1	30.8	22.3	23.9	18.9
U.S.A.	3.0	4.3	8.1	10.2	12.2	39.2	32.1	26.8	26.5	21.5
India	3.2a	2.4	3.6	3.4	4.4	34.9a	38.5	37.5	42.0	37.2
Japan	5.3	5.3b	5.2	7.3	10.8	33.7	36.5b	35.3	24.2	20.4
Korea	n.a.	n.a.	3.9c	3.5d	4.8	n.a.	n.a.	43.2c	28.1d	27.3
Taiwan	n.a.	2.4e	n.a.	3.2	5.3	n.a.	35.9e	39.0	37.1	28.6

(a) 1881; (b) 1920; (c) 1944; (d) 1975; (e) 1905. German figures in brackets exclude Berlin.
Source: OECD countries from OECD, *Labour Force Statistics*, various issues, OECD *Demographic Trends 1950–1990*, Paris, 1979, and B. Mueller, *A Statistical Handbook of the North Atlantic Area*, Twentieth Century Fund, New York, 1965. Asian countries from B. R. Mitchell, *International Historical Statistics: Africa and Asia*, Macmillan, London, 1982, World Bank, *World Development Report 1990*, and UN, *The Aging of Populations and Its Economic and Social Implications*, New York, 1956.

up. There has been a constellation of other influences which have generally had an adverse effect on savings — the oil shocks, the switch in policy emphasis towards anti-inflationary rather than full-employment objectives, the aberrant fiscal-monetary policy mix in the U.S.A., the greater caution in macropolicy which results from the great openness which has developed in international capital markets; see Maddison (1984 and 1991). These causal influences require very careful scrutiny before one can jump to conclusions about a "shortage" of world savings, or the efficacy of policy action specifically directed to enhance savings incentives.

Some of the savings literature stresses the possibility that the ageing of the population and the swelling cohorts of elderly citizens will reduce the incentive or capacity to save, or that the decline in the proportion of children will reduce the incentive to provide for posterity. It is clear from Table 5 that ageing has been important in the advanced capitalist countries and is starting in Asia, but the timing and pattern of change in savings ratios has not been very obviously affected by this.

Even more striking than the demographic changes of Table 5 are the changes in institutional arrangements that have led to the massive increase in the governmental role in the economy (see Table 6). On average, government spending on goods, services, and transfers accounted for 46 per cent of GDP in 1987 compared with 12 per cent in 1913. A significant

42   A. Maddison

Table 6. *Total government expenditures as a percentage of GDP at current prices, 1913–87*

	1913	1929	1938	1950	1973	1987
France	8.9	12.4	23.2	27.3	38.8	56.6[b]
Germany	17.7	30.6	42.4	30.4	42.0	47.3
Japan	14.2	18.8	30.3	19.8	22.9	33.9
Netherlands	8.2[a]	11.2	21.7	26.8	45.5	59.7
U.K.	13.3	23.8	28.8	34.2	41.5	45.2[b]
U.S.A.	8.0	10.0	19.8	21.4	31.1	37.0
Average	11.7	17.8	27.7	26.7	37.0	46.0

(a) 1910; (b) 1986.
Source: Maddison (1991).

proportion of these expenditures involve governmental takeover of provision for old age, or coverage of risks which were previously borne by individuals. This has obviously had an impact on the way savings are formed, but it is not so clear what the impact has been on overall rates of saving.

References

Agherli, B. B., Boughton, J. M., Montiel, P. J., Villanueva, D. & Woglom, G.: The role of national saving in the world economy. *Occasional Paper*, No. 67, IMF, Washington DC, 1990.
Blades, D.: Alternative measures of saving. *OECD Economic Outlook, Occasional Studies*, June 1983.
Dean, A., Durand, M., Fallon, J. & Hoeller, P.: Savings trends and behaviour in OECD countries. *OECD Economic Studies*, No. 14, Spring 1990.
Friedman, M.: *A Theory of the Consumption Function*. NBER, Princeton, 1957.
Horioka, C. Y.: Why is Japan's household saving rate so high? A literature survey. *Journal of Japanese and International Economies 4*, 1990.
Kuznets, S.: *Capital in the American Economy: Its Formation and Financing*. NBER, Princeton, 1961a.
Kuznets, S.: Long term trends in capital formation proportions. *Economic Development and Cultural Change*, July 1961b.
Kuznets, S.: Capital formation in modern economic growth. In his *Population, Capital and Growth: Selected Essays*, Heinemann, London, 1974.
Maddison, A.: *Economic Growth in the West*, Allen and Unwin, London, 1964.
Maddison, A.: Comparative analysis of the productivity situation in the advanced capitalist countries. In J. W. Kendrick (ed.), *International Comparisons of Productivity and Causes of the Slowdown*. Ballinger, Cambridge, MA, 1984.
Maddison, A.: *Dynamic Forces in Capitalist Development*. Oxford University Press, 1991.
Modigliani, F.: Life cycle, individual thrift, and the wealth of nations. *American Economic Review*, June 1986.
Sturm, P. H.: Determinants of saving: Theory and evidence. *OECD Economic Studies*, No. 1, Autumn 1983.

Saving and Capital Market Imperfections: The Italian experience*

Luigi Guiso

Bank of Italy, Rome, Italy

Tullio Jappelli

Instituto Universitario Navale, Naples, Italy

Daniele Terlizzese

Bank of Italy, Rome, Italy

Abstract

Italy's saving rate is high by international standards, even when differences in growth are taken into account. We argue that credit and insurance market imperfections provide a plausible explanation for the high Italian saving rate. We also reject the potential roles of the public sector, informal financial arrangements, bequests and the slope of the earnings profile as alternative explanations of the evidence.

I. Introduction

Two features characterize the Italian saving rate. First, by international standards, Italy is a "high-saving" country and second, the Italian saving rate has declined markedly in the last three decades. We provide a consistent framework for interpreting these facts. According to the life-cycle hypothesis, they should be explained mainly by differences in demographics and productivity growth between countries and over time; cf. Modigliani (1990). However, as we argue in Section II, the differences in growth rates between Italy and the other major OECD countries are rather small when compared with the large differences in their saving rates: growth appears to generate more saving in Italy than elsewhere. Thus, growth alone cannot account for the high Italian saving rate and for its sharp decline.

*We would like to thank two anonymous referees, the editors and the discussant for helpful comments on an earlier draft of this paper. The views expressed here are those of the authors and do not involve the responsibility of the Bank of Italy.

We argue that capital market imperfections provide a plausible explanation of the evidence. An economy in which households are liquidity constrained exhibits a higher saving rate than an economy with perfect markets, if the two economies grow at the same rate, and an identical reduction in growth leads to a greater reduction in saving in the economy with imperfect markets; see Jappelli and Pagano (1991). Thus, the interaction between growth and capital market imperfections may explain not only why Italy's saving rate is high; it may also explain why it declined so sharply in the 80s.

In Section III we present evidence to show that the level of development of the Italian consumer credit, mortgage and insurance markets is by far the lowest of the major industrial countries. Regulations, high down payments, wide interest rate spreads and limited competition make it more difficult to obtain consumer credit, mortgages and insurance in Italy than in most of the other industrialized countries. In Section IV we evaluate alternative explanations for the high Italian saving rate, and reject the role of bequests and the slope of earnings profiles as possible causes. In Sections V and VI we survey some recent empirical evidence on the effect of capital market imperfections on saving in Italy. It is suggested in Section VII that the approach taken in this study is also useful for analyzing inter-country differences in saving rates and the response of saving to a liberalization of financial markets.

II. The Italian Saving Rate in an International Perspective

Table 1 reports the private saving rates of the seven major OECD countries (hereafter the G7) and the three Nordic countries (Norway, Sweden and Finland). For each country we also report the average rates of growth of gross national product over ten-year periods. In terms of gross savings rates, Italy ranks first in all three periods. However, this measure of saving includes the erosion in purchasing power of the stock of nominally denominated debt due to inflation and depreciation of the capital stock.[1] Inflation adjustment is extremely important in Italy, on account of its high rate of inflation and its high level of public debt, especially in the past 15 years. Table 1 shows that in terms of net private sving rates adjusted for

---

[1] Any theory of consumer choice refers to net, rather than gross saving rates. However, income, consumption and depreciation are not strictly comparable across countries; cf. Hayashi (1986). Thus, some of the differences emerging from Table 1 may merely reflect differences in accounting practices. For brevity, net saving rates not adjusted for inflation are not reported. Italy's rank is unchanged, however; on average, depreciation, as measured by the national accounts, has not been higher in Italy than in the G7.

Table 1. *Private saving and growth in the G7 and the Nordic countries*[a]

| | Average 1960–70 | | | Average 1971–80 | | | Average 1981–87 | | | Differences (1980s–60s) | | Ratio of NSA of the growth rate of GNP | | |
	GS (1)	NSA (2)	ρ (3)	GS (4)	NSA (5)	ρ (6)	GS (7)	NSA (8)	ρ (9)	ΔNSA (10)	Δρ (11)	1960s (12)	1970s (13)	1980s (14)
Canada	18.1	8.0	4.7	20.7	11.5	3.8	22.5	12.1	3.1	4.1	−1.6	1.7	3.0	3.9
U.S.	17.7	8.3	3.5	19.2	8.2	2.9	18.7	6.8	3.1	−1.5	−0.4	2.4	2.8	2.2
Japan	28.7	18.1	9.5	29.9	20.0	4.9	26.8	15.4	3.7	−2.7	−5.8	1.9	4.1	4.2
France	22.5	14.5	5.0	22.0	11.5	3.4	18.8	5.4	1.8	−9.1	−3.2	2.9	3.4	3.0
Germany	21.1	13.8	4.1	20.2	11.0	2.8	20.0	8.8	1.6	−5.0	−2.5	3.4	3.4	5.5
Italy	25.8	17.6	5.2	29.4	14.5	3.7	28.1	11.0	1.9	−6.6	−3.3	3.4	3.9	5.8
U.K.	13.1	6.1	2.6	16.4	0.8	1.8	17.7	4.7	3.2	−1.4	0.6	2.3	0.4	1.5
G7 average	21.0	12.3	4.9	22.5	11.1	3.3	21.8	9.1	2.6	−3.2	−2.3	2.5	3.4	3.5
Finland	18.2	7.4	4.8	19.3	7.8	3.8	20.0	7.7	3.2	0.3	−1.6	1.5	2.0	2.4
Norway	19.4	8.5	3.8	18.8	5.5	4.8	19.2	2.4	3.9	−6.1	0.1	2.2	1.1	0.6
Sweden	—	7.6	4.2	14.2	8.0	2.1	15.5	5.5	2.4	−2.1	−1.8	1.8	3.8	2.3
OECD average	—	11.4	4.9	21.0	11.9	3.4	20.4		2.4	−2.4	−2.5	2.3	3.5	3.8

[a] Gross private saving-rates (GS) are expressed as a percentage of gross national product. Net private saving rates adjusted for inflation (NSA) are expressed as a percentage of net national product. The inflation adjustment is the product of the rate of change in the private consumption deflator and the stock of outstanding government debt at the beginning of each year. Growth (ρ) is the average rate of growth of gross national product. The source for gross saving rates is Dean *et al.* (1990); for net saving rates and growth, Modigliani (1990).

inflation, Italy ranked second in the 1960s (after Japan), second in the 1970s (again, after Japan) and third in the 1980s (after Japan and Canada). This brings us to the first fact: the Italian private saving rate is comparatively high.[2] In contrast to the unadjusted figures, inflation-adjusted private saving rates declined by 6.6 per cent from the 1960s to the 1980s (column 10). This reduction was more pronounced than in all countries shown in Table 1 (except France). Thus, the second feature of the Italian private saving rate is that it declined substantially in the last 30 years.

The life-cycle model points mainly to differences in population in productivity growth rates to explain why saving differs among countries and why it changes over time. However, the differences in the growth rates of Italy and the G7 are rather small when compared with the large differences in respective saving rates. The Italian net private saving rate (adjusted for inflation) in the 1960s was almost 5 percentage points higher than the G7 average, but its growth rate was only 0.3 per cent above average. In the 1970s the differences were 3.4 and 0.4 per cent respectively, while in the 1980s private saving in Italy was 2 per cent above average, but growth was actually below average (-0.7 per cent). Not even the stripped-down version of the Modigliani-Brumberg life-cycle model, which emphasizes the effect of growth on saving by assuming a flat earnings profile throughout the life of the individual, can explain these large differences in saving by relying only on differences in growth. According to this model, in fact, the predicted differences between the Italian and the G7 saving rates is only 0.6 per cent in the 1960s, 1.1 per cent in the 1970s and negative in the 1980s.[3]

---

[2] One possibility is that Italy has a higher than average private saving rate because it has a higher than average government deficit. This would be the prediction of the much debated Ricardian Equivalence Proposition which asserts that national saving should be taken as reference, since people incorporate the budget constraint of the government in their own budget constraint; see Barro (1974). Contrary to the Ricardian Equivalence Propositoin, however, private saving has not risen to offset the increase in government deficit in the postwar period; cf. Modigliani and Jappelli (1987).

[3] In this version of the model individuals live L years, work in the first M years and earn a constant income throughout their working life. The labor income of each generation grows at a rate γ. If the rate of interest and the rate of time preferences are equal to zero, the aggregate saving rate s can be written as

$$s = 1 - \frac{M}{L} \frac{(1+\gamma)^{L} - 1}{(1+\gamma)^{L-M}[(1+\gamma)^{M} - 1]}.$$

The calculation in the text assumes a value of 53 for L and 40 for M. The values of γ are given in Table 1. For Italy, the simulated rates are 19.0, 15.9 and 9.9 for the three decades. The corresponding values for the G7 are 18.4, 14.8 and 12.6.

One way of checking that growth alone cannot explain the difference in saving between Italy and the G7 is to compare the ratios between saving and growth among countries (Table 1, columns 12, 13 and 14). By this measure, Italy ranks first in the 1960s and 1980s and second in the 1970s. This ranking already shows that the Italian saving rate was high not only in absolute terms, but also relative to its growth rate.[4]

A more formal way of checking that growth cannot explain Italy's high saving rate is to predict its saving rate by running a pooled regression over countries and (ten-year) periods that excludes Italy. In all cases, and even when we add other OECD countries or other regressors — such as government saving and the dependency ratio — the coefficients tend to underpredict substantially the Italian private saving rate in all three decades. Two typical regressions for the period 1960–87, both excluding Italy from the sample, are as follows:

Sample: 18 observations of 6 G7 countries

$$S_p = 0.092 + 2.361 \, \rho - 0.178 \, S_g - 0.191 \, \text{Dep} \qquad \text{SE} = 0.038$$
$$ (0.048) \ (0.591) \quad (0.319) \quad (0.139) \qquad \text{d.v. mean} = 0.102$$

Sample: 60 observations of 20 OECD countries

$$S_p = 0.094 + 1.429 \, \rho - 0.486 \, S_g - 0.061 \, \text{Dep} \qquad \text{SE} = 0.042$$
$$ (0.048) \ (0.591) \quad (0.319) \quad (0.139) \qquad \text{d.v. mean} = 0.106$$

where S_p and S_g are net private and public saving adjusted for inflation, respectively, ρ is the rate of growth of GDP, Dep is the ratio of the population under 15 to the total population, and standard errors are reported in parentheses.[5]

In the first regression the difference between the predicted and the actual Italian saving rates are -3.3 per cent in the 1960s, -3.3 in the 1970s and -2.5 in the 1980s. In the second regression the differences are -4.8 in the 1960s, -3.4 in the 1970s and -1.1 in the 1980s. Regressions with national saving as the dependent variable yield similar results. The data tell us that, by international comparison, the Italian saving rate is high even when differences in growth and other variables are taken into account.

Since differences in growth cannot explain the evidence, we turn to other factors that could account for the high Italian saving rate. The issue

---

[4] The ratio is also high in Germany and Japan (in the 1970s and 1980s). On the other hand, the Nordic countries' private saving rate is low not only in absolute terms, but also with respect to their rate of growth, which was roughly in line with that of the other OECD countries.

[5] The data source is Modigliani (1990). The OECD countries not included in the estimation are Italy, New Zealand, Yugoslavia and Turkey.

that we think deserves the closest scrutiny is the possibility that the main difference between Italy and the G7 is the low degree of development of Italian capital markets. When credit and insurance markets are imperfect, young households are forced to save (or consume less) in response to borrowing constraints and engage in precautionary saving in reaction to insurance market imperfections. In the absence of population or productivity growth, capital market imperfections do not, of course, generate positive aggregate saving. But once one allows for growth, an economy with capital market imperfections exhibits a higher saving rate than an economy with perfect markets. In addition, the effect of growth on saving is greater in an economy with liquidity constraints: an identical change in growth — for instance, from zero to positive growth — generates a greater change in saving in an economy with liquidity constraints; see Jappelli and Pagano (1991).[6]

This interaction between saving, growth and liquidity constraints may also explain why Italy's saving rate declined so sharply in the 1980s. In the G7 the decline in growth was of the same order of magnitude as in Italy, but the decline in private saving was only 3.2 per cent (against 6.6 per cent in Italy). Thus, in Italy, the reduction in growth has been associated with a greater reduction in saving than in other countries. This pattern is consistent with the idea that liquidity constraints are more severe in Italy than elsewhere.

Besides liquidity constraints, however, other factors may explain the two features of the Italian saving rate: the Italian earnings profile may be flatter than elsewhere, or the bequest motive in Italy may be stronger. In the presence of growth, a strong bequest motive, or a flat earnings profile may induce a high saving rate. These issues are addressed in Section IV.

III.   Italian Capital Markets in an International Perspective

Table 2 reports figures for consumer credit and mortgages in the main OECD countries and in three Nordic countries (see columns 1 and 3). In Italy both markets are between one fifth and one tenth of the size of those in most other countries in the Table. The terms of consumer credit to

---

[6] Jappelli and Pagano (1991) illustrate this point in the context of a three-period overlapping generations model where the young are liquidity constrained and productivity growth is exogenous. In a closed economy, the saving rate is the product of the growth rate and the capital-output ratio; they show that for any given level of the growth rate, liquidity constraints raise the capital-output ratio and therefore saving. In a small open economy, saving is no longer the product of growth and the capital-output ratio, but the proposition that the saving rate is higher in the economy with liquidity constraints still holds. Liquidity constraints also generate higher saving in a version of the model with endogenous growth à la Romer.

Table 2. *Household liabilities and insurance premiums in the G7 and the Nordic countries*

	Consumer credit[a] (1)	Durables as a % of total consumption[b] (2)	Mortgage loans[c] (3)	Average down payment as a percentage of the housing price[d] (4)	Ownership (per cent)[e] (5)	Insurance premiums as a % of GDP[f] (6)
Canada	22	14	60	20	62	5.41
U.S.	23	10	61	20	65	9.07
Japan	18	5	25	40	60	8.90
France	8	12	44	20	47	5.06
Germany	15	–	–	30	37	6.40
Italy	4	11	6	50	59	2.36
U.K.	10	9	45	15	59	8.35
G7 average[g]	14	–	44	–	56	6.47
Finland	39	11	42	20	61	5.31
Norway	48	12	60	–	67	5.08
Sweden	39	10	61	20	57	4.49

[a] As a percentage of private consumption expenditures in 1988 (for Japan and France in 1987, for Sweden in 1987, for France in 1987, for Sweden in 1986). Consumer credit sources: OECD Financial Statistics Monthly, Section 2, Table D.4, December 1990. For Italy, Annual Report of the Bank of Italy, 1989, Table D23, p. 234. Data for Finland, Norway, Sweden and Japan have been provided by the Central Banks of Finland, Norway and Sweden and the Japan Information Centre Corporation, respectively.

[b] All figures refer to 1980. The "durable" aggregate excludes semi-durables. Source: OECD National Accounts.

[c] As a percentage of private consumption expenditures in 1982. Sources: Boleat (1987, Table 21.8, p. 218). For Italy, Annual Report of the Bank of Italy, Appendix, 1984, Table aD29. Data for Finland, Norway and Sweden were kindly provided by the Central Banks in each country.

[d] The average down payment is the amount of personal funds required to buy a home even when individuals are allowed to borrow from different institutions. For Canada, Finland, France, Germany, and the U.S. the figure refers to 1982–3 from Boleat (1987). For Japan the source is Hayashi, Ito and Slemrod (1988). For Italy, the numbers are our own estimates based on conversations with market specialists. The figure for the U.K. is the average ratio of mortgage advances to housing prices for first-time home buyers in 1988 from Lomax (1991).

[e] For Canada, Japan, France and Germany the figures refer to 1978; for the U.S., Italy, the U.K. and Sweden to 1981; for Finland and Norway to 1980. Source: Boleat (1987), Table 29.1, p. 460.

[f] Sources: Sigma, Zurich, March 1990, and Annuario Italiano di Statistica, Rome, 1989, Table 16.18.

[g] Average figures are unweighted averages of all countries.

households are a likely explanation for the small size of this market. Guiso, Jappelli and Terlizzese (1991) report that in Italy, the spread between borrowing and lending rates for personal loans and the down payment for purchases of durables is comparatively high. An alternative explanation for the low level of consumer credit is that Italian households have a low propensity to borrow, either because their demographic characteristics and earnings differ from those of other OECD households or simply because they are thrifty. However, simulations by Jappelli and Pagano (1989) suggest that the earnings profiles and age structure of the population fail to explain what is it that induces Italian households to borrow less than their OECD counterparts.

In countries with deep consumer credit markets, many households finance the purchase of durable goods by borrowing. An indirect indicator of the potential impact of borrowing constraints on consumption expenditures is provided in Table 2 (column 2), where we report the ratio of outlays on durables to total consumption expenditure. This ratio is no lower in Italy than in most OECD countries. Thus, if borrowing constraints exist in Italy, they do not prevent households from acquiring durable goods. But clearly, if credit finances only a very small share of consumption, most durables will be purchased by drawing on accumulated saving rather than borrowing.

Regulation plays an important role in mortgage markets. By law, the minimum down payment for first-time buyers is 25 per cent of the value of the house. In practice, however, the required down payment is 50 per cent, as opposed to 20 per cent in the U.S. and Canada, 15 per cent in the U.K., and 20 per cent in Finland and Sweden (Table 2, column 4). Short maturities place an additional burden on Italian households. The typical mortgage maturity in Italy ranges from 10 to 15 years, as opposed to 25 years in Canada, 28 years in the U.S., 25 to 30 years in Japan, and 15 years in France; cf. Lomax (1991).[7] In the U.S., Sweden, Canada and the U.K., loan applications are processed rapidly because specialized credit reference agencies provide information on the credit histories of borrowers; cf. Pagano and Jappelli (1991). Such agencies did not begin operating in Italy until 1990, so the problems associated with asymmetric information between lenders and borrowers are likely to be more severe and the cost of processing loans higher than in other countries.[8]

---

[7] In almost all European countries there is direct government involvement in the provision of mortgage loans, either directly or through the tax system; cf. Boleat (1987). In Italy, by contrast, government intervention in housing finance is very limited and government incentives have been reduced over the years; cf. Guiso, Jappelli and Terlizzese (1991).

[8] In January 1991 the spread between the variable mortgage interest rate and the 3-month inter-bank rate was 0.5 per cent in Germany, 1 in the U.S., 1.5 in the U.K., 2 in Japan and France; see Lomax (1991). In Italy it was 2.5 per cent.

Because of high down payments, high interest rate spreads and low maturities, it is not surprising that the Italian mortgage market is one of the smallest in the OECD. However, mortgage market imperfections have not prevented Italian households from becoming homeowners. The small size of the mortgage market cannot be attributed to a low percentage of owner-occupation, which is actually higher in Italy than in several OECD countries (Table 2, column 5). But since the mortgage market is small and the percentage of owner occupation high, many households borrow either very little or not at all in order to acquire their homes.

Column 6 of Table 2 indicates that the average Italian buys less private insurance than the average citizen of any other OECD country reported in the Table. In Italy insurance premiums as a percentage of GDP are 2.4 per cent, a figure between one half and one third that of any other major OECD country. This is largely attributable to regulation, which places strict barriers to entry on firms and strong restrictions on the types of contracts that individuals may buy. Premiums are set by a regulatory agency and strictly enforced. Although some progress towards liberalization has been made in recent years, regulation is considerably tighter than in any other major European country.[9]

Informal financial arrangements may serve as a form of insurance against risk. A similar argument applies in the case of credit markets, i.e., affluent parents may relieve the borrowing constraints of their children. The fact that Italians buy so little insurance and borrow so little may merely indicate that informal markets cover all types of risks and needs efficiently and at a low social cost; a network of informal markets may therefore overcome credit and insurance market imperfections. To be effective, transfers have to be timed correctly. They have to occur when they are most needed, i.e., in emergencies or when credit constraints are binding. Bequests are very unlikely to serve these purposes. Gifts or loans have to occur inter vivos.

However, all surveys of Italian households indicate that private transfers are not widespread. In a typical cross section, not more than 2 or 3 per cent of households report that they have received either gifts or loans from relatives and friends during the previous years. This contrasts with the U.S. (the only country where private transfers have received wide attention),

---

[9] Efficient social insurance programs may substitute for private health and life insurance. In principle, the government may provide the most efficient form of insurance because it has the largest pool of applicants. Guiso, Jappelli and Terlizzese (1991) report evidence showing that: (i) if anything, public coverage of most risks in Italy is lower than in the G7; (ii) the increase in public insurance has not been greater in Italy than in other countries; (iii) private insurance markets were small even before the public provision of insurance started to expand. They conclude that the role of the government cannot explain why Italian private insurance markets are so thin.

where more than 10 per cent of households report receiving transfers during a one-year period; see Cox (1990). Guiso and Jappelli (1991) report that in Italy some of these transfers are directed towards liquidity-constrained households. This finding is consistent with the hypothesis that informal markets help remove borrowing constraints. But such transfers are not widespread, and most households remain liquidity-constrained even after private transfers have been made.[10]

To sum up, Italian capital markets are significantly at variance with the paradigm of perfect capital markets that is required by rational consumers to smooth income fluctuation and acquire durable goods and homes without distorting the consumption profile. The markets for household credit and insurance are much less developed than those of other OECD countries at a comparable stage of economic development. Regulation, transaction costs and informational asymmetries are the likely reasons for these market failures.[11]

IV. Bequests and Earnings Profiles

One objection to our analysis is that the age-earnings profile may be flatter in Italy than in other countries. The life-cycle model suggests that in an economy with a flat earnings profile, the young save relatively more (or borrow less) than in economies where resources are more concentrated later in life. For any given growth rate, the resulting saving rate is higher than in an economy with a steep earnings profile. Data on earnings profiles in Italy, the U.S. and Japan — three countries with considerably different saving–growth experience — do not support this hypothesis (Table 3). The Italian cross-section profile is similar to the American, but flatter than the Japanese. Once we correct the cross-section profiles for the effect of productivity growth, it appears that the U.S. profile is the flattest, i.e., closest to that implied by the stylized version of the life-cycle model. In Italy, instead, households have been confronted with a relatively steep earnings profile, and even more so in Japan. Due to this, the saving rate should be highest in the U.S., followed by Italy and Japan, contrary to what has been observed.

A second possible objection is that Italians save because they have a strong bequest motive. If households pass on a fraction of their lifetime

---

[10] Some transfers are large and are likely to be made on "special" occasions, such as marriage and the purchase of a home. We return to this issue in Section V.

[11] A complementary explanation for the failure of credit markets· is that the costs of enforcing contracts and disposing of collateral are substantial. In Italy it takes an average of 4 years to repossess a house in case of mortgage foreclosure, as opposed to one year or less in the U.K., the U.S. and the Nordic countries (Source: Italian Bankers Association).

Table 3. *Earning profiles in Italy, the U.S. and Japan (age group 40–49 = 100)*

Age	Cross-section profiles[a]			Profiles adjusted for productivity growth[b]		
	Italy (1)	U.S. (2)	Japan (3)	Italy (4)	U.S. (5)	Japan (6)
20–29	65	65	32	30	50	11
30–39	87	92	79	59	81	47
40–49	100	100	100	100	100	100
50–59	83	85	104	97	97	174
60–69	25	42	45	54	54	126

[a] Sources: Italy: 1989 Survey of Household Income and Wealth. United States and Japan: Hayashi (1986, Table 3, p. 170). Data for Japan refer to 1980; data for the U.S. to 1972–73.
[b] The adjustment for the cohort effect is the average annual rate of growth of GNP per employed worker between 1960 and 1988, i.e., 3.9 per cent in Italy, 1.3 per cent in the United States and 5.3 per cent in Japan.

resources to future generations, an increase in the growth leads to higher aggregate saving; in this sense saving is an increasing function of the strength of the bequest motive. There is little direct evidence concerning the role of bequests in Italy. The specific importance of intergenerational transfers in the form of housing was studied by Barca, Cannari and Guiso (1991), who found that bequeathed wealth in 1987 accounted for 20–30 per cent of aggregate wealth, a value that is not high if compared with the share of inherited wealth in the U.S.; see, for instance, Kotlikoff and Summers (1988).[12]

Indirect information on the potential role of intergenerational transfers can be inferred from age–wealth profiles in Italy, the U.S. and Japan. The pattern of wealth decumulation, shown in Table 4, does not indicate that Italians have a particularly strong bequest motive. If anything, the Italian profile points to the presence of more wealth decumulation by the elderly than in the other two countries and is much more hump-shaped than in Japan, where bequests are thought to be very important.[13]

---

[12] This estimate is based on direct information relating to the years in which real estate was inherited and does not include financial wealth.
[13] The Japanese age–wealth profile is affected by the tendency of the elderly to merge with younger households. Wealth decumulation is more evident if one isolates nuclear families, which make up 50 per cent of Japanese households; see Hayashi (1986). The Italian and U.S. profiles would be more similar if extended families were more widespread in the U.S. But the proportion of individuals over 60 living with younger households is 5 per cent in Italy and only 3 per cent in the U.S.

Table 4. *Wealth profiles in Italy, the U.S. and Japan (age group 56–65 = 100)*

Age	Cross-section profiles[a]			Profiles adjusted for productivity growth[b]		
	Italy (1)	U.S. (2)	Japan (3)	Italy (4)	U.S. (5)	Japan (6)
<25	26	20	11	6	12	2
26–35	41	52	41	13	35	9
36–45	75	87	81	35	67	29
46–55	99	89	94	68	78	56
56–65	100	100	100	100	100	100
66–69	63	74	99	82	81	122
70–74	62	73	98	102	86	136
75–79	45	86	65	86	107	104
>80	31	40	74	67	52	134
Amount[c]	154	86	17	599	136	106

[a] Sources: Italy: 1989 Survey of Household Income and Wealth. United States: 1979 Household Pension Survey, Ando and Kennickell (1987, Table 7.1, p. 163, line NW79). Japan: 1979 National Survey of Family Expenditure, Ando and Kennickell (1987, Table 7.9B, line ARM, p. 195).
[b] The adjustment for the cohort effect is the average annual rate of growth of GNP per employed worker between 1960 and 1988, i.e., 3.9 per cent in Italy, 1.3 per cent in the United States and 5.3 per cent in Japan. In each case we assume that the average age for individuals in the first age-group is 20.
[c] Wealth is the sum of real and financial wealth, net of liabilities. The last row of the table indicates the values of net worth in the age class 56–64. For Italy this number is in millions of 1987 lire, for the United States in thousands of 1979 dollars, for Japan in millions of 1979 yen.

More formal analyses exist of the pattern of wealth decumulation. King and Dicks-Mireaux (1982) found that in Canada, the rate of wealth decumulation between the ages 65 and 85 ranges from 0.7 to 1.5 per cent per year. In the U.S., Hurd (1987) found a rate of decumulation of 1.5 per cent, and Hubbard (1986) found even lower values. On the other hand, Brugiavini (1987) found that the rate of wealth decumulation in Italy ranges from 1.5 to 8 per cent, according to the model specification. Both the (limited) direct information on bequests, and the indirect evidence from patterns of wealth decumulation by the elderly suggest that a strong bequest motive is not a valid explanation of the high Italian saving rate.

V. The Effect of Liquidity Constraints of Consumption

We now summarize some recent empirical evidence concerning the effect of borrowing constraints on consumption. According to the permanent income hypothesis with rational expectations, in the absence of liquidity constraints, consumption growth should not correlate with lagged disposable income or anticipated income growth.

Using aggregate annual data, Guiso, Jappelli and Terlizzese (1991) regress the growth rate of consumption on the expected growth rate of disposable income using a specification and estimation method similar to those adopted by Campbell and Mankiw (1991) for six OECD countries. The size of the excess sensitivity parameter is consistent with the hypothesis that borrowing constraints induce the failure of the Euler equation for consumption. In fact, when the results of four recent studies are combined, it appears that excess sensitivity is highest in Italy and France, reaches intermediate values in the U.K. and Japan, is low in Canada and the U.S., and lowest in Sweden and Denmark.[14] The ranking, which is also confirmed by panel data estimates, correlates negatively with the size of the consumer credit market (Table 2, column 1), which can be regarded as an indicator of the availability of credit, and is consistent with the hypothesis that liquidity constraints are more severe in Italy than elsewhere.[15]

The discussion in Section III implies that mortgage market imperfections may force households to save when young in order to finance the purchase of homes. With perfect markets, by contrast, households would borrow early in life, and repay the loan over a long horizon which is, in principle, their entire life. Figure 1 plots the incidence of owner-occupied dwellings by age groups. The proportion of owner-occupation increases slowly with age, and reaches a peak before retirement. The majority of Italian households own their first house in their late thirties or forties. This pattern contrasts sharply with the experience of other countries: the average of U.S. and U.K. first-time buyers was 28 and 29, in 1985, while it was 41 in Italy in 1988.

Even if the pattern of Figure 1 is consistent with the hypothesis that mortgage market imperfections distort households' optimal consumption

---

[14] See Jappelli and Pagano (1989), Giavazzi and Pagano (1990), Campbell and Mankiw (1991) and Guiso, Jappelli and Terlizzese (1991). The sample periods of the estimates are 1954–88 for Italy, 1972–88 for France, 1957–88 for the U.K., 1972–88 for Canada, 1953–85 for the U.S., 1972–88 for Sweden and 1966–87 for Denmark.

[15] If households wish to borrow but have no access to credit markets, an increase in disposable income increases current consumption with respect to future consumption, thus reducing consumption growth. In fact, in the two-year panel of the 1989 Survey of Household Income and Wealth, Guiso, Jappelli and Terlizzese (1991) found that the income coefficient is negative (-0.17) and significantly different from zero when regressed on consumption growth. The coefficient is larger (in absolute value) than that found in other countries. Zeldes (1989), using the PSID, estimated a coefficient that varied between -0.021 and -0.081, depending on the sample split; Hayashi (1986) found values ranging from -0.041 to -0.13 using Japanese (pseudo) panel data.

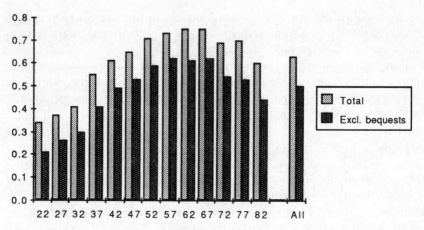

Fig. 1. Home ownership ratio by age-group in 1989 (age groups identified by average ages).

profile, one cannot rule out the possibility that intergenerational transfers in the form of housing eliminate the need for an organized mortgage market. If young households expect to receive a house as a bequest, they may choose to rent, rather than buy, while waiting to receive the bequest. This strategy avoids the need to save large amounts to meet high down payments.[16]

However, expected bequests are likely to affect the behavior of only a small section of the population, as shown in Figure 1, where we plot the proportion of owner-occupation excluding households that received their house as a gift or bequest. We note that: (i) only 13 per cent of the sample (22 per cent of homeowners) received their house as a bequest; (ii) the total sample profile and that of buyers are very similar, i.e., the timing of bequests does not affect the overall pattern of housing tenure.

To assess the impact of mortgage market imperfections on consumption, Guiso, Jappelli and Terlizzese (1991) used a strategy similar to that adopted by Hayashi (1985) and Zeldes (1989), and evaluated how much renters would consume if they were not subject to mortgage market constraints. They assumed that homeowners are not constrained in the mortgage market, estimated their desired consumption and used the estimated coefficients to predict the desired consumption of renters. With either formal or informal perfect markets, the gap between desired and actual consumption of renters should be zero. A positive gap can be

---

[16] The pattern of owner-occupation by age shown in Figure 1 may in fact be consistent with the choices of a large group of households that expect to receive a bequest around the age of 40.

interpreted as a symptom of fast accumulation of resources by renters in order to meet high down payments. Using data from the 1989 Bank of Italy Survey of Household Income and Wealth, renters are found to save 15 per cent more of their permanent income than if they obeyed the same consumption rule as owners. In the sample, removing borrowing constraints would reduce saving by 2 or 3 per cent of permanent income, depending on the model specification.

VI. Precautionary Saving

Since insurance markets in Italy are far less developed than in the other OECD countries, Italian households can be expected to engage in substantial precautionary saving. Ideally, we would like to test for the effect of a particular risk that is less insured in Italy than in other countries, such as health risk. The main problems are that health risk is difficult to measure, and that there is almost no evidence on the empirical relevance of health risk in any country.

Most studies that have confronted the issue of precautionary saving have limited the focus on earnings uncertainty, which is only one risk that households face and perhaps not even the most important one. The 1989 Italian Survey of Household Income and Wealth included questions about the subjective probabilty distribution of earnings in 1990. On average, the standard deviation of earnings is only 2 per cent of permanent earnings. Guiso, Jappelli and Terlizzese (1992) estimate a consumption function using this self-reported measure of uncertainty and find that earnings uncertainty raises saving and wealth accumulation. At sample means, however, precautionary saving is a modest 0.14 per cent of permanent income and the share of precautionary wealth in total wealth is only 1.8 per cent. These results suggest that earnings uncertainty, alone, does not explain the high Italian saving rate. However, they do not rule out the possibility that other risks, such as health risk, are important determinants of saving. At the moment, one can only speculate that these risks generate higher saving in Italy than in other countries.

VII. Conclusions

We have argued that capital market imperfections are the likely explanation for the high Italian saving rate and for its recent sharper decline. Italian credit and insurance markets are considerably thinner than those of other comparably developed countries. Credit finances a trivial share of household consumption and investment, and Italians buy very little insurance. The family does have a role in overcoming credit market imperfections, but a limited one. The role of the government in providing insurance against risks does not appear any more important in Italy than in other OECD countries. Wealth decumulation by the elderly is actually greater in Italy than in Japan or the United States, implying that Italians do not have a particularly strong bequest motive. The evidence suggests that Italians are not "different" in any major respect from other OECD citizens; rather, Italian capital markets are different.

The approach taken in this study may prove useful in the analysis of inter-country differences in saving rates. Previous literature, e.g., Modigliani (1990), has focused mainly on the role of productivity growth, demographic variables and fiscal policy to explain cross-country differences in saving rates but rarely explored the role of capital market imperfections. The international evidence in Table 2 suggests that the high degree of development of credit and mortgage markets in Finland, Norway and Sweden may be responsible for their relatively low saving rates. Similarly, as also shown by Hayashi, Ito and Slemrod (1988), mortgage market imperfections may partly explain the high Japanese saving rate. This country-study evidence is validated by Jappelli and Pagano (1991), who find that indicators of capital market imperfections, such as minimum down-payment ratios and the volume of consumer credit, are important determinants of the inter-country differences in OECD saving rates.

This study also has implications for the effect of European financial integration on the evolution of the Italian saving rate. In 1992 minimum down payments will be lowered to 25 per cent for all mortgages, restrictions on maturities will be abolished, legal costs reduced, and second mortgages introduced. These changes will sharpen competition among lenders, and cedit terms for consumers will improve accordingly. Financial deregulation will thus stimulate the convergence of the Italian saving rate towards those of the other major industrial countries.

References

Ando, A. & Kennickell, S.: How much (or little) life cycle is there in micro data? In R. Dornbusch, S. Fischer & S. Bosson (eds.), *Macroeconomics and Finance. Essays in Honor of Franco Modigliani*, MIT Press, Cambridge, 1987.

Barca, F., Cannari, L. & Guiso, L.: Bequests and saving for retirement. What impels the accumulation of wealth? Mimeo, Bank of Italy, Rome, 1991.

Barro, R.: Are government bonds net wealth? *Journal of Political Economy 81*, 1095–117, 1974.

Boleat, M.: *National Housing Systems: A Comparative Study*. Croom Helm, London, 1987.

Brugiavini, A.: Empirical evidence on wealth accumulation and the effects of pension wealth: An application to Italian cross-section data. Financial Markets Group, DP No. 20, London School of Economics, 1987.

Campbell, J. Y. & Mankiw, G. N.: The response of consumption to income: A cross-country investigation. *European Economic Review 35*, 723–56, 1991.

Dean, A., Durand, M., Fallon, J. & Hoeller, P.: Saving trends and behavior in OECD countries. *OECD Economic Studies,* 7–58, Spring 1990.

Giavazzi, F. & Pagano, M.: Can severe contractions by expansionary? Tales of two small European countries. *NBER Macroeconomics Annual,* MIT Press, Cambridge, 1990.

Guiso, L. & Jappelli, T.: Intergenerational transfers and capital market imperfections. Evidence from an Italian cross-section. *European Economic Review 35,* 103–20, 1991.

Guiso, L., Jappelli, T. & Terlizzese, D.: Why is Italy's saving rate so high? CEPR DP No. 572, 1991.

Guiso, L., Jappelli, T. & Terlizzese, D.: Earnings uncertainty and precautionary saving. CEPR DP, forthcoming, 1992.

Hayashi, F.: The effect of liquidity constraints on consumption: A cross-sectional analysis. *Quarterly Journal of Economics 100,* 183–206, 1985.

Hayashi, F.: Why is Japan's saving rate so apparently high? *NBER Macroeconomics Annual,* MIT Press, Cambridge, 1986.

Hayashi, F., Ito, T. & Slemrod, J.: Housing finance imperfections, taxation and private saving. A comparative simulation analysis of the United States and Japan. *Journal of the Japanese and International Economies 2,* 215–38, 1988.

Hurd, M. D.: Savings of the elderly and desired bequests. *American Economic Review 77,* 298–312, 1987.

Jappelli, T. & Pagano, M.: Consumption and capital market imperfections: An international comparison. *American Economic Review 79,* 1088–105, 1989.

Jappelli, T. & Pagano, M.: Saving, growth and liquidity constraints. CEPR DP, Dec. 1991.

King, M. & Dicks Mireaux, L.: Asset holdings and the life-cycle. *Economic Journal 92,* 247–67, 1982.

Kotlikoff, L. J. & Summers, L.: The contribution of intergenerational transfers to total wealth. In D. Kessler & A. Masson (eds.), *Modelling the Accumulation and Distribution of Wealth,* Oxford Unversity Press, New York, 1988.

Lomax, J.: Housing finance — an international perspective. *Bank of England Quarterly Bulletin,* 56–64, Feb. 1991.

Modigliani, F.: Recent developments in saving rates: A life-cycle perspective. Frisch Lecture, 6th World Congress of the Econometric Society, Barcelona, 1990.

Modigliani, F. & Jappelli, T.: Fiscal policy and saving in Italy since 1860. In M. Boskin, J. Flemming & S. Gorini (eds.), *Private Saving and Public Debt,* Basil Blackwell, London, 1987.

Pagano, M. & Jappelli, T.: Information sharing in credit markets. CEPR DP No. 579, 1991.

Zeldes, S.: Consumption and liquidity constraints: An empirical investigation. *Journal of Political Economy 97,* 305–46, 1989.

Inflation, Capital Markets and Household Saving in the Nordic Countries*

Erkki Koskela

University of Helsinki, Finland

Matti Virén

University of Turku, Finland

Abstract

Household saving ratios in the Nordic countries are very low by international standards and have declined markedly during the 1980s. Aggregate quarterly time-series data for the period 1970–89 are used to study the development of household saving behavior over time. The evidence suggests that the household saving ratio responds positively to both the inflation rate and real income growth. There is also some weak evidence to support the view that the rate of change in real housing prices has a negative effect on household saving ratios.

I. Introduction

Household saving ratios in the Nordic countries have two distinctive features. First, by international standards, the Nordic countries are "low" savers and second, household saving ratios have declined markedly during the 1980s. As regards first feature, the standard approach has been to use the life cycle hypothesis of saving (LCH) to explain cross-country differences in average household saving ratios. Early tests of the LCH — using data from the 1950s — to account for inter-country differences in average private and household saving ratios were successful, but tests using more recent data from the 1970s and 1980s have been less so; see e.g. Koskela and Virén (1989). While the reasons for the mixed and relatively poor performance of the LCH in the context of cross-country data may be

*This paper was written while both authors worked at the Bank of Finland. Financial support from the Yrjö Jahnsson Foundation and the Nordic Economic Research Council is gratefully acknowledged. We are indebted to Marco Pagano and two anonymous referees for helpful comments on an earlier version of the paper.

debatable and may include measurement problems, different accounting practices etc., the underlying assumptions should also be questioned.

Standard formulations of the LCH abstract from potential capital market imperfections and taxes. With perfect capital markets, households can dissave and borrow within the bounds of solvency at the same interest rates at which they can save and lend. For various reasons, however, borrowers may be subject to binding borrowing constraints. Casual observation suggests that liquidity constraints are a fact of life for many households. As for taxes, their level and structure differ widely across countries and it can be argued that they affect incentives to borrow and save, and thereby household saving ratios.

Turning to the development of household saving ratios over time, the "low" Nordic household saving rates have declined markedly during the 1980s, to the point where the household saving ratio as defined by national accounts has occasionally turned negative in Denmark, Finland, Sweden and Norway. This change in saving behavior in the Nordic countries occurred simultaneously with the liberalization of financial markets see Lehmussaari (1990b) for a description.[1] Therefore, it seems natural to try to associate the change in saving behavior with financial market liberalization. This conclusion may be premature, however. Other variables such as the inflation rate, the real income growth rate and interest rates also changed and may be able to account for changes in saving behavior.

Financial market liberalization was associated with rising housing prices and housing wealth in the Nordic countries. More generally it could be argued that windfall gains (losses) in housing prices cause declines (upturns) in household saving. One objection to this explanation is that a shift in the relative price of housing need not affect aggregate saving. Any relative price increase implies that some gain (those selling the good), while others lose (those buying the good). Anyway, this suggests that it might be useful to analyze household saving behavior and housing within a unified framework.

The purpose of this analyis is to study household saving behavior using aggregate quarterly time-series data from Denmark, Finland, Norway and Sweden for the period 1970–89. After looking briefly at the issue of why household saving ratios are comparatively "low" in the Nordic countries, the empirical part of the paper focuses on time-series evidence on the development of household saving ratios. We begin by estimating the kind of household saving functions which were reasonably successful in the 1960s and 1970s in order to see how well the "old" specifications work under

---

[1] Muellbauer and Murphy (1989) have argued that the decline in the U.K. saving ratio since 1980 is attributable to liberalization of financial markets.

somewhat different economic conditions and institutional circumstances. We then move on to account for the interaction between household saving and housing markets, and for the potential role of interest rates and taxes.

The paper proceeds as follows. A framework for empirical analysis is presented in Section II, starting from a basic saving function and extending it to allow for the housing market, interest rates and taxation. In Section III we introduce the data to be used, briefly discuss the issue of the level of household saving, and then concentrate on time-series analysis of household saving behavior in the Nordic countries.

II. Household Saving: Framework for Empirical Analysis

During the 1970s and early 1980s a considerable amount of effort was devoted to analyzing the relationship between inflation and household consumption and saving behavior. It was observed that high rates of inflation tended to be associated with high rates of personal savings in OECD countries. As usual in economics, numerous hypotheses were proposed to explain this phenomenon. One explanation was put forward by Deaton (1977). According to his misperception hypothesis, households may not have sufficient information to distinguish between relative and general price movements. If so, unanticipated inflation is misinterpreted as the rise in relative prices of goods which households currently buy, so that real saving increases. If one is prepared to assume constant income and inflation expectations, then one ends up with the following basic specification:

$$s_t = a_0 + a_1 s_{t-1} + a_2 y_t + a_3 p_t + u_t \qquad (1)$$

where s is the households' saving ratio, y the real income growth rate, p the inflation rate and u the error term. One may expect a_1, a_2, a_3 to be between zero and one, so that the savings ratio adjusts partially and "surprises" in inflation and real income will affect the saving ratio positively.

The observed relationship may largely be a statistical mirage, however. This is basically because income, as measured in national accounts, includes interest payments on financial assets, which do not really constitute income at all during inflation. Thus measured savings, i.e., the difference between measured income and consumption, tend to rise with inflation. In the empirical section we briefly consider the question of the proper interpretation of inflation.

Earlier we noted that financial market liberalization was associated with rising housing prices in the Nordic countries. Since housing wealth is widely distributed across the population and comprises the most important form of wealth for many households it is important to analyze interactions between saving behavior and housing. Elsehwere, we have developed a simple three-period model to illustrate the potential interaction between saving, capital markets, interest rates, the relative price of housing and inflation; see Koskela and Virén (1991). The qualitative features of the model can be briefly characterized as follows. One result is that the household saving ratio is positively associated with the binding down-payment ratio. This is important at least for two reasons. First, countries seem to differ in terms of down-payment ratios. Japan and Italy, for example, have high down-payment ratios; see Boleat (1987). These countries also happen to be "high" savers. Second, an aspect of financial market liberalization was that housing loans could be obtained at lower down-payment ratios than earlier. This is consistent with the negative relationship between saving and increased liberalization. According to the model, it can be shown, that the higher price of owner-occupied housing, the higher the saving of those households that plan to purchase. On the other hand, the future selling price (the expected capital gains from housing) affects neither consumption nor saving, but in the case of nonbinding down-payment requirements, the future selling price can be shown to have a negative saving effect. Another feature of the model is that the interest rate effect can be decomposed into offsetting substitution and income effects, leaving the total effect ambiguous *a priori*.

Earlier considerations suggest that in addition to the usual variables, the down-payment ratio, the relative price of housing and the real (or nominal) interest rate might affect household saving behavior.[2] It is here that taxation might play its role, mainly due to the deductibility of interest rate expenses in taxation. Unfortunately we do not have time-series data on down-payment ratios, so that we write the augmented specification for the household savings ratio s as follows

$$s_t = a_0 + a_1 s_{t-1} + a_2 y_t + a_3 p_t + a_4 ph_t + a_5 i_t + a_6 T_t + u_t, \tag{2}$$

where ph = the rate of change in the real housing price, i = the nominal interest rate, and T is the (average) marginal income tax rate. In the specification one may expect that $a_4 < 0$ if capital gains dominate capital losses, while a_5 and a_6 are ambiguous. If the (average) marginal income tax rate affects saving only via the tax deductibility of interest rate expenses, then the two last terms collapse to $a_5(1 - T_t)i_t$ and $a_5 > 0$. There is no reason, however, to suppose that tax deductibility is the only channel of influence of T_t.

---

[2] Wilcox (1989) has argued that the nominal interest rate may matter. As the nominal interest rate increases liquidity constraints, both bind previously constrained households more tightly and raise the number of constrained households. To the extent that financial institutions follow a practice of restricting borrowing so as to keep prevailing payment-to-current income ratios below some ceiling level, then a rise in nominal interest rates tends to increase liquidity constraints.

III. Empirical Results

Some Descriptive Statistics

Before turning to the empirical analyses with time-series data, it is useful to outline some descriptive data for the four Nordic countries under consideration in terms of household saving behavior and some of their likely main long-term determinants. Households' net saving rates for these countries are displayed in Figure 1 (along with housing prices). As noted earlier, there are two obvious facts regarding these saving rates: first, the overall level is rather "low" in an international perspective and second, they exhibited a dramatic fall towards the end of the 1980s. In fact, negative saving rates can occasionally be discerned in all of the sample countries.

We begin by presenting some aggregate data over the period 1985–1989 for the four Nordic countries and the rest of the OECD in Table 1. The table suggests that, except for Norway, the "growth rate effect" — so celebrated in the seminal formulation of the LCH — does not provide much help in explaining the "low" saving ratios in the Nordic countries. However, for most of the other variables, there is a rather clear difference between the Nordic countries and the rest of the OECD. This is true for the size of the public sector, social security expenditures, population aged 65 and over as a percentage of the total population and current transfers as a fraction of GDP. The Nordic countries are characterized by a high ratio of elderly people, and high social security expenditures and transfers, which should have a negative effect on the household saving ratio. The insurance role of the government seems to be larger in the Nordic countries. Finland, however, appears to be an exception; its values are rather close to the OECD averages, although the saving ratios in Finland and the rest of OECD differ dramatically. Moreover, the size of consumer credit markets in the Nordic countries seems to exceed the OECD average. This conforms with the view that Nordic capital markets are more developed than those of other OECD countries.

It can be argued that under income uncertainty, borrowing constrains and other capital market imperfections tend to increase saving, *ceteris paribus*; see Deaton (1991). Thus earlier observations suggest that very low saving rates in the Nrdic countries may reflect the absence of borrowing constraints or other capital market imperfections and the large insurance role of government.

A way to evaluate whether the low saving rates reflect the absence of capital market imperfections is to estimate the Euler equations suggested by Campbell and Mankiw (1990) and to test for a significance of the income term. The estimating equation is $\Delta c_t = \alpha + \lambda \Delta y_t + u_t$. The size of the

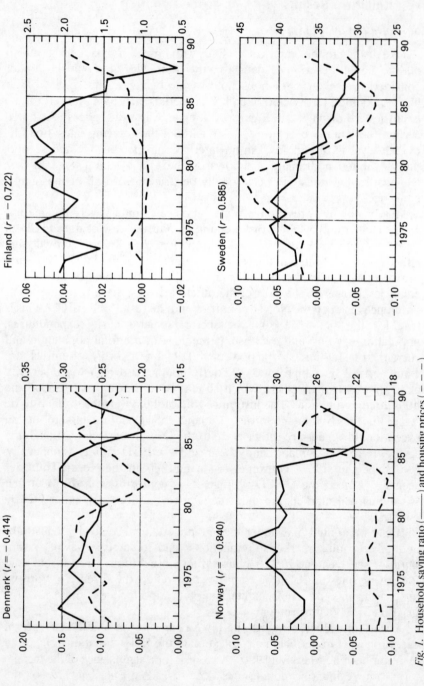

Fig. 1. Household saving ratio (———) and housing prices (– – –).

Table 1. *Some descriptive data for the Nordic countries*

	s	b	Δc	r	DEP	RET	SOS	Δy	tr	G
Denmark	0.7	37	1.4	6.8	18.1	15.2	27.7	2.5	18.7	57.2
Finland	1.2	39	4.3	4.3	19.4	12.7	21.9	3.7	12.9	40.3
Norway	−3.8	48	1.9	6.7	19.7	16.0	29.9	0.7	17.4	54.4
Sweden	−3.5	39	3.1	5.9	18.0	17.5	29.5	2.7	20.7	60.6
Rest of OECD	11.8	14	3.5	5.1	19.8	12.9	19.2	3.2	13.5	36.5

Notes: The figures are percentage sample averages for the period 1985–1989 (except for RET, DEP, SOS and G which are derived from the period 1984–88). s = households' net saving rate, r = the (*ex post*) real interest rate, DEP(RET) = population aged 0–15 (65 and over) as percentage of total population, SOS = social security expenditure as percentage of GDP, tr = general government current transfers (excl. subsidies)/GDP, and G = total government receipts as percentage of GDP, Δc = rate of growth of private consumption and Δy = rate of growth of households' real disposable income. Rest of OECD denotes unweighted average for 14 OECD countries not including the Nordic countries. In the case of Δc, Δy, and G, however, it denotes total OECD. b = consumer credit as percentage of consumer spending in 1988. Sources: Giavazzi and Pagano (1990) and Guiso, Jappelli and Terlizzese (1991).

income coefficient can be interpreted as the fraction of constrained consumers (or so-called "rule-of-thumb" consumers). The Instrumental Variable (IV) estimation results for the coefficient λ are: Denmark −0.019 (0.09), Finland 0.272 (0.97), Norway −0.023 (0.03) and Sweden −0.006 (0.07), where numbers in parentheses are t-ratios.[3]

The results are to a large extent consistent with the hypothesis that low saving rates reflect the absence of borrowing constraints; the estimates of λ are indeed rather low for Denmark, Norway and Sweden, and perhaps also for Finland; see e.g. Campbell and Mankiw (1990) and Jappelli and Pagano (1989) for international evidence. Thus, it may be concluded that the informal evidence on the insurance role of government and on the extent of consumer credit markets, as well as the estimates of the excess sensitivity parameter λ, go a long way in providing an explanation for the low saving ratios in the Nordic countries.

Inflation, Housing Prices and Saving Ratio: Nordic Countries

We continue the empirical analysis by estimating the household saving function specification (2) without the interest rate and tax factors for Denmark, Finland, Norway and Sweden for the period

---

[3] The instruments included were Δy_{t-1}, Δy_{t-2}, Δc_{t-1}, Δc_{t-2}, Δi_{t-1}, Δi_{t-2}. The sample period was 1971Q2–1989Q4.

1971Q2–1989Q4.[4] In the first place, we are interested in the performance of the "old specification" (1), given the changes in institutions and economic conditions which have taken place in these countries during the 1980s. The equations were first estimated by OLS, but the OLS estimator turned out to be inefficient. Thus, estimation was then carried out using the SUR estimator; the results are reported in Table 2.

The results indicate that the basic (i.e., Deaton's) saving function specification (1) performs rather well. The explanatory power of the estimated equations is fairly good for all countries, the coefficients have the expected sign in all cases and, moreover, they are estimated rather precisely. According to the estimation results, both income growth and inflation tend to increase household saving.[5]

As far as housing prices are concerned, the evidence is somewhat mixed. This might be expected given the difference among countries in the way housing prices have behaved during the sample period. These differences can be seen in Figure 1 which shows both household saving ratios and real housing prices are graphed. These differences show up in the estimation results. Although the housing price effect is systematically negative if the inflation variable is not allowed to enter the equation, the more general specification which includes both the inflation rate and the rate of change in real housing prices does not imply a significant negative housing price effect for all four countries. In fact, such an effect can be discerned only for Finland and Norway.

An obvious problem with real housing prices is their potential endogeneity in terms of the household savings ratio. We studied this possibility by calculating the cross-correlation functions between the household saving ratios and the rate of change in real housing prices for all four

---

[4] The data were constructed for Denmark, Finland, Norway and Sweden. The sample period is 1970Q1–1989Q4. In the case of Denmark, however, the sample period is 1971Q1–1989Q4. The data (with the exception of the interest rate variables and the demographic variables) are seasonally adjusted. The data were obtained mainly from the respective central banks. In the case of Sweden, however, the main data source was OECD Quarterly National Accounts. The demographic data are derived from OECD Labor Force Statistics.

[5] In order to evaluate stability of the saving functions, we calculated the Chow-test statistics for all the equations in Table 3, when these were estimated by OLS. With the exception of Norway, the null hypothesis that the parameters are stable across the estimation period could be rejected at the 5 per cent significance level. Lehmussaari (1990a) has examined household saving dynamics using annual data for the period 1971–85. He concluded that, with the exception of Sweden, structural changes have occurred for the other three countries in connection with the introduction of financial market deregulation. Later research based on qaarterly data and taking wealth (housing and liquid assets) variables into account has not supported Lehmussaari's results; see the findings of Brodin and Nymoen (1989) for Norway and Berg and Bergström (1991) for Sweden.

Table 2. *SUR estimation results for the Nordic countries*

	D	F	N	S	D	F	N	S	D	F	N	S
Const.	0.017	−0.003	−0.016	0.021	0.031	0.002	0.002	−0.002	0.018	−0.001	−0.014	−0.023
	(2.32)	(0.86)	(3.98)	(5.88)	(3.48)	(0.73)	(0.83)	(1.31)	(2.30)	(0.37)	(3.60)	(5.40)
y	0.644	0.451	0.427	0.978	0.576	0.461	0.423	0.917	0.641	0.459	0.458	0.977
	(10.21)	(4.38)	(3.88)	(23.80)	(7.86)	(4.59)	(3.57)	(19.88)	(10.16)	(4.62)	(4.34)	(23.72)
p	0.985	0.184	0.832	0.871					1.049	0.166	0.824	0.930
	(5.55)	(1.61)	(4.40)	(5.48)					(5.44)	(1.50)	(4.57)	(5.19)
ph					−0.074	−0.051	−0.138	−0.083	0.056	−0.047	−0.146	0.038
					(1.03)	(2.26)	(2.38)	(1.26)	(0.85)	(2.10)	(2.82)	(0.58)
s_{t-1}	0.672	0.860	0.862	0.871	0.728	0.857	0.856	0.896	0.651	0.846	0.856	0.865
	(11.78)	(13.85)	(22.61)	(23.92)	(9.90)	(14.72)	(21.32)	(22.01)	(10.18)	(13.98)	(23.48)	(23.26)
R^2	0.753	0.749	0.876	0.912	0.659	0.753	0.866	0.883	0.755	0.761	0.888	0.914
100*SEE	1.657	1.059	1.448	1.275	1.946	1.052	1.510	1.473	1.650	1.071	1.379	1.267
D-W	2.220	2.134	2.096	2.482	2.534	2.103	2.397	2.166	2.143	2.174	2.333	2.484
h	1.095	0.690	0.441	2.199	2.999	0.514	1.832	0.770	0.746	0.882	1.517	2.212

$\chi^2_6 = 20.344$ $\chi^2_6 = 19.503$ $\chi^2_6 = 20.755$
$\ln(L') = 878.437$ $\ln(L') = 853.065$ $\ln(L') = 884.059$

Notes: Numbers in parentheses under the estimates are (asymptotic) *t*-ratios. *h* denotes Durbin's *h*-statistic for first-order autocorrelation, χ^2_6 the test statistic for diagonal covariance matrix and $\ln(L')$ the maximized value of the log likelihood function. D = Denmark, F = Finland, N = Norway and S = Sweden.

countries. In all cases, the rate of change in real housing prices led rather than lagged the household saving ratios (the lead was between 2–6 quarters). Although the estimating equations here include the housing price variable, an almost identical result was obtained when this variable was replaced by the housing wealth variable. Only the explanatory power of the equations decreased slightly; the value of the maximized log likelihood function for the whole system of equations is 885.056, slightly less than the corresponding tabulated value for the equation with the housing price variable (i.e., 885.410). When evaluating this result, it should be kept in mind that conventional measures of the housing stock are very trend-like and thus the changes in housing wealth are clearly dominated by fluctuations in housing prices."

Even though the results are relatively good, the coefficient estimate of inflation is rather high for all other countries except Finland, particularly if it is compared with those obtained by Deaton (1977) for the U.S. and the U.K. It should be pointed out, however, that the interpretation of the inflation rate is not fully clear, although our preliminary tests suggest that the hypothesis according to which only unanticipated inflation matters should be regarded as suspect; see Koskela and Virén (1991). The reason for these high inflation rate coefficients is unclear and should be the subject for further research.

Thus far we have abstracted from the interest rate and taxation. Can a significant after-tax or before-tax nominal or real interest rate effect be detected for these countries? Table 3 contains the t-test statistics for the additional interest rate and the (average) marginal income tax rate terms. The coefficients of the interest rate terms could not be estimated very precisely. As far as nominal interest rates are concerned, only in the case of Finland can the hypothesis that the coefficient equals zero be rejected. With real rates, such a conclusion can be drawn at the 5 per cent level only in the case of Sweden, if the inflation rate is not included in the model. The coefficient estimates of the marginal income tax variable (as a single additional explanatory variable) are all positive, but the t-ratios are so low that one cannot really draw any strong conclusions about the role of the (average) marginal income tax rate.

The reason for this lack of uniformity cannot be determined on the basis of the aggregated time-series data. First, mixed results may have to do with measurement and simultaneity problems. It is not easy to ascertain

---

[6] Recently, Brodin and Nymoen (1989) on Norwegian data, Berg and Bergström (1991) on Swedish data and Christensen and Knudsen (1990) on Danish data have emphasized and shown the importance of (housing and financial) wealth variables in tracking household consumption behavior in those countries during the 1980s. Our results conform with both these results and those reported by Muellbauer and Murphy (1989) for the United Kingdom.

Table 3. *An analysis of the effects of interest rates and taxes*

	t tests in different country eqs.			
Additional variables	D	F	N	S
Basic specification containing p				
Nominal interest rate	−0.55	3.23	−0.69	−0.47
Real interest rate	0.49	1.09	−0.31	−1.28
Real after-tax interest rate	1.29	−0.01	−0.07	−1.37
Marginal income tax rate	0.56	0.36	0.29	1.07
Basic specification containing ph				
Nominal interest rate	1.20	2.78	−0.60	−0.13
Real interest rate	0.83	0.01	−0.79	−1.77
Real after-tax interest rate	−0.22	−0.68	−1.03	−2.53
Marginal income tax rate	0.17	0.14	1.36	2.69

Notes: *t*-ratios are based on OLS estimation for the period 1971Q2–1989Q4. The expected rates of inflation for the real interest rates were derived from ARIMA models reported in Koskela and Virén (1991).

the representative rate of return for saving. And although the interest rate may well affect saving, saving shocks can also affect interest rates, for instance via the current account and international capital markets. Second, there is no theoretical presumption about the sign of their correlation. Changes in the real interest rates have both income and substitution effects and can increase or decrease savings depending on the balance between the two. Third, the marginal income tax rate may have an effect both via deductibility of interest rate expenses and via the return on savings. Finally, the age distribution of the population as well as the distribution of financial assets by age group also have to be taken into account. An increase in the rate of return affects not just the return to current saving, but also the return to all stock of testing financial wealth. If a large share of this financial wealth is in the hands of older individuals, then the change in the real rate of return will increase the income of the very people who are likely to spend more. Via this mechanism, the response of the aggregate household saving rate to the real interest rate might be negative; see Sheshinski and Tanzi (1989.[7] Clearly, our findings are in line with an

---

[7] In the case of Finland, it turns out that there are striking differences among the age groups both in terms on their saving, on one hand, and their assets and liabilities, on the other. In particular, younger households were shown to have negative and the elderly positive saving in 1988. To be more precise, the following age profile of saving rates could be derived from Finnish cross-section data for households (the years refer to the age of the "head of household"): 15–24 years, −4 per cent; 25–34 years −2 per cent; 35–44 years −4 per cent; 45–54 years −1 per cent; 55–64 years 12 per cent; and 65 years and over 6 per cent; see Vilmunen and Virén (1991) for further details.

enormous body of research, which has failed to show any clear empirical relationship between interest rates and the saving ratio.[8,9]

IV. Concluding Remarks

As for the issue of why household saving ratios are low in the Nordic countries, the insurance role of government (measured in terms of social security expenditure and current transfers as a fraction of GDP), the extent of consumer credit markets as well as the estimates of the excess sensitivity parameter go a long way in providing an explanation.

Our main focus of interest in the empirical analysis, however, was to explain time-series development of household saving over two decades in the Nordic countries. We started by estimating the kind of household saving functions which were reasonably successful in the 1960s and 1970s in order to see how well the "old" specifications work under different economic conditions and institutional circumstances of the 1980s. While not without problems, the results were relatively good for the specification according to which the saving ratio adjusts partially and responds positively to the inflation rate and which favours including the rate of change in the real housing price as an additional explanatory variable.[10]

This means that falling inflation rates, rising real housing prices (and housing wealth) — associated with financial market liberalization — as well as falling real income growth have contributed to the decline in household saving ratios in the Nordic countries during the 1980s, with some modifications for Sweden. As for the role of the real (or nominal) interest rate and the (average) marginal income tax rate, the results were relatively imprecise and mixed across countries. The reason for this cannot be determined on the basis of the aggregate time-series data.

References

Berg, L. & Bergström, R.: A quarterly consumption function for Sweden 1970–1989. Mimeo, University of Uppsala, 1991.

---

[8] Given declining household saving rates, it might be interesting to see whether the slowly moving time-trend variables could also contribute to the explanation of this behavior. Clearly, the demographic variables DEP and RET — presented in Table 1 — as well as the fraction of self-employed workers in total civilian employment are potential candidates. When these variables were introduced into the specification (2) as additional explanatory variables, they performed rather poorly; see Koskela and Virén (1991).

[9] We also looked at the evidence for Finland in a more detailed way in terms of various estimation methods and a battery of diagnostic tests. The results did not change qualitatively from those reported above; see Koskela and Virén (1991) for details.

[10] This conforms with the weak (and somewhat mixed) evidence on the relationship between household saving and real estate prices in the U.S.; see Skinner (1991) for a recent survey.

Boleat, M.: *National Housing Systems: A Comparative Study*, Croom Helm, London, 1987.

Brodin, P. A. & Nymoen, R.: The consumption function in Norway: Breakdown and reconstruction. Research Department, Bank of Norway, 9189/7, 1989.

Campbell, J. Y. & Mankiw, N. G.: Permanent income, current income and consumption. *Journal of Business and Economic Statistics 8*, 265–279, 1990.

Christensen, A. M. & Knudsen, D.: MONA — A quarterly model of the Danish economy. Symposium on Economic Modelling, Urbino, July 1990.

Deaton, A.: Involuntary saving through unanticipated inflation. *American Economic Review 67*, 899–910, 1977.

Deaton, A.: Saving and liquidity constraints, *Econometrica 59*, 1221–1248, 1991.

Giavazzi, F. & Pagano, M.: Can severe fiscal contractions be expansionary? Tales of two small European countries. In O. J. Blanchard & S. Fischer (eds.), *NBER Macroeconomics Annual*, MIT Press, 75–111, 1990.

Gruiso, L., Jappelli, T. & Terlizzese, D.: Saving and capital market imperfections: The Italian experience. Conference on Saving Behavior: Theory, International Evidence and Policy Implications, Helsinki, May 1991.

Jappelli, T. & Pagano, M.: Consumption and capital market imperfections. *American Economic Review 79*, 1088–1105, 1989.

Koskela, E. & Virén, M.: International differences in saving rates and the life-cycle hypothesis: A comment, *European Economic Review 33*, 1489–1498, 1989.

Koskela, E. & Virén, M.: Inflation, Capital Markets and Household Saving in the Nordic Countries. Conference on Saving Behavior: Theory, International Evidence and Policy Implications, Helsinki, May 1991.

Lehmussaari, O.-P.: Deregulation and consumption: Saving dynamics in the Nordic countries. *IMF Staff Papers 37*, 71–93, 1990a.

Lehmussaari, O.-P.: Why saving fell in the Nordic countries. *Finance & Development*, 15–17, 1990b.

Muellbauer, J. & Murphy, A.: Why has UK personal saving collapsed? Mimeo, Credit Suisse First Boston, 1989.

Sheshinski, E. & Tanzi, V.: An explanation of the behavior of personal savings in the United States in recent years. NBER WP No. 3040, 1989.

Skinner, J.: Housing and saving in the United States, NBER WP No. 3874, 1991.

Wilcox, J.: Liquidity constraints on consumption: The real effects of "real" lending policies. *Federal Reserve Bank of San Fransisco Economic Review*, 39–51, Fall 1989.

Vilmunen, J. & Virén, M.: Saving and indebtedness Among Different Age Groups in Finland, *Bank of Finland Bulletin 65*, (4), 8–13, 1991.

Comment on L. Guiso, T. Jappelli and D. Terlizzese, "Saving and Capital Market Imperfections: The Italian Experience" and E. Koskela and M. Virén, "Inflation, Capital Markets and Household Saving in the Nordic Countries"

Marco Pagano
University of Naples, Italy

One learns a great deal from a comparative reading of these two valuable case studies on saving in Italy and the Nordic countries. I shall try to summarize what I learned from these two papers, with no pretense of being exhaustive or balanced in my assessment. I shall also mention a direction in which further research might prove fruitful.

The first lesson of these two studies is that the traditional wisdom goes some way towards explaining both the international differences in saving rates and their movement over time. In different ways, in fact, they reinforce a basic insight of the life-cycle theory: that the growth rate is a key determinant of the saving rate. The decline in the growth rate appears as the main reason for the fall of the private saving rate in Italy as well as the Nordic countries, and differences in growth rates help to explain why Italian households have traditionally been high savers and Nordic households low savers.

The second lesson is that this is not the whole picture. These papers suggest that considerable progress can be made by supplementing the stylized model of life-cycle theory with information on the functioning of capital markets: households' saving behavior can be considerably affected by their ability to borrow and share risk via capital markets. I would add that government policies that redistribute income among households and alter the allocation of risk are equally important for the analysis of saving, especially in the presence of capital market imperfections.

Most of the evidence, especially in the study on Italy, concerns the functioning of capital markets. Life-cycle theory, as well as the permanent income hypothesis, proceeds under the assumption of perfect credit and insurance markets. But in practice these markets can fail, resulting in intermediaries rationing their services to households or providing them at noncompetitive rates. If these market failures are not common to all countries, capital market imperfections help to explain cross-country differences in saving rates.

This point, in spite of its simplicity, had been widely neglected so far, and the two papers at hand provide compelling evidence to support it. Guiso, Jappelli and Terlizzese show that credit and insurance markets cater inefficiently to Italian households, especially as a result of regulation and lack of competition among intermediaries; Koskela and Virén report instead that Nordic households borrow considerably from financial intermediaries. Taken together, this evidence points to an additional explanation of inter-country differences in saving, on top of differences in growth rates.

It should be mentioned that these findings have an impressive counterpart in the results of excess sensitivity tests provided by the two papers: in Italy aggregate consumption seems to track predictable changes in disposable income much more closely than in Scandinavian countries. Although Deaton (forthcoming) has argued that estimates of excess sensitivity based on aggregate data cannot be taken as a measure of liquidity constraints because of aggregation bias, the estimates reported in these two studies agree strikingly with much other macro- and microeconomic evidence that excess sensitivity is higher in countries where consumer credit is less developed (see the references quoted in the two studies).

While both papers are quite persuasive in bringing out the potential role of capital market failures in the explanation of cross-country variation in saving rates, they pay less attention to the effects of government transfer and insurance schemes on saving, except for occasional hints (see footnote 9 in Guiso, Jappelli and Terlizzese and the discussion of Table 1 in Koskela and Virén).

There are three channels through which the social security system can lower private saving. First, the pension system transfers income towards the old, with a negative effect on private saving (in the absence of an operative bequest motive). Second, public transfers may redirect income towards liquidity-constrained households, even within the same generation. Third, the government can replace the market in the provision of insurance (for instance by offering public health insurance), which can result in a lower level of precautionary saving. In the latter two cases, government policy affects private saving precisely because of the failure of private capital markets.

These effects of government intervention could be relevant for the countries analyzed in these two studies. The all-encompassing nature of the social security system in the Nordic countries may help to explain why their household saving rate is so low by international standards. In Italy, instead, the growing coverage of the social security system has probably contributed to the large decline in the private saving rate, and to its partial convergence towards the average OECD level. Evidence in this direction has in fact been provided in a recent study by Rossi and Visco (1991).

References

Deaton, A.: Macroeconomics and microeconomics. Chapter 5 in *Understanding Consumption*, forthcoming.

Rossi, N. & Visco, I.: Private saving and government deficit in Italy. Workshop on Savings in Italy: Past and Future Trends, Household and Government Behavior, Rome, January 1992.

Saving among Young Households. Evidence from Japan and Italy*

Albert Ando

University of Pennsylvania, Philadelphia, PA, USA

Luigi Guiso

Bank of Italy, Rome, Italy

Daniele Terlizzese

Bank of Italy, Rome, Italy

Daniel Dorsainvil

University of Pennsylvania, Philadelphia, PA, USA

Abstract

The tendency of both young and old households to save or dissave a very small fraction of their total resources is inconsistent with a strict life cycle model. We concentrate on young households and document their behavior, drawing on Italian and Japanese data. The theoretical structure we propose is broadly consistent with the spirit of the life cycle theory, while at the same time capable of accounting for the observed facts without relying on assumptions about credit markets or the degree of consumer foresight.

I. Introduction

The earnings profile appears to rise steeply with age in most countries, especially those with rapid growth such as Italy and Japan. It is therefore natural to expect that, because of the consumption smoothing principle, young people will dissave. Using microdata for Japan and Italy, we show that families and single individuals both save and accumulate net worth

---

*This paper is a shortened version of an article that is part of a research project on savings sponsored by the Bank of Italy. Basic computations using Japanese data and the construction of the cohort means were completed in 1986–87 at the University of Osaka, when Ando was given access to data from the 1979 and 1984 national surveys of family income and expenditure. We wish to thank Angus Deaton for helpful discussion, the participants in the Helsinki conference and two referees for their comments. We are also grateful to Luigi Sciamplicotti for very valuable research assistance.

throughout their working lives, even while they are quite young and their current incomes are lower than future incomes.

We are thus faced with the question as to why young people do not dis-save. This is a shift in emphasis from recent literature, where much effort has been devoted to devising modifications to the life cycle theory that could accommodate the relatively low propensity to dissave by older, retired families.

The mere lack of dissaving by very young households may be explained by the presence of liquidity constraints or myopia. The ingenious interaction of liquidity constraints with uncertainty recently proposed by Deaton (1991) can, within a buffer stock context, explain a limited amount of saving; it is, nonetheless, probably inadequate to explain the significant saving by very young households with relatively low incomes observed in the data.

We propose instead an explanation based on the hypothesis that, for very young households, due to the expectation of (future) consumption opportunities not available today, higher future income might be accompanied by larger needs. This creates a situation in which, at a later period, the marginal utility of income is higher even though expected income is higher than current income.

The increase in current consumption induced by an expected increase in future income might then be small (or even negative). According to this interpretation, consumption will be concentrated in periods with better opportunities. In contrast to the smoothing of consumption, we obtain what might be called a "consumption lumping" principle.

Consumption lumping can also be obtained if the marginal utility is higher in middle age because of the evolution of family size. Attanasio and Browning (1991) show that controlling for demographic changes within households considerably smoothes the age consumption profile. However, close association between consumption and income at a young age still characterizes the data.

In Section II we present evidence that young families and individuals with relatively low current earnings, who anticipate rapidly increasing future earnings, nevertheless save a significant proportion of their current income. We show that the reaction to anticipated changes in income is negligible for very young families, and that it becomes sizeable and significantly different from zero for older cohorts. We also find that the level of net worth has a positive effect on consumption, significant and smaller than one, indicating that families do follow a fairly long-term plan of asset accumulation. This casts doubt on the hypothesis of myopic behavior.

In Section III we outline a theoretical explanation and offer an illustrative example. We conclude with a general discussion which contrasts our theoretical explanation of young consumers' behavior with alternative explanations from recent literature.

II. The Saving Behavior of Young Households: An Empirical Assessment

In a recent paper Carroll and Summers (1991) presented a composite and well-documented picture of consumption behavior that is difficult to square with standard versions of the permanent income or life cycle theories. In particular, they use microdata to show that the basic implication of a simple life cycle model is not borne out. On the contrary, there seems to be little evidence of low frequency consumption smoothing, as both young and old households dissave too little. The behavior of the second group has been thoroughly investigated, both empirically by e.g. Ando and Kennikell (1986) and Hayashi, Ando and Ferris (1988) as well as theoretically by e.g. Davies (1981).

Our focus here is on the behavior of young consumers, which is interesting for at least two reasons. First, the predictions of the life cycle theory at the individual level are characterized by, among other features, zero lifetime saving and negative correlation between current saving and expected future income, while the main features of macrodata are positive and sizeable total saving and positive correlation between the saving-income ratio and the growth rate of aggregate income. They are usually reconciled with each other by aggregating consumers at different points in the life cycle. However, the effects of aggregation are unambiguous only when the preferred age pattern of consumption and the lifetime earnings profile are such that families do not dissave before retirement. If young individuals dissave significantly, the larger weight assigned to them in a growing economy by the process of aggregation could result in a negative correlation between total saving and growth. The saving behavior of young consumers is therefore crucial in assessing the consequences of aggregation for the level of total savings and its correlation with the growth of income[1].

Second, whereas simple extensions of the life cycle theory have been able to account for the low level of dissaving among the old, the behavior of the young has proved more difficult to rationalize. Liquidity constraints and myopia are often invoked to explain the lack of borrowing against a higher future flow of income. These hypotheses are suggestive, but they

---

[1] To be sure, the reference to aggregation could in principle be avoided, as both positive savings and a positive correlation with the growth rate of the economy are consistent, in general equilibrium, with a representative agent model. However, the latter seems to require a higher level of sensitivity of consumption decisions to interest rates than is usually estimated (or larger movements in interest rates than those currently observed); see also Carroll and Summers (1991). Aggregation of consumers at different points in the life cycle thus appears to be the most reliable mechanism to explain the macrocorrelation between savings and growth.

are not entirely convincing (see Section IV). In our view, greater emphasis on young people will eventually make it easier to discriminate between the alternative interpretations of savings behavior.

Descriptive Evidence: High Saving Rate by the Young and a Potential Sample Selection Bias

Table 1 shows saving rates by age for Italian and Japanese households, along with cross-section earnings profiles, which appear to be increasing with age. Given the high growth experienced by both countries, the adjustment for increases in productivity would make the two profiles extremely steep, especially at the beginning of life.[2] Consequently, the strict life cycle theory would suggest that young consumers decumulate substantial amounts of wealth (if they have any at the beginning of their working lives) or run negative saving.

The evidence points in the opposite direction. Young households save a considerable proportion of their current income. Combining cross-section data for different years and looking at the annual change in net worth of the average household in a specific age cohort, while giving a rather different measure of net accumulation, nonetheless confirms the basic fact: in spite of steep earnings profiles, young households, both in Italy and Japan, accumulate wealth.[3]

A potentially important bias might arise from the fact that young consumers still living as dependents within their families do not appear as independent households in the surveys. If (for whatever reason) they tend to consume more of what they earn (or, similarly, if the young consumers who become independent are thriftier), the observed "oversaving" of the young might be a statistical illusion. Given the tendency for the young consumers in both Japan and Italy to live in their parents' homes long after they start working, this sample selection problem could be important.

Before proceeding with a more elaborate analysis, we check in the simplest possible manner whether the household status of young adults makes a significant difference. Table 2 shows mean values of some key variables for a number of relevant groups. Our comments refer to Japan but, as can easily be seen, the same conclusions apply to Italy. Row A

---

[2] Assuming a rate of growth of productivity of 4 per cent in Italy and 5 per cent in Japan (approximately equal to the average growth of GDP per worker in the last 30 years in the two countries), the adjustment for growth would lead to a level of earnings in the highest age bracket 2.2 times as large as that in the youngest age bracket in Italy, and 2.6 times that in Japan.

[3] The larger estimate for saving implied by the change in net worth is due partly to capital gains on housing, which were substantial in both Japan and Italy between the two years used to construct the figures in the table.

Table 1. *Younger households' saving, disposable income, wealth accumulation and earnings by age: Italy and Japan*

Age of head of household	Italy				Age of head of household	Japan (3)			
	Saving (1)	Annual change in wealth (2)	Disposable income	Earnings		Saving (4)	Annual change in wealth (5)	Disposable income	Earnings
20–23	2,744	—	21,391	15,253	20–24	405.2	584.4	1,640.5	1,577.1
24–27	3,504	9,267	23,229	17,232	25–29	404.6	745.9	2,252.9	2,101.9
28–31	5,076	12,238	27,109	20,103	30–34	391.4	952.5	2,943.1	2,713.9
32–35	6,205	10,103	29,613	23,488	35–39	478.3	1,090.7	3,579.1	3,251.9
36–39	5,611	16,387	31,786	25,505	40–44	586.1	1,143.4	4,044.3	3,620.7
40–43	7,903	9,531	33,856	26,971					

(1) Defined as households' disposable income minus households' consumption expenditure.
(2) Annualized change is net worth between the end of 1987 and the end of 1987 prices.
(3) These figures represent a weighted average for ordinary families (married couples, their children and other members such as retired parents), single person households, and working male adults living in another household. See also the explanation in the text on the construction of cohorts.
(4) Defined as household disposable income minus (economic) consumption.
(5) Weighted average of the annualized change in net worth for ordinary and single households between the fourth quarter, of 1979 and the fourth quarter, of 1985, in 1987 prices, and the saving of male, working dependent adults (mostly living with their parents). For the last group, we use saving defined as income minus consumption since we do not have information on their assets and liabilities. This concept includes real capital gains and losses, especially on values of residential property.

Table 2. Disposable income, consumption and net worth by type of household: Italy (I) and Japan (J)

	Age of head		Disposable income		Consumption		Net worth		Saving rate	
	I	J	I	J	I	J	I	J	I	J
A Pure nuclear families	58	52	30,880	4,661	23,947	4,029	162,140	22,104	0.22	0.14
B Extended families with one working adult aged 25–29	58	54	48,234	5,556	33,133	4,334	194,379	23,879	0.31	0.22
C Single person families aged 25–29	27	27	19,741	2,113	17,332	1,667	47,467	4,083	0.12	0.20
D Combined household (A+C)			50,621	6,733	41,279	5,696	209,607	26,187	0.72	0.15

Source: *Italy:* Indagine sui bilanci delle famiglie, Banca d'Italia, 1988. Thousands of 1987 lire.
Japan: National survey of family income and expenditure, 1979, Status Bureau, Government of Japan. Thousands of 1979 yen.

corresponds to pure nuclear families;[4] row B corresponds to pure nuclear families extended to include one, and only one, working dependent adult male aged 25–29[5] (extended families); and row C corresponds to a single, working adult male aged 25–29 and living alone.[6] For row B the saving-income ratio is 0.22, while for the sum of rows A and C, which represents a fictitious family comparable with that in row B, it is 0.15. Thus, the saving-income ratio is 7 percentage points higher for the extended families. The conclusion that we draw from this table is that, if anything, young working dependents save proportionately more than independent consumers of comparable age. It is thus difficult to interpret the overall behavior of young households within a standard consumption smoothing paradigm. However, the issue deserves further scrutiny, especially as regards the question of the response of young consumers to (expected) future changes in earnings.

Young Consumers and Future Income Changes

If longitudinal data on both earnings and consumption were available, it would be possible to construct measures of expected future earnings for each single consumer and test their effect on current consumption. Unfortunately, longitudinal data are usually not available for either consumption or earnings. However, by combining cross-section data at different points in time, cohort average data can be constructed for consumption and current and future earnings.

The basic idea is illustrated in Fig. 1, which shows two cross-section patterns of earnings for individuals (heads of households) with specific characteristics (occupation, education, etc.) over all ages. Suppose that the cross-section age-earnings profile aa was observed in year t, and bb was observed in year $t + h$ (to be specific, let t be 1979 and $t + h$ be 1984, the two years covered by the available Japanese surveys). Suppose then that the position p represents the actual earnings of a group of individuals aged 35 in 1979. They will be aged 40 in 1984, and hence will occupy the position s in that year. We let this position represent, for 1979, the

---

[4] That is, either couples, possibly with nonworking children, or one of the members of a former couple with nonworking children.

[5] In most cases the additional working dependent adult is the son or daughter of the head of household, although we allow for all other possible cases. For Japan, only households with male dependent adults where selected.

[6] To correct for a possible bias in saving propensity because the age of the pure nuclear families is lower than that of the extended families, for Italy we randomly draw a subsample from the pure nuclear families that has the same (head of household's) age distribution as that observed among the extended families. For Japan we select pure nuclear families in the age bracket 50–54, approximately matching the average age of the extended families.

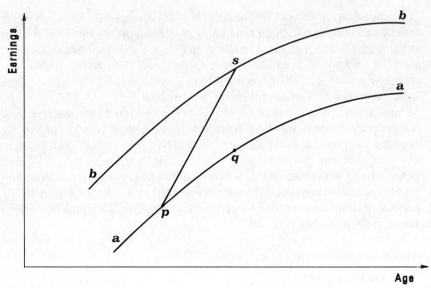

Fig. 1.

expected earnings five years ahead of individuals who, in 1979, occupy position *p*. Note that this group's lifetime earnings path is considerably steeper than either *aa* or *bb*[7] and is generally quite different from the path that would be obtained by adjusting *aa* for the growth in the overall productivity of the economy.

The principal problem when using a sequence of cross-section data to approximate panel data stems from the possibility that, between 1979 and 1984, the household in question changed type. For example, single persons get married, married couples divorce and so on. Since the mean income of these different household types is different, careful handling of the type changes is required in order to obtain reasonable estimates of expected future income. Clearly, the issue is of particular relevance for young consumers, who are the focus of our attention.[8]

---

[7] The movement from position *p* to position *s* consists of two components. The first, from *p* to *q*, is the age effect, which might include improvements in skills and, therefore, an increase in productivity that cannot be distinguished from other effects of age. The second component of the movement, from *q* to *s*, is the productivity increase specific to calendar year, and is common to all members of the work force, regardless of age. An empirical distinction between these two reasons for a change in earnings could be important since changes due to calendar year productivity increases are more likely to be subject to surprises. Thus, the distinction is potentially useful in assessing the explanation of the observed savings-growth correlation in rapidly expanding economies based on a "surprise" element.

[8] A similar problem, arising when older people merge into one of their children's households, was tackled by Hayashi, Ando and Ferris (1988).

Consider then the population of ordinary households (husband and wife, their children and perhaps other members), aged between 30 and 35, living in 1984. Let us focus our attention on the male head of each household. He could have come from one of four groups. He may have already been the head of the same household; he could have been a single person living independently; or he could have been a working dependent adult in someone else's household, most probably his parents'. The fourth possibility, a nonworking dependent adult in someone else's household, can be dismissed for our purposes since there are very few nonworking dependent adult males over the age of 25.

We refer to type i families, $i = (OF\ SF, DA)$, and type j families, $j = (GOF, GSF, GDA)$, where the symbols represent, respectively: ordinary families with married couples at the core, male single-person families, and working male dependent adults in 1979 (i) and 1984 (j), and G is a mnemonic for grown. All are aged 25–29 in 1979 and 30–34 in 1984.

We have no information that can precisely match each type i family with a type j family. By making strong assumptions, however, we can deduce the transition probabilities. We assume, first of all, that every family in OF will move to GOF. Since the divorce rate in Japan is extremely low and the mortality rate at these ages is also low, this seems a reasonable assumption. We also assume that families in SF will be either in GSF or GOF and families in DA will be either in GDA or GOF; in other words, we assume tha a single person does not become a dependent adult, or a dependent adult a single person. This may not be a reasonable assumption, but without it, it would become extremely hard to proceed. The possible transition paths are illustrated in Figure 2. From the number of families and individuals in each group, obtained from the 1980 and 1985 censuses,

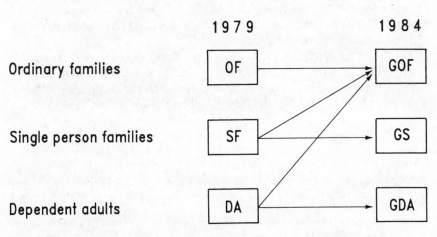

Fig. 2.

we estimated the transition probabilities, which were then used to compute the expected future earnings of each type i family. We verified that the number of corresponding families and individuals in the samples of the National Survey of Family Income and Expenditure, multiplied by sampling ratios, approximates the census figures fairly well.

The last step was to divide the family types into smaller groups in order to construct a set of cohort means to be used in the estimation. We used occupation, location, and the number of children as classificatory variables, and managed to obtain about 70 cohorts for each age group.

As mentioned above, in this study we have departed from the standard approach to constructing expected earnings, which adjusts the cross-section pattern of earnings of similar families for the general productivity gains over time. The level of future expected earnings for each 1979 cohort is defined as the mean earnings of the corresponding cohort in 1984, using as weights the transition probabilities computed as shown above. In other words, we assume a perfect foresight forecast.[9]

Empirical Findings

The regression results relating to the 1979 survey are shown in Table 3[10]. Regressions were run by dividing all the variables by earnings in 1979 (Y79). For ease of interpretation, the results are shown in level form. The two columns refer to households whose head was aged 25–29 and 30–34, respectively, in 1979.

Considering first the group of young consumers, we note that the coefficient of current earnings (after the terms KID and MEM are taken into account), is 0.584, against 0.052 for expected future earnings (denoted as EY84). Further, the coefficient of EY84 is not at all significant. This result appears to confirm the contention of Carroll and Summers (1991) and Carroll (1989) that expected future income does not have much effect on either consumption or savings.

On the other hand, the coefficient of net worth in 1979, W79, is significantly different from zero (0.05, with a t-ratio of 4.58), but considerably smaller than one. This means that, in contrast to the myopia hypothesis, young consumers plan for the future, although they adjust very slowly if

---

[9] This procedure has the shortcoming that it covers only five years. For the young groups dealt with here, the relevant expected earnings should cover the major portion of their working life of some 30 years or so.

[10] Space limits prevent us from presenting similar regressions relative to Italy, where we had access to a short panel. The results are highly consistent with those obtained for Japan.

Table 3. *Dependence of younger households' consumption on current earnings, expected future earnings and net worth (dependent variable: consumption in the 1979 survey)*

A	Age of household head in 1979	
	25–29 no. of cohorts = 62	30–34 no. of cohorts = 71
constant	454.4 (5.17)	1,082.8 (7.15)
Y79	0.506 + 0.049 KID + 0.016 MEM (2.57) (5.45) (0.38)	0.198 + 0.048 + 0.125 MEM (2.34) (7.61) (3.78)
EY84	0.052 (0.79)	0.169 (3.65)
W79	0.05 (4.58)	0.025 (2.55)
R^2	0.64	0.72
Mean of	{C79 = 2,517.1; KID = 1.47; MEM = 0.41}	{C79 = 2,880.6; KID = 1.52; MEM = 0.41}

Legend:
KID = Number of children aged 17 or younger;
MEM = Number of members in the family, other than husband, wife and their children.

they find a significant gap between their current and planned patterns of asset accumulation.

For the older age group, the coefficient of current income is considerably smaller (0.294, taking into account the terms KID and MEM), and the coefficient of expected income is both large, 0.169, and significant. This is a clear indication that the older group takes future earnings into account in determining consumption. Net worth has a somewhat smaller coefficient, but remains an important variable.[11]

It is difficult to square these results with the hypothesis of myopic behavior. Further, simple models of consumption associated with liquidity constraints appear to contradicted.[12] It is interesting, in our view, that the effect of future earnings on current consumption becomes significant only for households that are at a later stage of the life cycle, albeit still relatively young.[13] One possible explanation is that liquidity constraints, while

---

[11] According to the classification in footnote 7, we ran a regression splitting the changes in EY84 into calendar year increases in productivity and changes due to the age effect. Unfortunately, this distinction was possible only for the young group; in this case both components turned out to be not significantly different from zero.

[12] A positive effect of future expected income on current consumption might be consistent with the presence of liquidity constraints in Deaton's model, in which anticipation of higher future income reduces the need for precautionary saving.

[13] This finding is confirmed in the regressions run on Italian data.

binding for very young households, cease to bite fairly soon. In Section III, after introducing our theoretical framework to account for the saving behaviour of young households, we return to this issue, arguing that the age dependency of sensitivity to expected future income finds a natural explanation in our approach.

III. The Life Cycle of Opportunities

In the conventional approach, economic agents are identified by a given preference relation defined over a given consumption set. Although this description is inherently static, some goods could be interpreted as being available only in the future, and the preference relation could be dependent on the state of the environment, as the description of each good involves the contingencies on which it will be consumed.

However, in the absence of a complete set of markets in which, at the beginning of the agent's life, all the commodities so defined can be exchanged, it seems more natural to define not only agents' decisions but also their "identities" as the result of a sequential process.

At the start, each agent has a preference relation involving a (usually small) set of commodities, i.e., those with which he is most familiar, perhaps because of his parents' behavior. But he probably does not have a clear opinion concerning other goods, certainly those not yet invented but also, and more significantly, those consumed in different socioeconomic levels.

As the agent grows older and pursues his career, his position on the socioeconomic ladder changes, he moves to different places and the composition of his family evolves. He becomes acquainted with new people, observes new habits and discovers new consumption patterns. Indeed, the agent's own social identity, as defined by his relationships with other people, can be said to evolve with age.

At the beginning of their working lives, individuals face a wide range of possible paths, all of which might involve not only different patterns of lifetime earnings but also a different structure of needs and preferences. As they grow older, either by choice or by chance some of the original possibilities will no longer be feasible, and each individual will eventually settle down in what might be called a "social niche".

The social niche to which an individual belongs entails, to some extent, a preferred consumption structure. For this reason, we interpret the discovery of the niche as providing an opportunity to improve consumption choices. It is then intuitive that people have an incentive to postpone some of their purchases until they have discovered in which social niche they will end up.

In more formal terms, we are describing a situation in which utility is the joint product of consumption and (social) environment. The two "factors" are complementary, so that a better environment entails higher marginal utility of consumption.

An Example

Several models exemplifying these ideas could be constructed. The social niche, for instance, could be identified with the agent's "true tastes", which are unknown at the beginning of his life and are progressively discovered.

It can be shown that the opportunity to learn about his real preferences leads the young consumer to accumulate resources against the day when, having grown up and "discovered himself", he will be able to derive greater utility from consumption; see Ando, Guiso and Terlizzese (1991). If the evolution of preferences over the life cycle is ignored, saving by young cohorts will be underestimated, or their borrowing overestimated.

In another example, analyzed here in more detail, an individual's niche is identified with his job position. Let us suppose that the various jobs in an economy are associated with different incomes, working conditions and overall social environments.[14] They can often be ranked according to a dominance criterion, as some involve both a higher income and a more agreeable environment. For example, let us consider a mine worker and a university teacher. A switch from the former's to the latter's job, quite apart from giving a higher income, implies a dramatic improvement in health conditions and in the cultural and social quality of life. Similar though less marked differences usually accompany the progression from a job as an unskilled worker to one as a skilled craftsman and from the latter to a managerial position, or, more generally, whenever there is a change in the type of job.

We believe it is reasonable to assume that the better the working conditions and the stronger the positive externalities generated by relationships with colleagues and by the social circle associated with a given job, the higher the utility derived from each unit of consumption; on this point, see also Arrow (1974).

Let us take an economy in which there are two types of jobs, σ_h and σ_l, corresponding to two rungs on the social ladder (high and low, respectively). σ_h dominates σ_l, since it entails both a better environment and a higher income ($y_h > y_l$). Consider also an agent whose life is divided into two periods, who consumes c_i in period i ($i = 1, 2$) and works, in the first period, in job σ_l. The future, however, also holds the possibility of social

---

[14] The idea of a strict connection between a consumer's job position and his social niche, i.e., his social status, is emphasized by Solow (1990).

promotion and the agent anticipates that, with probability p, he will be offered a better job. Reflecting the idea that there is little social downgrading, we assume that the agent never drops below the social ranking from which he starts.[15]

On the basis of our previous discussion, we can assume that

$$u_1(c, \sigma_h) > u_1(c, \sigma_l) \tag{1}$$

where $u(\cdot)$ is the instantaneous utility function, and the subscript on the $u(\cdot)$ denotes a partial derivative.[16]

The agent then solves:

$$\max \quad u(c_1, \sigma_l) + (1 - p) u(c_{21}, \sigma_l) + p u(c_{22}, \sigma_h)$$

$$\text{s.t.} \quad c_1 + s = y_l$$
$$c_{21} = y_l + s$$
$$c_{22} = y_h + s$$

where s represents saving and, for the sake of simplicity, the subjective discount rate is set equal to the interest rate and both are set equal to zero. This problem, under assumption (1), will be labeled (A).

In order to have a benchmark, let us now consider the case where the only difference between the two jobs is the income they offer, so that the utility function is independent of σ and assumption (1) is replaced by:

$$u_1(c, \sigma_h) = u_1(c, \sigma_l). \tag{2}$$

We label this modified problem (B). It is useful to write down the first-order conditions of both problems, for the sake of simplicity assuming interior solutions:

$$(\text{FOC1}) \quad u_1(y_l - s, \sigma_l) = (1 - p) u_1(y_l + s, \sigma_l) + p u_1(y_h + s, \sigma_h)$$

$$(\text{FOC2}) \quad u_1(y_l - s, \sigma_l) = (1 - p) u_1(y_l + s, \sigma_l) + p u_1(y_h + s, \sigma_l).$$

For a given p, let us call $s^*(p)$ the solution to (FOC1) and $\hat{s}(p)$ the solution to (FOC2); the latter is the one usually considered in the literature.

If we now take (FOC1) combined with assumption (1), it is simple to

---

[15] Some partial but clear evidence supporting this assumption can be obtained from the Italian Survey of Households' Income and Wealth; for details on the SHIW see Guiso, Jappelli and Terlizzese (1991). In the Italian case we computed that 80 per cent of the job changes led to earnings at least as high as those in the original job.

[16] We assume that the agent's utility is directly dependent on his position on the social ladder. An alternative assumption might be that utility depends only on goods, some of which are not marketable but can be acquired through status. A similar approach is taken by Cole, Mailath and Postlewaite (1991), who also emphasize the interaction between agents' social status and savings decisions in a general equilibrium context.

prove that $s^*(p)$ is larger than $\hat{s}(p)$ and, provided that the gain from social promotion is large enough, s^* can be positive even when $\hat{s}$ is negative.

As shown by Ando, Guiso and Terlizzese (1991), a second interesting implication of this model is that the effect of an increase in future expected inncome on saving can be positive and, even if negative, has a smaller absolute value than that usually assumed. This is true when the increase in expected income is assumed to be the result of an increased probability of the better job. This follows from the fact that a rise in p entails, along with the increase in income, a greater probability of the better opportunity: a larger future income goes hand in hand with a better future environment for consumption, which to some extent offsets the incentive to borrow against the larger income and increases current consumption.

The savings behavior that is motivated by the anticipation of future consumption opportunities, geared to the discovery of one's social niche, has an intrinsic dynamics that is difficult to capture fully with the overly simple model presented here. Indeed, discovery of the social niche is a learning process that we believe is faster at a young age, slows down as the agent pursues his chosen career and virtually comes to a halt at some time in the middle of the life cycle. Some calculations made on the 1989 Italian Survey of Households' Income and Wealth, although far from representing conclusive evidence, lend support to this presumption. The probability of changing job for different age classes has the following features: it peaks at young age (before age 30) with a value close to 12 per cent, falls slightly between 30 and 35 (to about 10 per cent), halves between 35 and 40 and hovers somewhat below 4 per cent thereafter. We interpret these findings as suggestive of the fact that the flow of new opportunities which the consumer can reasonably anticipate drains away as he grows older. As a result, the reaction of consumption to expected future income might be negligible at a very young age, when changes in income are expected to be offset by changes in consumption opportunities; at a somewhat older age, standard life cycle behavior would tend to prevail.[17] As anticipated in the preceding section, the age dependence of the reaction to future income finds a natural explanation in our framework.

IV. Discussion

Simple versions of the life cycle hypothesis are unable to explain fully the observed facts regarding the savings of young consumers. An amendment

---

[17] In the regression run on the Italian panel data we included a dummy, representing changes in job position, interacted with expected future income. When the latter is significantly different from zero, the coefficient of the dummy is significant and negative, lending some support to our theory.

to the theory appears to be called for, and two main directions have been explored in the literature: the possibilities of liquidity constraints and of myopic behavior.

Liquidity constraints represent a somewhat obvious explanation for the relatively small amount of borrowing by young generations, as it is simply postulated that they are unable to borrow. Although this explanation merely shifts the question one step back, since the presence of borrowing constraints should itself be justified theoretically , it does capture some important features of the actual working of markets. There are, however, grounds for doubting whether credit market imperfections are enough to explain the observed deviation of young people's behavior from that postulated by the life cycle theory.

First, taken literally, the borrowing constraint assumption would imply that agents should be "on the constraint", consuming all their income, whereas we observe nonnegligible savings, even in the early part of their working lives. To be sure, Deaton has recently shown that the existence of positive savings can be made compatible with binding liquidity constraints when there is uncertainty and the consumers are either "impatient" or "imprudent".[18] Both assumptions are somewhat unusual, and their nature implies that the savings thus generated are not likely to be large.[19]

Second, and more importantly, the consumption pattern of young generations follows closely that of income in countries where the level of development of financial markets is quite different and where the incidence of liquidity constraints is therefore also likely to differ widely.

The second explanation proposed in the literature, i.e., shortsightedness, simply implies that people do not borrow against future income, because they do not think of it. The status of this hypothesis is not clear, however. It would seem to be an interpretation superimposed on models whose structure has little to do with myopic behavior. On the empirical side, shortsightedness is invoked to explain a low (or zero) coefficient on expected future income in regressions explaining current consumption; see Carroll

---

[18] The role of prudence is not directly examined by Deaton, but a simple extension of his argument establishes the claim.

[19] In Deaton's simulations the amount of saving that can be generated is generally less than 1 per cent of (mean) income, a relatively small amount when compared with the actual saving of young households. We should note, however, that sizeable savings by the young can be obtained if imperfections in the market for consumption loans are coupled with imperfections in the market for mortgages; cf. Artle and Varaiya (1978). Saving for the future purchase of a house can also be interpreted within our framework, with no constraints assumed for the credit market. It can be shown that there is an incentive to increase current saving, postponing the purchase of a house, if (a) homeownership enhances the marginal utility of consumption; (b) there are transaction costs in the secondary market for houses; (c) there is uncertainty about future income flows but learning takes place.

(1989). In the same regressions, however, current wealth appears to have a coefficient significantly different from zero and smaller than one, which is not consistent with short-sighted consumers.

In this study we have provided evidence that young people's current consumption responds to some extent to future earnings. We have also offered an explanation for the apparently low responsiveness that preserves the forward looking feature of the life cycle theory. We have outlined a theory in which current savings can be interpreted as a choice of flexibility, since the existence of future opportunities may be an incentive to postpone consumption until those periods in which it yields greater utility.

The life cycle theory starts with the notion that the temporal distribution of resources is different from the optimal allocation of consumption over the life span, and that savings are needed to reallocate resources over time. In its original version, it emphasized the feature that, by and large, earnings are less than the optimal level of consumption after retirement (and perhaps at the beginning of life) and that they tend to be more than the optimal level of consumption during the middle range of a family's life. We have emphasized the possibility that the optimal consumption pattern may be rising more sharply than earnings at a very young age. This might lead to large savings at the beginning of working life, when earnings are relatively low, and to consumption lumping rather than consumption smoothing behavior at a relatively young age.

References

Ando, A. E. & Kennickell, A. B.: How much (or little) life cycle is there in micro data? The cases of the United States and Japan. In R. Dornbusch, S. Fischer & J. Bossons, (eds.), *Macroeconomics and Finance. Essays in Honor of Franco Modigliani.* MIT Press, Cambridge MA, 1986.

Ando, A., Guiso, L. & Terlizzese, D.: Young household saving and the life cycle of opportunities. Evidence from Japan and Italy. Mimeo, Bank of Italy, 1991.

Arrow, K. J.: Optimal insurance and generalized deductibles. *Scandinavian Actuarial Journal*, 1–42, 1974.

Artle, R. & Varaiya, P.: Life cycle consumption and homeownership. *Journal of Economic Theory 18*, 38–58, 1978.

Attanasio, O. & Browning, M.: Consumption over the life cycle and over the business cycle. CEPR Meeting, Madrid, June 1991.

Carroll, C.: Uncertain future income, precautionary saving and consumption. Mimeo, MIT, 1989.

Carroll, C. & Summers, L. H.: Consumption growth parallels income growth: Some new evidence. In B. D. Bernheim & J. B. Shaven (eds.), National Saving and Economic Performance, University of Chicago Press, Chigaco, 1991.

Cole, H. L., Mailath, G. J. & Postlewaite, A.: Social norms, saving behavior and growth. Caress WP 91–14, University of Pennsylvania, 1991.

Davies, J.: Uncertain lifetime, consumption and dissaving in retirement. *Journal of Political Economy 89*, 1981.

Deaton, A. S.: Saving and liquidity constraints. *Econometrica 59*, 1221–1248, 1991.

Guiso, L., Jappelli, T. & Terlizzese, D.: Earnings uncertainty and precautionary saving. Mimeo, Bank of Italy, 1991.

Hayashi, F., Ando, A. & Ferris, R.: Life cycle and bequest savings. *Journal of the Japanese and International Economics 2*, 450–491, 1988.

Solow, R. M.: *The Labour Market as a Social Institution*. Basil Blackwell, Cambridge MA, 1990.

Comment on A. Ando, L. Guiso, D. Terlizzese and D. Dorsainvil, "Saving among Young Households. Evidence from Japan and Italy"

T. N. Srinivasan

Yale University, New Haven, CT, USA

The purpose of the paper is to show that young households in Japan and Italy save a significant proportion of their current income. Such behavior is not consistent with a strict life-cycle model. The authors propose a theoretical structure that is meant to be consistent with the observed behavior. This theory is based on the notion that, if in the future not only an individual's income is higher than his present income, but his social status is also higher, and if higher social status raises the marginal utility of consumption at all levels of consumption, then such an individual will consume more of his present income than another individual who experiences the same rise in future income without any change in his social status. To the extent the young are more likely to experience future changes in their social status, presumably this theory is consistent with their saving part of their current income. It would seem that the changes in social status have to be exogenous to the decision-making of the individual — in any case the simple two-period model in Section III of the paper explicitly treats the indicators of social status as exogenous.

Whatever the plausibility of the theory, without a workable definition of social status and a data set in which the changes in income as well as in social status are documented, a direct empirical test of the theory is ruled out. Even identification of the effect of social changes may be infeasible in such a case — for example, if income and social status are positively related, the effect of social status is indistinguishable from nonconvexities in preferences. What the authors in fact do is test whether expected future income significantly influences current consumption in addition to current income. They find no significant (resp. significant) effect for households headed by individuals in the age group 25–29 (resp. age group 30–34). For both sets of households, the effect of an increase in net worth on current consumption is significant, though the effect is smaller for age group 30–34.

The dependent variable in the regression is the *mean* consumption in 1979 of a *cohort* of households with the age of the head in the relevant age group, where cohorts are defined using occupation of the head, location of the household and the number of children in it as classificatory variables. The expected future earnings (i.e., in 1984) for each cohort is computed by first dividing families into three types according to status of its *male* head: married, living with wife, children and others; single person living independently; and a working dependent adult living in someone else's household. By making some strong assumptions, transition probabilities from one type to another between 1979 and 1984 are estimated from survey data for the two years. For each 1979 cohort, the level of future expected earnings is defined as the mean earnings of the corresponding cohort in 1984, using the transition probabilities as weights.

There are two econometric problems with the regression. First, if the number of households in each cohort varies across cohorts, there could be heteroscedasticity on the error terms. Second, even if perfect foresight is assumed as the authors do, since the data relate to two *separate* cross sections rather than a panel of households, the estimated future earnings are subject to measurement error, in part due to sampling errors in the estimated transition probabilities and in part due to the fact that the 1984 earnings do not relate to the same set of households. Unless corrected for heteroscedasticity, the estimated standard errors of coefficients would be incorrect and measurement error would bias the estimated coefficients.

To sum up, while explaining the apparent inconsistency with the life-cycle hypothesis of the behavior of young households in Japan and Italy is of interest, the authors have not tested their particular explanation of it. At best, they have confirmed the inconsistency through their regression.

Household Saving in LDCs: Credit Markets, Insurance and Welfare*

Angus Deaton

Princeton University, Princeton, NJ, USA

Abstract

Some ways in which farmers in LDCs can protect their living standards against fluctuations in income are discussed. After considering the theory of consumption under uncertainty when there is no or limited borrowing, the case where some borrowing is allowed is also examined. Empirical evidence from some LDCs is used to look at (i) household borrowing and lending, their importance and timing, and their role in smoothing consumption, and (ii) the life-cycle behavior of consumption and income. The results suggest that "hump" life-cycle saving is not likely to be a very important generator of wealth in LDCs and provide further evidence on the limited role of credit markets.

I. Introduction

Agricultural income is inherently uncertain. Weather, pests, disease and fires make yields uncertain, and the notorious variability of agricultural prices can generate fluctuations in farmers' incomes even when output is stable. In poor countries, most of the population earns its living from agriculture, either directly or indirectly. For many of these people, a poor harvest or a low harvest price can threaten disaster, even if, on average, agricultural incomes are sufficient to provide a sustainable standard of living. In such circumstances, the protection of living standards requires that resources be transferred across time, from good years to bad years. For this to work, someone, farmers, communities, or governments, have to be able to look ahead, and make adequate provision for the future. Until

*The original, longer version of this paper, Deaton (1991b) can be obtained from the Research Program in Development Studies at Princeton University. I should like to thank Kristin Butcher for splendid research assistance, and the Lynde and Harry Bradley Foundation for financial support. Some of the results reported here come from a research project on saving behavior supported by the World Bank; the views expressed here are those of the author and should not be attributed to the World Bank or its affiliated organizations.

recent years, much of the development literature, and in particular the literature on project evaluation in developing countries, UNIDO (1972), Little and Mirrlees (1974) and Squire and van der Tak (1975), supposed that individuals were unlikely to be able to make adequate intertemporal plans, so that the government should do so on their behalf. In practice, there are many government policies that play such a role, at least in part. Many governments, particularly in Africa, set agricultural procurement prices that do not vary with world prices, and argue that such schemes help stabilize farm incomes. Governments in many developing countries are involved in the provision of credit, which can also play a role in insuring consumption in the face of income variability. There are also a wide range of relief policies, from *ad hoc* famine relief to more regular food for work schemes, which can provide some minimum living standards in bad times.

This paper is concerned with non-governmental consumption insurance schemes. I discuss some of the ways in which farmers can protect their living standards against fluctuations in income. Where there are credit markets, individuals can borrow and lend, and there is no need for consumption to be tied to income in the short run. But even without credit markets, or with limited credit facilities, money or goods can be put by in good years to provide a buffer against the bad times that will sooner or later follow. Knowledge of the extent to which poor households use these mechanisms is necessary if we are to assess the appropriate role, if any, for programs provided by the state.

Section II of the paper considers the theory of consumption under uncertainty when there is no borrowing, or limited borrowing at penal rates. The starting point is the model of liquidity constraints in Deaton (1990a, 1991a). I consider the effectiveness of simple rules-of-thumb of the type that agents could easily implement, and evaluate the welfare consequences of these against fully optimal strategies. I also look at the case where some borrowing is allowed, albeit in limited amounts, and at high rates of interest. In this model with "money-lenders", agents can pay to avoid the worst outcomes in a pure buffering model, when a succession of low incomes, which has exhausted precautionary assets, is followed by a further bad year.

Section III considers some empirical evidence from Côte d'Ivoire, Thailand and Ghana. I look at two separate issues: (i) household borrowing and lending in Côte d'Ivoire and Ghana, their importance and their timing in an attempt to assess the part they play in smoothing consumption, and (ii) the life-cycle behavior of consumption and income, here using data from Thailand and Côte d'Ivoire. As argued by Carroll and Summers (1991), if credit markets are good enough to support long-term (low-frequency) consumption smoothing, and if the life-cycle hypothesis is true, then the ratio of young people's life-time resources to those of old people is larger in fast growing countries (Thailand) than in slow-growing countries (Côte d'Ivoire), so that consumption profiles should be more tipped towards the young in the former than in the latter. In fact, the opposite is true, and I show that, in contrast, consumption tracks current income very closely. There results suggest that "hump" life-cycle saving is not likely to be a very important generator of wealth in these countries, and provides further evidence on the limited role of credit markets, at least for long-term consumption smoothing. Section IV provides some brief conclusions.

II. Theory: Saving with Borrowing Constraints

Individuals in poor countries borrow and lend money, and perhaps do so to prevent shortfalls in consumption. However, it remains implausible that agents can always borrow as much as they like for consumption purposes, so that it is important to examine behavior when borrowing is not permitted. The essential point to note is that the inability to *borrow* does not imply that the consumer cannot *save*. Indeed, the fact that borrowing may be unavailable when most needed is itself a reason to set aside something when times are good; liquidity constraints reinforce the precautionary demand for assets. Many consumers may never wish to borrow; people who are patient, or for whom the return on assets is sufficient to overcome their impatience, will tend to postpone consumption, building up assets as they go, so that temporary short-falls of income are unlikely to pose a problem, except perhaps early in life. But for those who are impatient, or who are poor enough to feel that future consumption is an inadequate reward for postponing current consumption, lack of borrowing facilities will be a real disadvantage. For such consumers, it is essential to hold some assets that can be used to buffer consumption when incomes are low.

A simple model of optimal buffering is constructed in Deaton (1991a), and is summarized here as a starting point. Preferences take the standard form,

$$u = E_t \left\{ \sum_{\tau=t}^{\infty} (1+\delta)^{t-\tau} v(c_t) \right\} \tag{1}$$

where $\delta > 0$ is the rate of time preference, and $v(c_t)$ is the instantaneous (sub) utility function, assumed to be increasing, strictly concave, and differentiable. The evolution of assets is given by

$$A_{t+1} = (1+r)(A_t + y_t - c_t) \tag{2}$$

where y_t is labor income, A_t is real assets and r is the real interest rate. I assume that $r < \delta$, so that the agent's impatience outweighs the incentive to accumulate. The real interest rate is treated as fixed and known, and all the uncertainty is focussed on labor income y_t. Labor is inelastically supplied, and y_t is a stationary random variable with support $[y_0, y_1]$, with $y_0 > 0$ and $y_0 \le y_1 \le \infty$, so that income cannot fall below the positive floor y_0. I start from the most obvious form of the borrowing restriction, viz.

$$A_t \ge 0. \tag{3}$$

The simplest way to solve the consumer's problem is to start from the modification of the usual Euler equations that is brought about by the presence of the borrowing constraint (3). Define the state variable x_t "cash on hand", by

$$x_t = A_t + y_t. \tag{4}$$

x_t is the maximum that can be spent on consumption in period t. Consumption in periods t and $t + 1$ must satisfy

$$\lambda(c_t) = \max [\lambda(x_t), \beta E_t \lambda(c_{t+1})] \tag{5}$$

where $\lambda(c)$ is the marginal utility of c, i.e. $\lambda(c) \equiv v'(c)$, $\beta = (1 + r)/1 + \delta)$, and $\beta < 1$ since $r < \delta$. If the consumer is constrained, consumption can be no higher than x_t, and the marginal utility no lower than $\lambda(x_t)$. The constraint will bind if marginal utility at x_t is higher than the discounted expected marginal utility next period, otherwise the two marginal utilities are equated in the usual way. Note that the expectation itself takes account of the possibility of future constraints.

The solution to (5) depends on the stochastic structure of the income process y_t. Here, since my interest is in extending the model in other directions, I deal with only the simplest case where income is independently and identically distributed over time. Deaton (1991a) discusses cases where income is a first order autoregressive or moving average process. In the i.i.d. case, the optimal rule is to make consumption a function of cash on hand, i.e.

$$c_t = f(x_t) \tag{6}$$

where, by virtue of (4) and (2), x_t evolves according to

$$x_{t+1} = (1 + r)\{x_t - f(x_t)\} + y_t \tag{7}$$

and y_t, labor income, is an i.i.d. stochastic process.

In general, it is not possible to write down an analytical form for the function $f(x)$. However, the theory can be used to infer its general properties, and in practice, given specifications for the utility function and the distribution function of incomes, as well as the interest rate and time-preference parameters, the function can be calculated numerically. Given his cash on hand, the consumer should spend everything if the total is below some critical value x^*, say. Above x^*, something is put by for the future, and the marginal propensity to retain cash, although always less than unity, is an increasing function of cash on hand. If the consumer follows the optimal rule, consumption can be very much smoother than income; if the income process is normally distributed with mean 100 and standard deviation 10, if utility is isoelastic with a coefficient of relative risk aversion of 3, and if the interest and time-preference rates are 5 per cent and 10 per cent respectively, the standard deviation of consumption is 5, which is half that of income. This can be achieved with very low average levels of "buffer" assets, averaging only 7 and rarely more than 10. However, consumption fluctuations are necessarily asymmetric. It is always possible to prevent consumption being too high, since resources can be kept for the future. But if assets are exhausted, as must happen from time to time, there is always the *possibility* of low income immediately thereafter, and the unprotected consumer has no choice but to cut consumption to match. Of course, these outcomes are no worse than would be the case if consumption were equal to income, and the optimal buffering strategy much reduces their likelihood. When they occur, the shadow price of the borrowing constraint, the shadow price of loans, will rise to high levels; for the same parameter values, rates of 30 per cent occur every twenty years or so, and rates of well over 100 per cent are possible. There is a demand for loans at even very high rates of interest.

The calculation of the optimal policy (11) from the conditions (5) and (7) is not a trivial task. The function has to be approximated by points along a grid, or by some suitable polynomial, and then values or parameters chosen to satisfy the functional equations as closely as possible. The question then arises as to whether consumers could reasonably be expected to solve this problem for themselves, and if not, whether there might not exist simpler, more intuitive rules of thumb that might do nearly as well. In Figure 1, the broken line shows the optimal policy for a consumer with the preferences and income process described above, while the piecewise linear function shows the simple rule of thumb: "spend all cash on hand up to mean income, and 30 per cent of any excess". (The third function on the graph will be discussed below.) My choice of rule of thumb is not arbitrary, but was guided to some extent by knowledge of the optimal function. However, the critical point at which saving begins was taken to be mean income rather than any approximation to the optimal critical point. Note also that the rule-of-thumb function is never below the optimal function, so that the consumption is always too high, and I have made no attempt to achieve a better approximation. My concern is more that the rule should be simple, simple enough to have plausibly evolved from trial and error.

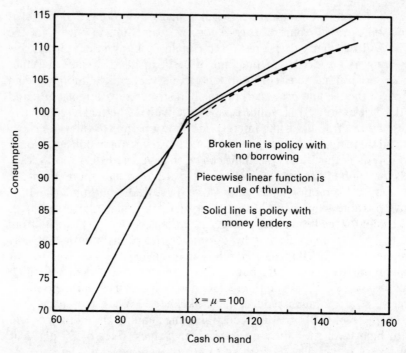

Fig. 1. Three consumption policies.

There are various ways of assessing the performance of such a rule. Figure 2 is one; it illustrates a 200-year realization of income, consumption, and assets under the rule of thumb. Income values are random independent draws from $N(100, 10)$, the agent begins with no assets, and the process is allowed to run, governed by (6) and (7) with $f(x_t)$ in (6) taken to be the piecewise linear function, i.e.

$$f(x_t) = x_t - 0.7(x_t - \mu)I(x_t > \mu) \tag{8}$$

where $I(.)$ is the indicator function. The outcomes in the figure are very close to those generated by the optimal policy, indeed there seems to be no practical difference between the two. Not only does the rule-of-thumb reproduce all the characteristics of the stochastic equilibrium under the optimal policy, but there is no perceptible welfare difference. Figure 3 shows value functions for various policies, and that for the rule of thumb in Figures 1 and 2 is not visibly different from that for the optimal policy. (These value functions are calculated from the following procedure. Start from a grid on x, $\{xx_1, xx_2, \ldots, xx_N\}$ and corresponding grid on c, $\{c_1, c_2, \ldots, c_N\}$, with $c_i \equiv f(xx_i)$. Then the transition rule (7) is used to calculate a

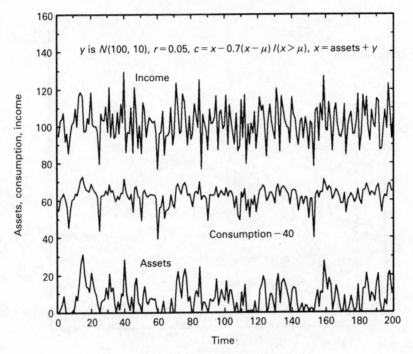

Fig. 2. Buffering without borrowing and rule of thumb behavior.

transition matrix T with element t_{ij}, the probability that, given x is xx_i in t, it is xx_j in $t+1$. We also have a grid of subutility values $v_i = v(c_i) = v\{f(xx_i)\}$, so that the expected utility associated with xx is the infinite sum of terms of the form $(1+\delta)^{-i} T^i v$ or $\{I-(1+\delta)^{-1} T\}^{-1} v$. Figure 3 also shows the value functions associated with a number of other possible consumption strategies. The next best after the optimal strategy and the rule-of-thumb is a second rule of thumb where, instead of saving 70 per cent of the excess above μ, only 50 per cent is saved, so that there is even more excess consumption than by the first rule. Quite some way below comes the value function that comes from the simplest policy of all, that associated with setting consumption equal to income and accumulating no assets. Finally, the worst policy shown is the ultra-conservative one of spending no more than mean income, and spending less if cash on hand is less. These rankings show that, at least for these parameters, the rules of thumb do well capturing most of the benefits of the more complicated optimal policy, and that any sensible rule of this form does a great deal better than the "obvious" policy of never saving anything. These results are not surprising given earlier results in the commodity storage literature,

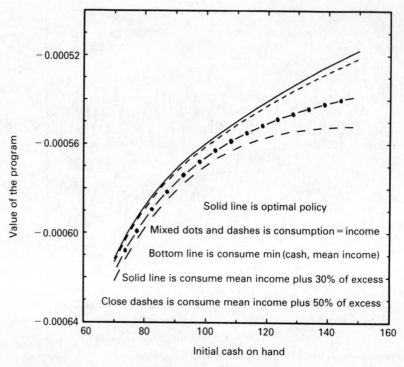

Fig. 3. Value functions for alternative policies.

where piecewise linear storage functions are known to perform well relative to fully optimal policies; see Newbery and Stiglitz (1981, Chapter 30).

One feature of these results that is perhaps surprising is the small values that are attached by consumers to any form of consumption smoothing. Figure 3 can be used to read off the amount that a "consumption equals income" consumer would pay to be instructed in the optimal buffering policy, and the answer is close to 10, which is one tenth of mean income, or one standard deviation of income. This amount is the *discounted present value* of the improvement, not a continuing per period gain, and seems a very small amount to pay for the consumption stream in Figure 2 rather than the income stream immediately above it. Of course, the agent who buffers consumption loses utility by holding assets, as well as gaining from the greater stability of his consumption and the net gain appears to be rather small. The low value attached to consumption smoothing is a standard result from other research, for example in the theory of commodity price stabilization; the continuing income equivalent of a reduction in variance is approximately the reduction in the coefficient of variation multiplied by half the coefficient of relative risk aversion, an approximation that accords well with the results in Figure 3. But as has often been noted, these standard evaluations generate answers that reflect neither intuition nor the urgency with which policy-makers and agents in LDC's approach the stabilization issue.

It is also possible to calculate how much these consumers would pay to be rid of the uncertainty altogether, and how much to be rid of the liquidity constraints, In this context, it is the liquidity constraints that hurt, much more than the uncertainty. If there is no uncertainty, the optimal policy is derived from equation (5), but without the expectation. If we insert the isoelastic form $\lambda(c) = c^{-\rho}$, invert and take logarithms, we have

$$\ln c_t = \min[\ln x_t, \ln c_{t+1} - \rho^{-1}(r - \delta)]. \tag{9}$$

Since impatience dominates, $\delta > r$, so that, if initially, the consumer has assets, they will be run down along a declining consumption path until consumption equals income, at which value it will remain thereafter. The value of this policy is the middle line in Figure 4, higher than the value of the optimal policy with borrowing restrictions and uncertainty, but much lower than the function for the case where there are neither borrowing constraints nor uncertainty. If there are no borrowing constraints, then these impatient consumers will plan a falling consumption trajectory, with initial consumption set to satisfy the long-run budget constraint. In the case illustrated, which has the same parameters as before, initial consumption is 84 per cent higher than mean income, so that very substantial use is made of the borrowing facility, consumption is brought forward, and there are large utility gains. (I have been unable to calculate the fourth value function, for the case where there is uncertainty, but no restrictions on borrowing, but I conjecture that it lies not far below the top curve in Figure 4.)

In practice, while agents in LDC's do borrow and lend, it is unlikely that they would be able to borrow the very large sums that their impatience might dictate, and certainly not at rates that are the same as those at which they can lend. To consider a more realistic situation, I computed one further policy function, with the same parameters as before, but now allowing a limited amount of borrowing, up to 10, which is 10 per cent of income and one standard deviation, but at the "usurious" rate of 25 per cent. The Euler equation (5) is modified fairly straightforwardly to include four "regimes" instead of two. In the worst possible states, when cash on hand is very low, the maximum of 10 is borrowed from the moneylender, consumption is cash on hand plus 10, and consumption moves one for one with resources. This is the bottom segment of the function in Figure 1 above. As resources increase, less is borrowed from the moneylender until a segment is reached on which consumption is equal to cash on hand, and

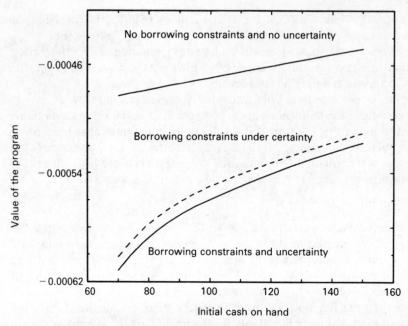

Fig. 4. The costs of uncertainty and borrowing constraints.

for this segment the policy function runs along the 45-degree line. At yet better positions, we get the same qualitative behavior as in the original model, with something being saved, and the original and "moneylender" policy functions asymptote to one another as the level of cash on hand becomes very large, and the probability of ever having to resort to the moneylender becomes correspondingly small.

Figures 5 and 6 illustrate the differences in behavior and value functions generated by the presence of the moneylender. Given the penal borrowing rate, it is not surprising that the moneylender is rarely used. However, there is a noticeable effect on the downward peaks in consumption, which are much less severe in the presence of the moneylender than without. Note too that the presence of the borrowing facility means that the consumer holds fewer assets; the precautionary need for assets is less when borrowing is available, even in limited amounts and at unattractive rates. The value functions hold no great surprises and once again, the evaluation of the gain in Figure 6 is small given what appears to be the marked usefulness of borrowing in Figure 5.

It is no simple matter to turn the theory of this section into fully articulated econometric specifications that could be confronted with the data. The lack of explicit functional forms for the optimal policy functions

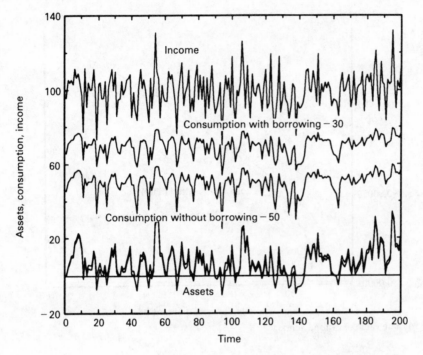

Fig. 5. Consumer behavior with and without a moneylender.

presents computational difficulties, which would be made worse if the income process were allowed to be temporally dependent, a generalization that would certainly be required by the data. It is also unclear whether the quality of the microeconomic data on income and saving is sufficient to support the estimation of complex non-linear models. At this stage, it seems better to use these models as a guide for data exploration, and that is the purpose of the empirical section below. Note, however, the broad implications of the sort of models discussed here:

(i) The dynamics of consumption and income are such as to detach consumption from income in the short-term, but not in the long-term. There is "high-frequency" consumption smoothing, but no "low-frequency" smoothing, over the life-cycle, nor over longer secular periods. The model is consistent with some lending and borrowing for buffering purposes, but not with the existence of long-term loans for consumption purposes. Agents look ahead in an entirely rational manner, but their horizons are naturally truncated at periods when they run out of assets, beyond which there is no point in planning. Even so, rational agents would save in anticipation of short-term falls in income, and vice versa.

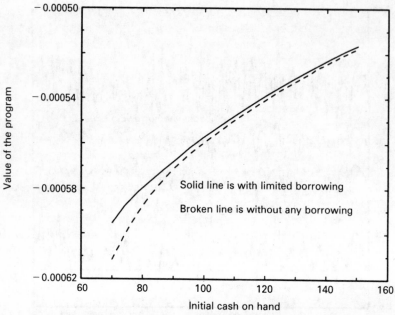

Fig. 6. The value of a moneylender.

(ii) In the cross-section, dissaving is likely to be common. If income is stationary, there will be as much dissaving as saving in the long run, and depending on the point in the agricultural cycle, large fractions of households may spend more than their income. The relationship between consumption and cash in hand depicted, for example, in Figure 1, will not be observed directly in the data, because income processes will differ from agent to agent. Abstracting from short-term buffering behavior, consumption will match income across agents, so that the implications of the theory for cross-sectional behavior are essentially identical to those of the standard permanent income theory, and consumption rises less rapidly than income because of the increasing proportion of transitory income as income rises.

(iii) Unlike the life-cycle model, buffering models do not provide an explanation for wealth holding in the society as a whole. There is no "hump" retirement saving and alternative explanations must be sought for the wealth that is actually observed. A crucial assumption in the buffering model is that consumers are *impatient*, so that assets are a necessary evil, lost consumption opportunities that must be held as insurance against an uncertain and dangerous future. In fact, it is reasonable to suppose that impatience is a characteristic that varies from individual to individual in the population, and that while most are too impatient to accumulate, there are a minority of patient accumulators, who save to finance higher consumption later, either for themselves or for their heirs. In such a model, we have the opposite of Irving Fisher's contention that poverty generates high rates of time preference. It is high rates of time preference that make it optimal for agents to remain poor, and low rates of time preference that generate individual fortunes and long-lived dynasties. But patience, unlike wealth, is not easily bequeathable from parent to child, so that fortunes do not last for ever. To adapt the saying, families go from liquidity constraints to liquidity constraints in three generations. In this world, most individuals have little or no wealth, they smooth consumption in the short-run, but there are no long-standing deviations of consumption from income, and no room for accumulation. Wealth is owned by a small minority of individuals who are abnormally patient, who had access to abnormally large rates of return, or who were fortunate enough to inherit wealth from patient parents and grandparents who were in such a position. Whether or not this picture describes the United States is still being hotly debated; see Kotlikoff and Summers (1981), Modigliani (1988) and Kotlikoff (1988). That wealth transmission is governed by the sort of process discussed here has previously been argued by Bevan and Stiglitz (1979).

III. Empirical Evidence from LDCs

Patterns of Lending and Borrowing

I begin with evidence from West Africa. The World Bank, in collaboration with the Governments of Côte d'Ivoire and Ghana, has been collecting household data on a wide range of variables since 1985 in Côte d'Ivoire and 1987/8 in Ghana. The Living Standard Surveys (LSS) have relatively small samples by the standards of many household surveys in developing countries, but are distinguished by their range and depth, enquiring into the whole range of economic and social activities of the household members. Both data sets contain panel elements, with a half of the households surveyed in each year retained for one subsquent appearance in the next; the results here are based on the three years 1985, 1986, and 1987 from Côte d'Ivoire, and the single year 1987/8 from Ghana.

Table 1 summarizes the information on the extent of debts and credits in all three years of the Ivorian survey and the first year of the Ghanaian one. A little more than a third of the survey households on Côte d'Ivoire owe loans, while closer to a half have made loans that are still outstanding. Note that the same loans may be counted in more than one year, although two-thirds of loans are for durations of twelve months or less. Since there may be more than one lender or borrower in each household, and since there are lenders who are not private individuals (but 89 per cent of rural

Table 1. *Fractions of households with outstanding debts and credits*

	Rural		Urban	
	Creditors	Debtors	Creditors	Debtors
Côte d'Ivoire				
1985	0.474	0.399	0.487	0.396
1986	0.502	0.364	0.525	0.373
1987	0.441	0.386	0.484	0.333
Ghana				
1987/88	0.272	0.286	0.315	0.352

Notes: Creditors are those households who have at least one member who is a creditor for an outstanding loan, and debtors those households who have at least one member who have a loan outstanding. Even in the absence of measurement error, fractions of creditors and debtors need not be the same because there are lenders other than households, and because there can be more than one creditor and debtor in each household.

and 68 per cent of urban loans are from private individuals) the number of households who are creditors need not be the same as those who are debtors. Even so, it is surprising that there are so many more creditor households than debtor households in Côte d'Ivoire, and it may well be that respondents are more willing to report assets than liabilities. The Ghanaian figures are a little lower than the Ivorian ones, and there is a closer match between the numbers of creditors and debtors. Again, informal arrangements dominate the picture. Only about 7 per cent of loans in both urban and rural come from private banks, government banks, or cooperatives, about the same fraction from private moneylenders, and three quarters from private individuals, a third of whom are relatives among rural borrowers, and a fifth among urban borrowers. Very few loans carry interest payments or require collateral, and in most cases do not involve regular, pre-specified payments. There is clearly an active market in informal credit.

The survey data cannot be used directly to assess the role played by these loans in smoothing consumption. The size of the loans is not very large, especially in the rural sector, where the need for consumption smoothing would seem to be largest. For urban Ivorian households who have any loans at all, the average amount owed is around ten per cent of average consumption. For the forest zones, the ratio is closer to 5 per cent and for the Savannah it is only 1.5 per cent. For Ghana, the proportions are even smaller, between one and two per cent of average consumption. Moreover, not all loans are for consumption purposes. The survey distinguishes loans for farm, for business, for school, and for other purposes and the last category, which presumably includes borrowing for consumption, comprises little more than half of all loans in Côte d'Ivoire

Table 2. *Distribution of loans by season of contract and termination (percentage)*

	Season in which loan began		Season in which loan terminated	
	Rural	Urban	Rural	Urban
Côte d'Ivoire				
Off season	16.8	22.8	44.3	20.3
Planting season	13.0	13.8	3.2	9.9
Growing season	30.5	24.7	5.7	22.5
Harvest season	15.2	21.7	6.3	17.7
Missing	25.6	17.1	40.6	30.0
Ghana				
Off season	26.6	25.2	19.5	14.7
Planting season	18.3	23.1	11.5	9.4
Growing season	37.2	33.6	24.3	22.6
Harvest season	17.9	18.1	19.0	16.8
Missing	—	—	25.8	36.5

Notes: The Ivorian data are pooled over the three years 1985–87; those from Ghana are from the single year 1987/88. Since there are many different crops in Côte d'Ivoire and Ghana, the seasons correspond only loosely to actual agricultural seasons which vary from place to place and crop to crop. Here the off season is December, January, and February, the planting season is March and April, the growing season is May, June, July, and August, and the harvest season is September, October, and November. The figures are percentages of all loans in each sector by season. Missings include some genuinely missing observations, Côte d'Ivoire in the first two columns, but also loans that are still outstanding in the last two columns.

and 60–70 per cent in Ghana. These figures do not suggest that loans play a major role in consumption smoothing, although even such small amounts may be helpful, as for example in Figures 5 and 6 above.

Another way of looking at the role played by loans is to examine their seasonal pattern, and the way in which loans are linked to the agricultural calendar. Table 2 shows the distribution of loans contracted and terminated by seasons, defined in terms of calendar months as detailed in the notes to the table. In the urban sectors of both countries, loan contracts and terminations are relatively evenly distributed throughout the year, but this is much less true in the rural areas, particularly for loan repayments. The χ^2 tests that the two distributions are the same are, for Côte d'Ivoire, 49.1 for contracts and 370.3 for terminations, and for Ghana, 6.0 for contracts, and 22.6 for terminations, all with three degrees of freedom. In Côte d'Ivoire, a large fraction (40 per cent or so) of loans in the rural sectors are taken out in the growing season, in the months before the harvest, and are repaid in the off-season, after the harvest (75 per cent). The pattern is much less clear in Ghana, but in general is quite consistent with loans being used to smooth consumption, even though the amounts are quite small. However, if such was the case we should expect changes in income between one year and the next to be positively associated with the net credit position (loans owed to less loans owed by) of the household. This can be tested in Côte d'Ivoire but not on the single year of data in Ghana. The predicted correlation exists in the 1985–86 panel, but is replaced by a *negative* correlation in the subsequent 1986–97 panel perhaps because of a different pattern of common shocks in the two years. In spite of the difficulties, the data from these two countries are perhaps consistent with a modest role for credit markets in smoothing consumption and as such are consistent with Udry's (1990) evidence from northern Nigeria.

Note finally that if borrowing restrictions are a problem for many households, assets, particularly liquid assets, should play a role in guaranteeing future consumption. A simple way of testing the role of these cash balances is to regress consumption in year t on assets in year $t-1$, including consumption and income in $t-1$ in an attempt to control for individual fixed effects. Lagged income has no predictive power for consumption conditional on lagged consumption, so the role of assets can be assessed by regressing consumption on its lag and on the amount of liquid assets in hand at the end of the previous period, nearly always cash, since few households report holdings of other financial assets. In the 1985–86 panel, this experiment generates a significant positive role for lagged assets in predicting consumption in the rural zones, but not in Abidjan or in other urban areas, but the 1986–87 panel shows no significant results for any of the five regions. Again we have the uncomfortable fact that the two panel data sets do not have the same structure.

Life-Cycle Patterns of Consumption and Income

If a large fraction of individuals are impatient and liquidity constrained, their consumption will track their incomes fairly closely over time. In cross-sectional data, there typically is such a close relationship, and Figures 7 and 8 show plots of average household consumption and household income by age of household head using household survey data for Côte d'Ivoire for 1985, 1986, and 1987, and for Thailand in 1986, distinguished by level of urbanization (sanitary districts are intermediate between urban (municipal areas) and rural (village) Thailand). The data have been smoothed over age groups, with each point showing averages for the age and the two (Thailand) or three (Côte d'Ivoire) ages on either side, with declining triangular weights. The Thai sample is larger, so it needs less smoothing, but five points are still required because people tend to report rounded ages (ending in 5's and 0's) and because those who do so have lower average consumption and income levels.

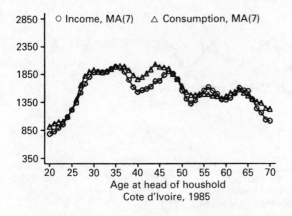

Age at head of houshold
Cote d'Ivoire, 1985

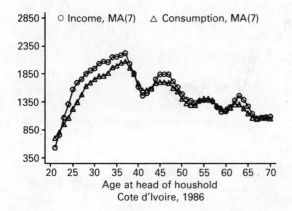

Age at head of houshold
Cote d'Ivoire, 1986

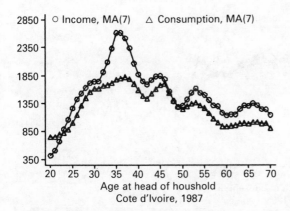

Age at head of houshold
Cote d'Ivoire, 1987

Fig. 7. Consumption, income and age: Côte d'Ivoire.

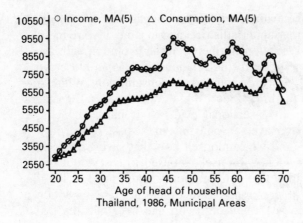

Age of head of household
Thailand, 1986, Municipal Areas

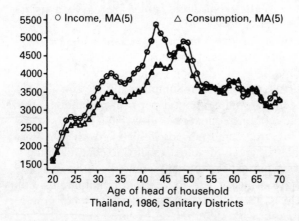

Age of head of household
Thailand, 1986, Sanitary Districts

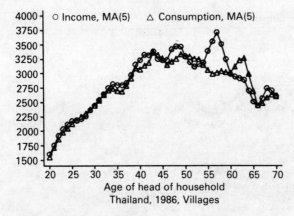

Age of head of household
Thailand, 1986, Villages

Fig. 8. Consumption, income and age: Thailand.

Although there is some evidence of "hump" saving in urban Thailand, and to a lesser extent in the sanitary districts and in Côte d'Ivoire in 1987, there is generally a close relationship between the evolution with age of consumption and income. Indeed, the relationship is even closer when purchases of durable goods are included in consumption. While such evidence casts doubt on the importance of life-cycle saving in the generation of national wealth, cross-sectional evidence is hardly conclusive. These households may have saved at some time in the past, or will do so at some time in the future, and we cannot tell how that saving may evolve with age. Nor can this evidence, by itself, by used to cast doubt on the central life-cycle proposition that consumption is determined by life-time wealth and the pattern of preferences, not by the life-time evolution of income. Tastes may vary systematically with age in a manner that is correlated with income. Indeed, as has long been recognized, the explanation is a plausible one, because the evolution of family size and responsibilities is similar to that of income.

However, the combination of the Thai and Ivorian evidence does provide evidence against the life-cycle hypothesis, and in favor of the proposition that consumption tracks income. The argument is due to Carroll and Summers (1991). According to Summers and Heston (1988), the Thai economy has been growing at about 4 per cent per annum over the last 25 years, while the Ivorian economy has grown at a little less than 1 per cent per annum over the same period. If such growth rates are reflected in individual incomes, and if they are expected to continue, then a 25 year old in Côte d'Ivoire has expected total lifetime resources that are two-thirds larger than those of his or her 75 year-old grandparents. For Thailand, the 25 year old is 7.1 times better off than his or her grandparent. Hence, if consumption is determined by life-time resources, consumption by age patterns should be more tipped in favour of young households in Thailand and more tipped in favor of the old in Côte d'Ivoire. Precisely the opposite is true. Consumption peaks at a much earlier age in the slow-growing Côte d'Ivoire than it does in the rapidly growing Thailand. Of course, tastes and preferences may be different in the two countries, but there is a much simpler explanation, which is that the patterns of income are different in the two countries, and consumption tracks income. Indeed, if the taste explanation is to be relied upon, then . family size is not the relevant variable, because family size peaks much later in Côte d'Ivoire, rising steadily from head's age 25 to 50 or later, than in Thailand, where the peak is reached by age 40.

In Figure 8, for Thailand, note that the vertical scales for the three regions are not the same, and that the range of variation of life-time consumption in the municipal areas, from 2550 to 7550 baht, is much larger than the range in the villages, from 1500 to 3250 baht. Again, the difference is more plausibly linked to the similar paths in income than to any difference in taste variation between urban and rural regions. It is also reasonable to suppose that incomes in urban areas have been growing more rapidly over time than those in the villages. Income differences between the two areas are very large, Bangkok is a rapidly growing city that accounts for much of Thailand's urban population, and there is a limit to the rate of growth of agricultural productivity. Yet there is no evidence in Figure 8 that consumption patterns are relatively tipped towards the young in the urban areas. Once again, the simplest hypothesis, that consumption tracks income, is the most plausible. Even if this is not the case, and the life-cycle hypothesis works in each country individually, with the tracking of income by consumption largely coincidental, the comparison of the two countries must reject any model that relies on common tastes across countries, as does the standard life-cycle explanation for the positive international correlation between saving and growth.

IV. Conclusions

The results of this study should be read in conjunction with the evolving literature on saving in developing countries, and are placed in more extensive context in the full version of this paper, Deaton (1991b). My own earlier work for the Côte d'Ivoire, Deaton (1990b), and Paxson's (1991), (1992) work for Thailand, confirm some but not all aspects of life-cycle theory. In particular, these papers provide evidence that farmers (and others) look ahead at least some way when deciding how much to consume and to save, but they do not support the cross-equation restrictions generated either by the full permanent income hypothesis, nor by any simple modification based on the way liquidity constraints might work. More general reviews of the undoubted progress in the area can be found in Gersovitz (1988) and Deaton (1990a). However, it will also be clear that much remains to be done. Although the data and the models generate what appear to be real insights, we are far from a really satisfactory understanding of all the evidence. The data themselves are difficult to use. Income is not a concept that is easily measured, particularly for people who are self-employed (in agriculture or elsewhere), and it is in the analysis of saving that data deficiencies are probably at their most acute. Except for the fact that there are more self-employed workers in LDC's, I do not believe that saving data are any worse in developing than in developed economies; indeed, high response rates and the willingness of "fresh" interviewees to spend a great deal of time with survey staff suggests the reverse. Even so, there is a great deal of measurement error in both income and saving, and the measurement error in each is almost certainly correlated, facts that must be recognized in any credible econometric analysis. The theories examined in the paper are useful, but none is strongly supported by the evidence. The model without borrowing is a useful benchmark and shows that it is possible for consumption to be very much smoother than income even without the intermediation of credit markets. However, there are important elements of reality that are not captured by such a formulation, and it is difficult to use the model to derive empirical predictions that can be readily tested on the data.

References

Bevan, D. & Stiglitz, J. E.: Intergenerational transfers and inequality. *Greek Economic Review 1*, 8–26, 1979.
Carrol, C. & Summers, L. H.: Consumption growth parallels income growth: Some new evidence. In B. D. Bernheim & J. B. Shoven (eds.), *National Saving and Economic Performance*. Chicago University Press for NBER, Chicago and London. 305–47, 1991.
Deaton, A. S.: Saving in developing countries: Theory and review. *Proceedings of the World Bank Annual Conference on Development Economics 1989; The World Bank Economic Review*, Washington, DC, 1990a.
Deaton, A. S.: Saving and income smoothing in Côte d'Ivoire. Research Program in Development Studies, Princeton University (processed), 1990b.
Deaton, A. S.: Saving and liquidity constraints. *Econometrica 59*, 1221–48, 1991a.
Deaton, A. S.: Household saving in LDC's: Credit markets, insurance, and welfare. Research Program in Development Studies WP No. 153, Princeton University, 1991b.
Gersovitz, M.: Saving and development. In Hollis Chenery & T. N. Srinivasan (ed.), *Handbook of Development Economics 1*, North-Holland, Amsterdam, 381–424, 1988.
Kotlikoff, L. J.: Intergenerational transfer of saving. *Journal of Economic Perspectives 2*, 41–58, 1988.
Kotlikoff, L. J. & Summers, L. H.: The role of intergenerational transfers in aggregate capital accumulation. *Journal of Political Economy 89*, 706–732, 1981.
Little, I. M. D. & Mirrlees, J. A.: Project Appraisal and Planning. Heinemann, London, 1974.
Modigliani, F.: The role of intergenerational transfers and life-cycle saving in the accumulation of wealth. *Journal of Economic Perspectives 2*, 15–40, 1988.
Newbery, D. M. G. & Stiglitz, J. E.: *The Theory of Commodity Price Stabilization*. Oxford University Press, Oxford, 1981.
Paxson, C. H.: Consumption seasonality and consumption smoothing. Research Program in Development Studies WP No. 150, Princeton University, 1991.
Paxson, C. H.: Using weather variability to estimate the response of savings to transitory income in Thailand. *American Economic Review 82*, 15–33, 1992.
Squire, L. & van der Tak, H. G.: *Economic Analysis of Projects*. Johns Hopkins University Press, Baltimore, 1975.
Summers, R. & Heston, A.: A new set of international comparisons of real product and prices for 130 countries. *Review of Income and Wealth 34*, 1–26, 1988.
Udry, C.: Credit markets in Northern Nigeria: Credit as insurance in a rural economy. *World Bank Economic Review 4*, 251–69, 1990.
UNIDO (United Nations Industrial Development Organization) *Guidelines for Project Evaluation*. Project Formulation and Evaluation Series, No. 2, United Nations, New York, 1972.

Comment on A. Deaton, "Household Saving in LDCs: Credit Markets, Insurance and Welfare"

Costas Meghir

University College, London, and Institute for Fiscal Studies, London, England

I particularly enjoyed reading this paper by Deaton which follows on his now well-established work on LDCs. Reading the literature on LDCs, it is quite clear that there is a need for a systematic analysis of the behaviour of individual agents and of the institutional framework which they operate. Recognition of the importance of microeconometric work for understanding how the overall economy works has stimulated such research for LDCs, and Deaton's work has been particularly influential in this respect. The important development on this front is the availability of panel data that follow the same households for some periods of time. The overall motivation of this paper is to provide a framework for analysing household saving in LDCs; the particular country considered in both setting up the model and looking at empirical evidence is the Côte d'Ivoire (and to a lesser extent Ghana). I would like to review what I perceive to be the most important results and raise a set of questions that should be part of the research agenda in LDCs.

Deaton begins by developing the theory of savings with borrowing constraints. The world set up here is one of constant real interest rates. Income is assumed to be independently (and identically) distributed over time. Crucially, there is no growth in this economy and moreover the individual discount factor is higher than the fixed real interest rate. The economy is characterised by an absence of institutions that could smooth consumption across time and/or across states of the world. Agents are forward looking and they maximise an additive intertemporal utility function over time. The period utility function is isoelastic. Apart from the intertemporal budget constraint, the agents face a borrowing constraint where assets are not allowed to fall below zero. Since there is no growth, and assuming that the interest rate was always kept below the discount rate, consumers would plan a falling consumption path if markets were complete. In the presence of borrowing constraints and in the absence of insurance markets, Deaton shows that individuals use a buffer stock policy to protect consumption against sudden drops in income. In periods of bad income draws, assets (cash in hand) are run down, sometimes to zero; in good times savings occur and assets are built up. No wealth is accumulated because of impatience (high discount factors); this inhibits growth and traps the agents into perpetual poverty.

This model was simulated and compared to a world with no income uncertainty and no liquidity constraints, where consumers use a simple rule of thumb by which, above a threshold, they save a fixed proportion of income. The results of these simulations are quite interesting in themselves. In this world, given that the rate of time preference is higher than the interest rate, the costs of liquidity constraints are very high; in contrast, households would pay very little to rid themselves of uncertainty, while rule-of-thumb consumers would pay practically nothing to be taught the full optimisation problem. The implications of these results are very important since they imply a low value of stabilisation policies. Nevertheless the way the simulations were performed seems to have given a very high weight to the role of time preference, while it seems to me that uncertainty would be a rather important driving force behind any observed savings behaviour in a rural area of an LDC. In the model, households implement a buffer stock policy which is presumably driven by the precautionary motive and not by the discount rate which would motivate them to borrow.[1] Yet the cost of this policy seems to be very low, particularly when compared to the benefits of being allowed to plan the optimal declining path of consumption. It seems to me that an interesting exercise would be to set the discount rate equal to the rate of time preference and to identify the level of income uncertainty that could generate the observed consumption behaviour in, say, Côte d'Ivoire. This could then be compared to actual income dispersion.

Another important assumption is that of constant relative risk aversion. A high-wealth household has the same attitude to risk as the low-wealth household in the simulations. Yet the low-wealth household is much more vulnerable to further bad income draws since it has very low assets with which to buffer consumption. In practice, it is very hard to model the behaviour of individuals at subsistence levels of consumption. Yet one feels that the behaviour of such rural households would be driven at least in part by the (small) probability of a series of bad events. Perhaps an interesting representation of preferences would be a quasihomothetic representation. To implement such a program, it would have to be assumed that income is bounded below so that utility is never allowed to go to minus infinity. If all risk is idiosyncratic (as it is in this model), this

---

[1] In the absence of uncertainty, with a constant income and no borrowing constraints, these consumers would borrow to implement a declining consumption path.

assumption could be justified by assuming that the village will provide subsistence insurance as an informal social security system. With such preferences, individuals become much more risk averse at low levels of consumption and never drive their cash in hand to zero. A similar issue is taken up by Gersovitz (1983), who also suggests that relaxing inter-temporal additivity would be a useful way of capturing the behaviour of households at very low consumption levels. Such modifications could lead to the implication of some moderate wealth accumulation, which may lie partly behind the 1 per cent growth rate in Côte d'Ivoire.

This brings us to the next question: is the main source of risk in these economies aggregate or idiosynchratic? One would believe that the presence of idiosynchratic risk would lead to formal or informal risk-pooling activity among households. In fact, evidence presented by Udry (1990) for Northern Nigeria implies that this is the case. His study indicates that households enter into loan agreements where the value of the repayment is contingent on the income outcome of the two partners. In his data, borrowers with bad income draws had a borrowing cost (*ex post*) of − 0.6 per cent, while households that did well paid on average 20.4 per cent interest. Udry's results can be interpreted as implying that risk pooling is a pervasive activity and hence risk is an important consideration for these villagers. They also imply that more detailed work is needed to uncover the informal arrangements that possibly exist in rural areas of LDCs. Deaton does present evidence of loan transactions and shows that loans are quite prevalent; moreover, their timing seems to follow the agricultural production cycle quite closely although the amounts involved are small. It would be interesting to know whether these loan contracts are a mechanism of risk pooling. On the other hand, if most of the risk is aggregate, this would explain the absence of risk-pooling mechanisms. The absence of markets to insure against aggregate uncertainty could be an important reason behind the low growth rates of some developing countries. After all, the dependence of an economy such as the Ivorian one on the world price of cocoa is quite well documented.[2]

An interesting observation made by Deaton is that there are practically no collateralised loans. If the utility costs of borrowing constraints are as high as implied by the simulations, individuals could be expected to use their property as collateral for loans that would serve to smooth consumption and come close to the unconstrained optimum declining path. To the extent that property such as land can be used as collateral, this should bypass the moral hazard problems and lead to a supply of loans at

---

[2] The Ivorian government implements a price stabilisation policy which protects cocoa farmers from price fluctuations. Nevertheless such a policy can be costly and the macro-economic effects could be considerable for most of the economy.

relatively low interest rates. This would be particularly true in non-Muslim societies where interest-bearing loans are not illegal. So why do we not observe more of this type of loan?

An important question facing anyone wishing to analyse such issues empirically is that of measuring all assets and activities that the household may be involved in for the purposes of insurance and/or consumption smoothing. Presumably a large part of savings is channeled to investments in both agricultural tools and, more importantly, education. Most households, at least in the Côte d'Ivoire, are large extended families. In itself this form of social organisation reduces exposure to risk by diversifying the activities of its members: at a point in time, some work on the land owned by the household, some work for pay on other farms, others migrate to the city to obtain jobs with secure pay, while others are sent to school. In this context remittances from migrant members of the family are a very important source of income with greater stability (or with risk not necessarily correlated with agricultural risk).

Alessie *et al.* (1992) have documented that in rural Côte d'Ivoire, children as young as seven years are taken in and out of school and work depending on economic conditions. In good times, saving presumably takes place by investment in education. To the extent that this is not measured, this will lead to lower observed savings rates and to the illusion of high rates of time preference. In addition, it is probably hard to measure and value savings in kind and investment in agricultural equipment.

The difficulty of measuring assets and savings in practice leads to an empirical strategy that uses Euler equations of consumption; the latter can usually be measured more accurately, although problems of definition and valuation are important here as well. Unfortunately, this version of Deaton's paper does not contain the detailed empirical work he has carried out to test a version of the PIH on Ivorian data. He does present a summary of his conclusion, however, where he says that liquid assets matter for consumption (conditional on lagged consumption) in rural areas only in one of the waves of the panel. Although it is hard to discuss conclusions based on research presented elsewhere, it is still worth raising the issue of the length of the panel: each set of data spans only two years. This raises an identification question in the presence of aggregate shocks (correlated across clusters). Even in the absence of aggregate shocks, a slightly longer panel would be useful for the appropriate choice of instruments. Since the data are organised at cluster level, all four years of data could be put together to form a pseudo panel at the expense of some of the cross-section variation. This would give a longer panel and would probably lead to less measurement error by averaging over households. Moreover, village level variables would be quite good instruments for household expectations since village level information is bound to be in the information set of the households.

Deaton briefly discusses the patterns of life-cycle consumption and income and compares fast growing Thailand to the slow growing Côte d'Ivoire. He reiterates the Caroll and Summers argument that the high level of Thai growth and the low level of Ivorian growth should imply (by the LCH) that consumption should be tipped much more in favour of the young in Thailand since the latter are much richer in a life-cycle sense. The reverse is true. I am not sure what this proves; if the Thai households have very low discount rates relative to interest rates and if income is very noisy in Thailand, one may expect that the young households do not borrow against future growth. Such behaviour may have led to the observed growth rates. Perhaps this last point emphasises the need for detailed microeconometric work which takes into account important measurement problems, the potential complexity of preferences, income risk and the institutional framework when analysing savings behaviour. We should also be rather cautious regarding simple cross-country comparisons without due reference to preference and institutional differences.

References

Alessie, R., Baker, P., Blundell, R., Heady, C. & Meghir, C.: The working behavior of young people in rural Côte d'Ivoire. *World Bank Economic Review 6*, (1), 139–154, 1992.

Gersovitz, M.: Savings and nutrition at low incomes. *Journal of Political Economy 91*, 841–855, 1983.

Udry, C.: Risk, insurance and default in a rural credit market: An empirical investigation in northern Nigeria. Mimeo, Northwestern University, April 1990.

The Impact of the Demographic Transition on Capital Formation*

Alan J. Auerbach

University of Pennsylvania, Philadelphia, PA and NBER, Cambridge, MA, USA

Laurence J. Kotlikoff

Boston University, Boston, MA and NBER, Cambridge, MA, USA

Abstract

The population of the United States is aging. We review a variety of the implications this has for U.S. national saving rates, and discuss the policy issues that they raise. After reviewing what different models would predict for household saving over the next several decades, we consider how the demographic transition may also affect national saving through changes in government behavior. Ways in which the composition of household saving might change as individuals age are also analyzed along with the implications of changes in government fiscal policy for asset composition.

I. Introduction

The population of the United States is aging. As of 1990, about one fifth of the total U.S. population was over 55 years old. In fifty years that figure will be close to one third.[1] This aging will be particularly acute among the older old. Currently, those over age 75 represent only 5 per cent of Americans. By 2040 this figure is projected to grow to about 12 per cent.

At the same time that the elderly fraction of the population is increasing, the relative population of young people will be declining. While well over half the population was under age 35 in 1990, this figure is projected to drop to just over 40 per cent by the year 2040.

*This is an abbreviated version of Auerbach and Kotlikoff (1991). An earlier version of this paper was presented in May 1991 at the Wharton Pension Research Council Symposium, "Demography and Retirement, the 21st Century", and the Conference on Savings Behavior, Espoo, Finland. We are grateful to our discussants, Alicia Munnell and David Weil, respectively, and other conference participants for comments.
[1] This and other projections for the U.S. and other countries are from Auerbach *et al.* (1989), and were compiled from Social Security Administration projections for the United States and comparable statistics for other countries.

This aging of the population, which is attributable to declining rates of fertility and mortality, has a range of implications for the level and composition of national saving and capital formation in the United States over the next several decades. In this paper, we review a variety of these implications and discuss the policy issues that they raise.

II. What are the Issues?

The demographic transition affects capital formation because of differences in household behavior over the life cycle. In the simple life-cycle model of household saving, individuals engage in a pattern of "hump" saving, drawing down resources in childhood and again in old age, with both of these periods of net dissaving financed by saving during pre-retirement adulthood.

Perhaps the simplest measure of how saving should be affected by the demographic transition is the *dependency ratio* of children and the elderly to the remainder of the population. According to midrange forecasts of the Social Security Administration, reported in Aaron *et al.* (1989, Table 1–1), the dependency ratio (those over 64 and under 20 to those between 20 and 64) of the United States will rise from 0.695 in 1990 to 0.806 in 2040, with the growth in the share of elderly swamping the reduction in the share of children in the overall population.

From this very simple trend, a decline in the saving rate might be predicted, as a smaller fraction of the population will be savers and a greater fraction of the population will be dissavers. However, this conclusion is sensitive to the exact specification of saving behavior and the pattern of the demographic transition. Therefore, the first issue we address is what different models of saving would predict for household saving over the next several decades.

The demographic transition may also affect national saving through changes in government behavior. An increasing share of government spending is in age-related categories, and spending on old-age pensions and health care would be expected to rise with the increase in the elderly population. The implications these spending increases will have for national saving depend not only on how the spending is financed, but also on how the private sector reacts to the government's fiscal policy. This relates to not only the horizons of households (the extent to which they are "Ricardian" consumers), but also the extent to which government social insurance programs may reduce household precautionary saving.

The interaction of government and household saving has another, political dimension, relating to the increasing political power of the elderly. A growing elderly population will not only increase the need for certain types of social insurance spending, but may also be able to shift the burden of such spending onto other generations, including those not yet alive. This, in turn, may have a further, depressing effect on the rate of national saving.

The pay-as-you-go method by which we calculate the budget of the social security system may contribute to such as shift in the burden, as short-run "surpluses" may increase the pressure to reduce current social security taxes or increase benefits. This is but one example of the problems of measuring "government saving." We discuss these problems and how they are influenced by the demographic transition.

As individuals age, they may alter not only their level of wealth but also its composition. Only under restrictive circumstances would one expect the saving and portfolio choice decisions to be independent. As the horizon of a household becomes shorter and its size and composition changes, we would expect changes in the riskiness of the assets it holds as well as changes in the size and type of housing, which represents about half of the U.S. private capital stock. The changes in government fiscal policy may also have implications for asset composition.

III. Capital Deepening and the Demographic Transition

As discussed in Auerbach and Kotlikoff (1991), there is considerable uncertainty about the "correct" model of saving, and no model has succeeded very well in predicting the rate of U.S. national saving in the 1980s. This does not necessarily imply that the models we have are useless for considering the changes which might be expected from future demographic change. We are, after all, conducting a *ceteris paribus* experiment, attempting to measure the effects of demographic change, other factors held constant. In any event, economic models of demographics, saving, and capital deepening (increases in capital per worker) are informative if only for demonstrating the potential effects that demographic change could have on the accretion of American wealth. With this objective in mind, we consider the results from a variety of models.

General Equilibrium Analysis

We begin with results from our earlier paper comparing demographic transitions in the United States and Canada; see Auerbach and Kotlikoff (1990b). The simulation results are from the Auerbach-Kotlikoff Demographic Simulation Model, henceforth the AK model. The AK model is a numerical simulation model for studying the general equilibrium effects of the demographic transition. The model's agents live for 75 years, the first 20 of which are spent as children. At age 21 each individual in the model becomes an adult and a parent. Adults in the model have to decide how much to work, how much to spend on their own and their children's consumption, how much to bequeath to their children at the end of their lives, and when to retire. These households view the present value of net social security benefits as wealth, although they do adjust bequests in response to this wealth. The decisions of these adults, when aggregated over the different generations of adults alive at a point in time, determine the total supplies of labor and savings to the economy.

Solution of the model requires that the time path of wage rates and interest rates be such as to make the supplies of labor and savings in each year equal to the demands for these productive factors by the model's firms. The model is solved over a 250 year period and also has an elaborate specification of the government sector. Most parameter values of the model are based on empirical studies of household behavior, while remaining free parameters are adjusted to make the model fit the observed postwar data for the U.S. as closely as possible. In addition, the model's annual birth rates are chosen to reproduce the past and projected demographic structure of the U.S. population.

For every simulation, projections begin in 1960, with the assumption that a steady state (including a steady-state population) existed in that year. We then run the model forward through a historical period (ending in 1985), benchmarked to actual data, in order to allow simulations from the present onward to incorporate the current nonsteady-state population structure. The results of three simulations are reported in Table 1. We discuss the alternative simulations below, and concentrate on the "base case" results provided in the first column of the table.

The base case assumption includes a continuation of current fiscal policy, by which we mean that each component of government spending will remain fixed per member of the group covered by the spending program. Changes in required tax revenue are assumed to come from variations in the rate of consumption taxes. For purposes of these simulations, we have also assumed that the social security system will run on a pay-as-you-go basis without any significant trust fund accumulation.

The model is benchmarked to the actual national saving rate in 1960. It predicts a rise in the saving rate during the 1980s. Thereafter, the model predicts a steady decline in the national saving rate, falling from 12.2 per cent in 1985 to 5.8 per cent in 2050, before increasing slightly to a steady-state value of 6.3 per cent.

This predicted gradual decline in the saving rate is to be expected given the gradual increase in the dependency ratio. A declining saving rate means slower growth in the accumulation of the U.S. wealth, and, ignoring the import of foreign capital, it also means slower growth in the accumulation of capital (plant, equipment, inventories and improved land). The

Table 1. *Demographic simulations from the AK (1990b) model*

	Base Case	No Age-Specific	2 Yr. Inc. in Soc. Sec.
Nat. Saving Rate			
1960	9.8	9.8	9.8
1985	12.2	12.2	12.2
1990	11.7	11.7	12.0
2010	9.5	9.4	10.1
2030	6.5	6.6	7.2
2050	5.8	5.9	6.3
Long Run	6.3	6.3	6.6
Consumption Tax Rate			
1960	9.8	9.8	9.8
1985	8.3	8.3	8.2
1990	8.6	8.6	8.4
2010	5.7	5.5	5.2
2030	5.8	5.2	4.9
2050	5.5	4.8	4.5
Long Run	5.3	4.6	4.1
Social Security Tax Rate			
1960	7.1	7.1	7.1
1985	7.6	7.6	7.5
1990	8.0	7.9	7.9
2010	10.2	10.2	8.0
2030	12.8	12.8	10.2
2050	12.8	12.8	10.1
Long Run	12.3	12.3	9.9

reduced rate of growth of U.S. capital over the next 50 years would be more troublesome were it not also the case that the supply of labor will also grow at a reduced rate. This slower growth of labor supply should not be surprising since the aging of the population means that an increasing fraction of the population will be retired. On balance, it turns out that the growth rate of labor supply will fall by more than the growth rate of capital, and the ratio of capital to labor is predicted to rise. Hence, the drop in saving rates notwithstanding, economic models in general, and the AK model in particular, predict capital deepening associated with the demographic transition. Perhaps a more intuitive understanding of this point arises from considering that in 2040 there will be more older people relative to young and middle-age workers and it is the older members of society who own the most wealth (capital).

The fact that capital will become increasingly abundant relative to labor means that the return to capital (real interest rates) will decline over time, while the return to labor (real wage rates) will increase over time. Beyond the model's normal growth in wages due to total factor productivity, the simulation predicts an increase of about 7 per cent in the after-tax real wage between 1990 and 2050. This implication of the demographic transition is good news for future workers, but bad news for the current baby boom generation. It means that when the baby boomers retire they will earn a smaller return on their accumulated savings, while their children and grandchildren are earning higher real wages (the return to labor).

The increase in pre-tax wages will also improve the government's fiscal position by expanding tax revenues. As a consequence, the government will be able to cut nonsocial security tax rates. As Table 1 indicates, in the AK model, the demographic transition will permit a drop in consumption tax rates by four percentage points. Alternatively, had we kept consumption tax rates constant, the AK model would have permitted almost a three percentage point drop in the income tax rate.

The good news for our children and grandchildren with respect to real wages and nonsocial security tax rates is offset by the bad news on social security tax rates. As the table shows, the social security tax rate in the Base Case, which does not take into account the 1983 Social Security Amendments, rises from 8.0 per cent in 1990 to 12.8 per cent between 2030 and 2050.[2] While the accumulation of a social security trust fund will obviate the need for such a future rise in social security tax rates, the trust fund is being accumulated through higher tax rates today. In either case, the demographic transition has necessitated a rise in payroll tax rates to maintain the viability of the social security system, although the incidence of the burden on different generations is quite different.

How robust is the central prediction of this model, that the saving rate will decline steadily for several decades from the 1980s? An alternative general equilibrium modelling approach, in Cutler *et al.* (1990), provides quite similar predictions. Their simulations are based not on the aggregation of life-cycle households, but rather on the assumption of a single, infinite-horizon family that chooses its optimal consumption path. For simulations that begin in 1970 (i.e., that start the household's consumption response to the demographic transitions in 1970, compared to the AK model's start in 1960), they find a saving rate that peaks in 1980, falls by about 5 percentage points to a low just before 2030, and then recovers slightly. Given the differences between the models, these predicted patterns are quite similar.

---

[2] These social security tax rates should be viewed as the sum of employer plus employee social security taxes. The reason that the model's social security tax rates are lower than the actual social security tax rates is that the model assesses social security taxes on all earnings; i.e., there is no earnings ceiling in the model.

Partial Equilibrium Models

The previous models study the effects of demographics on saving using general equilibrium simulation analysis. Other estimates from our own work, using a partial equilibrium approach (fixed interest and wage rates) predict that the saving rate will first rise for several years before beginning the decline that is common to all models. In our study based on fixed earnings and consumption profiles, we found that the savings rate should begin to fall around the year 2010; cf. Auerbach and Kotlikoff (1990a). Our alternative simulations, also based on actual consumption and earnings profiles, but imposing additional constraints implied by either the infinite horizon or life-cycle consumption model predicted that saving rates would peak sometime between 2000 and 2010; see Auerbach, Cai and Kotlikoff (1991).

There are many potential sources for the differences between the general equilibrium models' predictions of an immediate decline in the saving rate and the partial equilibrium models' prediction that saving rates first increase for several years. One explanation is the absence of general equilibrium changes in factor prices from the partial equilibrium models. In a previous study in which we imposed the partial equilibrium constant-factor-price assumption on some of the simulations with our general equilibrium model, we found a smaller predicted drop in the saving rate between 1985 and 2010 (1.5 versus 2.8 percentage points); cf. Auerbach *et al.* (1989). This may be due to the fact that with rising real future wages, households in the general equilibrium models save less at the onset of the demographic transition. However, this effect explains only part of the difference in predicted saving rates between the general and partial equilibrium analysis.

A second explanation may have to do with the consumption profiles used. While the general equilibrium simulations are based on consumption and earnings profiles generated by the assumption of household utility maximization, the partial equilibrium studies use actual consumption and earnings data by age to generate the consumption and earnings profiles. It is not immediately clear why this difference should be responsible for the difference in predicted savings behavior, but it deserves further investigation.

IV. Saving and Changes in Government Policy

Thus far, we have focused on changes in household saving that are likely to come about as a result of the current demographic transition in the U.S., and have ignored changes in government policy that may alter national saving directly or the saving behavior of households.

Many government spending programs, in addition to old-age pensions, are targeted toward the elderly; Medicare is the most prominent example. On the other hand, a significant share of local government spending is on schools, targeted towards the young. Hence we would expect offsetting pressures on different components of the overall government budget as the population ages.

In the "base case" simulations in the first column of Table 1, we assumed that all government spending remained fixed (except for normal productivity growth) relative to the targeted population; for example, Medicare spending per qualifying individual is kept constant. Hence, increases in the elderly as a fraction of the population increases Medicare expenditures per capita, overall.

To see how much pressure this maintenance of services places on the budget, we considered an alternative simulation, presented in the second column of the table, where overall spending was kept fixed per capita. As a comparison of the columns indicates, the extra expenditures necessitated by maintenance of services is not great, forcing a rise in the consumption tax of about 0.7 percentage points in the year 2050. The reason the increase is this small is that, while the elderly receive a considerable level of government spending per capita, so do the young, who become a smaller fraction of the total population as the transition proceeds. In addition, our simulations assume unchanging relative prices. To the extent that health care costs continue to rise relative to other expenditures, the shift towards an elderly population could be considerably more expensive to finance.[3]

Even more significant, however, are the expenses of maintaining the old-age survivors and disability insurance (OASDI) pension program of the Social Security system. Our base case simulations indicate that, under pay-as-you-go financing, maintenance of benefit levels would require an increase of 60 per cent in the payroll tax rate associated with OASDI. The third column of the table presents a simulation of the impact of increasing the retirement age gradually from 65 to 67, as called for by the 1983 changes in the social security system. As a comparison of the first and third columns of the table shows, this reduction in the present value of benefits is projected to increase national saving noticeably, while at the same time reducing the necessary increase in payroll tax rates. By the year 2010, for example, the saving rate is projected to be 0.6 percentage points higher as a result of the increased retirement age.

---

[3] Aaron *et al.* (1989; p. 50) report that, from 1974 to 1985, overall HI (Medicare) spending would have risen by 177 per cent had the cost of hospitalization payments risen at the same rate as the general price level. In fact, HI spending rose by more than 400 per cent over this period.

Even with the planned increase in the retirement age, the payroll tax will need to rise to finance benefits. In the simulations presented, this rise is timed to satisfy pay-as-you-go balance in the system. In reality, payroll taxes have already risen, and the economy has been accumulating a considerable trust fund to help pay for future benefits, with annual increments in the neighborhood of $100 million per year recently.

What effect will this accumulation have on saving? The answer depends on whether the trust fund accumulations have additional effects on fiscal policy. In isolation, they represent a powerful government saving program, as households currently alive are being forced to help pay the cost of future benefits. Although we have not performed simulations of this exact pattern of trust fund accumulation, trust fund simulations in Auerbach and Kotlikoff (1987) do suggest that accumulations of this magnitude would have a considerably larger impact on the national saving rate than would the gradual rise in the retirement age.[4]

The key issue, however, is whether the presence of such a large accumulating trust fund will lead to reduced levels of goverment saving in other areas. Given the practice of using the budget deficit as a measure of fiscal policy, the presence of such a large "surplus" may lead to a belief that fiscal policy is relatively "tight" and that taxes may be cut or spending raised, either in the social security system itself or elsewhere in the budget. This is an issue of both politics and measurement, issues to which we turn next.

V. Misreading Fiscal Policy during the Demographic Transition

While our nation's aging may not change our government's objectives, the aging process may wreak havoc on traditional measures of fiscal policy and, if more appropriate measures are not developed, lead to a misreading and misdirection of fiscal policy (see also Auerbach, Gokhale and Kotlikoff in this volume). The U.S. deficit is a case in point. In the next two decades the U.S. is projected to run significant surpluses arising, in the main, from an influx of social security receipts. Had the U.S. historically chosen different labels (words) for its social security receipts and payments, the projected surpluses in the next two decades would not necessarily arise.

The government accounts for social security each year by measuring the cash-flow surplus or deficit of each year's contributions over benefits. If, instead, we viewed the social security system as a combination of fair annuities plus net (positive or negative) additional transfer payments to

---

[4] For alternative simulations of the impact of the trust fund accumulation on national saving and welfare, see Aaron *et al.* (1989).

benefit recipients, contributions themselves would not be included in budget calculations, for they would be offset by the liability to pay future annuities that the government incurs simultaneously. Only the excess benefits being received by current beneficiaries would appear. Since current benefit recipients are, in the aggregate, receiving substantial lifetime transfers (net of the present value of payroll taxes), this would result in a major *increase* in the deficit that includes social security, instead of the massive surpluses currently reported.

The arbitrary nature of accounting conventions affects the deficit in many ways. As the preceding example indicates, however, the demographic transition influences the signal that any particular accounting convention provides. The use of a cash-flow approach to accounting for social security leads to the incorrect message that current generations, including those about to retire, are generating large surpluses for the current young and future generations.

These "surpluses" (of the social security system) of the 1990s may lead politicians to view fiscal policy in the 1990s as tighter than in the 1980s and provide them with an excuse to loosen fiscal policy. "Loosening" fiscal policy here means either increased government consumption spending or increased intergenerational transfers from future generations towards current generations, as would normally be provided by a tax cut.

Indeed, since social security revenues have been included in the deficit measure in evaluating compliance with the Gramm-Rudman deficit targets, these revenues have already provided politicians with an excuse for running looser fiscal policy than if social security receipts and expenditures were left out of the Gramm-Rudman calculus. The implications of the spending of such "surpluses" for capital formation is discussed further in Aaron *et al.* (1989).

Loosening of U.S. fiscal policy over the next two decades is likely to be detrimental to U.S. capital formation and leave fewer resources available to ease the burden of rising dependency ratios in subsequent decades.

VI. Implications of a Shift in Political Power Toward the Elderly

Even with a correct assessment of fiscal policy, the fiscal policy that is actually chosen could be greatly influenced by the growing political power of the elderly. Today 28 per cent of the voting age population is over 55; in 2010 the figure will be 36 per cent; and in the 2040 it will be 42 per cent. The recent passage and almost immediate repeal of a program to tax the elderly to pay for new catastrophic insurance coverage that would benefit them demonstrates that the elderly have an effective political voice. So does the record of the elderly over the past two decades in raising their relative income positions.

Between 1970 and 1984 the median real income of elderly households rose by 35 per cent. In contrast, the average real income of households aged 25 to 64 rose by less than one per cent. Boskin, Knetter and Kotlikoff (1985) point out that much of this improvement in the relative income position of the elderly reflects an increase in social security benefits.

Increasing transfers to the elderly by increasing the burden on future generations will, under all but the purest view of Ricardian equivalence, reduce national saving. Even if these transfers are from younger generations currently alive, the effect is likely to be a decline in national saving: the life cycle hypothesis suggests that the elderly have higher marginal propensities to consume than the young, and some recent evidence confirms this; see Abel, Bernheim and Kotlikoff (1991).

In addition to garnering larger government transfers, the elderly may affect the accumulation of U.S. capital by altering the composition and level of government consumption. There are numerous government consumption programs geared toward the elderly that could be initiated or expanded. The government could, for example, initiate a retraining program for the elderly to get them back into the labor force. Or it could provide the elderly with free transportation for shopping, etc. The list of reasonable sounding ways to redirect the government's consumption toward the elderly is, indeed, quite long.

To consider the potential impact of such political shifts on saving, we conducted two simulation experiments in our study assessing the effects of demographics on saving using earnings and consumption profiles; cf. Auerbach and Kotlikoff (1990a). In one experiment, we considered the effect of an increase in consumption by those over 65 by 5 per cent and a decrease in consumption by those under 45 by 5 per cent. Roughly speaking, this may be viewed as simulating the effect of cutting taxes on the elderly by 5 per cent of income and raising taxes on the young by 5 per cent of income. Aside from the effect of generally lowering saving rates, this policy would, according to our simulations, also sharpen the decline in the national saving rate as the elderly fraction of the population increases, by abot 6 percentage points in the year 2010.

A second, admittedly extreme, simulation exercise considered the impact of focusing *all* age-specific spending on the elderly. In particular, we asked what would happen to national saving if all age-specific spending were on programs for individuals over age 65 and if the level of such spending per elderly individual were constant through time. In this case, the large growth of the elderly fraction of the population leads to a huge increase in projected government expenditures, with a decline in the national saving rate of several percentage points. While considering an extreme case, this simulation does illustrate the potential importance of politically driven shifts in the composition of government spending.

The extent and type of government investment might also be altered in a government largely controlled by elderly voters. For example, given their shorter time horizons, the elderly may be less interested in longer-term government investments for such items as environmental preservation.

VII. Aging and the Composition of National Wealth

One may identify several effects that the changing age structure of the population may have on the composition and ownership of national wealth. These include the changing portfolio choice of households over the life cycle and the financial policy of government as it reacts to the changing demographic structure. We consider the household effects first.

Household Portfolios

Household portfolios would be expected to change over the life cycle. As age increases and time horizons shorten, there might be an increase in liquid assets and annuities in household portfolios, with households seeking to finance current and near-term consumption. Moreover, with the decline in family size associated with children reaching adulthood and, frequently, a spouse's death, households might also reduce their demand for housing.

There is some evidence that households shift from less liquid assets, such as private businesses and real estate, to more liquid assets, such as checking accounts and marketable securities, as age increases. Such results were obtained for the United Kingdom by Shorrocks (1982), using Inland Revenue data from the mid-1970s. Ioannides (1989), who studied the Federal Reserve Board's 1983 Survey of Consumer Finances, estimated quadratic relationships between wealth shares and age, and found that holding of "other real estate" decline with age while holding of "business assets" had an inverted U-shape holding pattern with respect to age. Holdings of money market funds increased strictly with age, while holdings of checking accounts and stocks and bonds all followed a U-shape pattern.

Individually purchased annuities do not represent a major share of household portfolios. This does not include the annuities provided by social security and private pensions, which represent a significant fraction of household wealth that increases as households approach retirement. However, an important question is how households would react to reductions in these provided annuities. For example, if social security benefits were cut substantially, how much of this reduction in annuities would households replace through their own purchases? The evidence on the responsiveness of private wealth to changes in public and private pensions ranges from full to only partial offsetting. Given that a significant fraction of households have very low wealth aside from their social security benefits, as reported by e.g. King and Dicks-Mireaux (1982) and Diamond and Hausman (1984), the responsiveness of the private sector would, presumably, depend on how benefits were cut; a move to means-testing might elicit a greater private response than an across-the-board cut in benefits. The response would also depend on the degree to which these public annuities are perceived as substitutes for available private sector assets.

One particular area in which annuity markets have not developed as fast as might have been predicted is "reverse annuity" mortgages, where the household uses its housing equity to support an annuity, with the seller of the annuity receiving the house in payment upon the death of the purchaser. As the household ages, one may distinguish two reasons for it to reduce its ownership of housing. First, it requires less housing consumption. Second, it may wish to hold its wealth in more liquid and/or annuitized form.

Although there are life-cycle effects of home ownership, the transactions costs associated with moving may limit the ability of aging households to reduce housing consumption. In light of this, households might still be expected to convert their illiquid housing wealth into more liquid form, as through remortgaging the house. For the elderly, a reverse annuity mortgage appears to be the ideal vehicle for this conversion, but little such conversion occurs. Recent research by e.g. Venti and Wise (1990) argues that this is because elderly households do not really wish to reduce their housing equity: even when they move, their equity does not typically go down. While there may be a decline in housing equity in the few years before death, households appear to retain a significant amount of housing equity until death, cf. e.g. Sheiner and Weil (1990).

Even if the elderly do not reduce housing demand significantly, the aging of the population may still affect total housing demand through a decline in the formation of new families by young adults. Based on cross-section estimates of housing demand, Mankiw and Weil (1989) argue that the rapid increase in real housing prices in the 1970s can be attributed to the postwar baby boom's transition to adulthood. They infer that housing demand and prices should fall in the coming decades.

In summary, the aging of the U.S. population may lead to an increase in the fraction of wealth held in liquid assets, although this should depend on the level of annuities provided by public and private pensions in the future. In addition, when all effects are considered, the share of housing in household portfolios is likely to fall as well.

Government Assets

The mirror image of the growth of publicly provided annuities is the growth of government's liability to pay these annuities. Many have argued that the growing social security trust fund may have important implications for asset markets, as this massive accumulation must be invested until it is eventually run down in the middle of the next century. However, the importance of this trust fund for the composition (as opposed to the level) of national saving may easily be overstated.

First of all, one has to recognize the ability of the private sector to shift its portfolio in response to government portfolio choice. As government shifts its purchase of assets, the incipient changes in relative rates of return will bring forth offsetting private sector responses. This factor alone has led others to conclude that how the surplus is invested is not a particularly important issue; see e.g. Aaron *et al.* (1989). However, as in the case of private pensions, it is also necessary to look beyond the assets that the trust fund holds to the liabilities that the trust fund is intended to offset.

If it is assumed that future benefit payments do not depend on the contemporaneous balance of the trust fund (a problematic assumption itself, but a useful starting point), then a change in the composition of the trust fund's assets also changes the nature of the implicit liability of future taxpayers. If taxpayers take this into account, they may wish to offset the government's portfolio shift with one of their own. For example, if the trust fund shifts to a riskier portfolio of assets, this might initially be expected to lead to a greater social assumption of risk. However, this government shift implicitly saddles the private sector with the added risk of the residual needed to pay benefits in excess of trust fund accumulations. Forward looking households might then wish to purchase the safer assets the government disposed of, without any increase in yield, in order to restore the character of their expanded portfolio, inclusive of the future implicit tax liabilities.

This argument is nothing more than an application of the Modigliani-Miller theorem to government finance. It is vitiated by several factors. A change in the trust fund balance may have real effects on benefits actually paid. Perhaps more important, the horizon of taxpayers may be considerably shorter than would be needed for a significant offset to occur. However, to ignore this effect completely also seems unjustified.

VIII. Conclusions

The demographic transition underway in the United States may have a significant effect on our national saving rate. Analysis of these effects is difficult because it requires projections far into the next century based on models of behavior for which historical validation is limited. However, research has shown that demographics may have powerful effects on national saving.

Although there is considerable uncertainty about the "right" economic models to use for analysis of household behavior, one of the greatest unknowns is how the political process will change as an increasing fraction of the voting population becomes elderly.

References

Aaron, H. J., Bosworth, B. P. & Burtless, G.: *Can America Afford to Grow Old?* Brookings Institution, Washington, 1989.

Abel, A., Bernheim, D. & Kotlikoff, L. J.: Do the average and marginal propensities to consume rise with age? Manuscript, Fall 1991.

Auerbach, A. J., Cai, J. & Kotlikoff, L. J.: U.S. demographics and saving: Predictions of three saving models. *Carnegie-Rochester Series on Public Policy,* 1991.

Auerbach, A. J. & Kotlikoff, L. J.: *Dynamic Fiscal Policy.* Cambridge University Press, Cambridge, England, 1987.

Auerbach, A. J. & Kotlikoff, L J.: Demographics, fiscal policy, and U.S. saving in the 1980s and beyond. In L. H. Summers (ed.), *Tax Policy and the Economy,* vol. 4, University of Chicago Press, Chicago, 1990a.

Auerbach, A. J. & Kotlikoff, L. J.: Tax aspects of policy towards aging populations: Canada and the United States. NBER WP3405, July 1990b.

Auerbach, A. J. & Kotlikoff, L. J.: The impact of the demographic transition on capital formation. Mimeo, 1991.

Auerbach, A. J., Kotlikoff, L. J., Hagemann, R. P. & Nicoletti, G.: The economic dynamics of an aging population: the case of four OECD countries. *OECD Economic Studies,* 1989.

Boskin, M., Knetter, M. & Kotlikoff, L. J.: Changes in the age distribution of income in the United States, 1968–1984. Mimeo, Oct. 1985.

Cutler, D. M., Poterba, J. M., Sheiner, L. M. & Summers, L. H.: An aging society: Opportunity or challenge? *Brookings Papers on Economic Activity 21* (1), 1–73, 1990.

Diamond, P. A. & Hausman, J. A.: Individual retirement and savings behavior. *Journal of Public Economics 23,* 81–114, Feb./March 1984.

Ioannides, Y. M.: Dynamics of the composition of household asset portfolios and the life cycle. Mimeo, Oct. 1989.

King, M. A. & Dicks-Mireaux, L.: Asset holdings and the life-cycle. *Economic Journal 92,* 247–67, June 1982.

Mankiw, N. G. & Weil, D. N.: The baby boom, the baby bust and the housing market. *Regional Science and Urban Economics 19,* 235–258, May 1989.

Sheiner, L. & Weil, D. N.: The housing wealth of the aged. Mimeo, Harvard University, Aug. 1990.

Shorrocks, A.: The portfolio composition of asset holdings in the United Kingdom. *Economic Journal 92,* 268–84, June 1982.

Venti, S. & Wise, D.: But they don't want to reduce housing equity. In David Wise (ed.), *Issues in the Economics of Aging,* University of Chicago Press, Chicago, 1990.

Comment on A. J. Auerbach and L. J. Kotlikoff, "The Impact of the Demographic Transition on Capital Formation"

David N. Weil

Brown University, Providence, RI, U.S.A.

Both theory and examination of data suggest a relation between people's age and the amount they save. It is thus natural to examine how changes in demographics will affect saving rates. I would like to take up the questions of whether the theories of saving that we have at our disposal are sufficient for such a task, and whether a more satisfactory answer could be provided by making better use of the available data.

Auerbach and Kotlikoff (AK) begin their exercise by measuring age-specific saving coefficients in cross-section data. Given such estimates, one way to forecast future saving would be simply to multiply these coefficients by the number of people in each age group, and see how saving would be altered over time.

Why might this exercise not work? Clearly, the answer is that in the future, the cross-section age/saving profile may be different from the one observed today. To see why this might be, consider the reasons for saving. Some determinants of the age/saving profile may not vary systematically with demographic factors such as an individual's stage of life cycle, receipt of bequests, tastes, health status, etc. But many other factors which affect saving will change as the age structure of the population changes. For example:

(1) Since people of different ages hold different amounts of capital, the capital/labor ratio should change as demographics change. This will change wages rates and interest rates, and in turn affect saving.
(2) If the social security system is funded on a pay-as-you-go basis, then as the population ages the burden of social security taxes on the young will change. This will reduce after-tax wages and affect labor supply.
(3) As the number of children that each old person has declines, a change might be expected in the size of the bequest left by each old person and/or the amount of bequest received by each child.

(4) Policy changes may also be correlated with changes in demographics. For instance, the generosity of government programs for the elderly may be related to the fraction of the population that is elderly.

If these kinds of problems are present, then as demographics change, the cross-section age/saving profile will change. So what can we do in order to forecast savings? The route taken by AK is to try to fit a model which replicates the current age/saving profile, but which can then be run forward to see how that profile will change over time. The model derives saving by people in each age group as optimal responses to given paths of interest and wage rates (and these interest and wage rates themselves as functions of the supplies of capital and labor). Similarly, bequest behavior and social security taxes and payments are incorporated as endogenous variables of the model.

Using a model in this manner, it is possible to forecast not only the change in the age/saving profile over time, but also the aggregate saving rate. Of course, this process will not produce accurate forecasts unless the theory used in building the model is the correct one for explaining the saving rate. Thus the question of whether the forecasting exercise conducted in this paper is useful comes down to the question of whether the theory used — in this case an extended life-cycle model (or sometimes the infinite horizon model) — is correct. While I think that this model is a useful pedagogical device, it is worth pointing out that several of its components are extremely at variance with the world as we observe it:

(1) No uncertainty. Whether excluding uncertainty is important depends on how much it contributes to overall saving. Deaton (at this conference and elsewhere) has made a convincing case that for most people, precautionary saving is very important. Carroll and Summers' (1991) finding that consumption tracks income very closely over the life cycle casts doubt on how important nonprecautionary saving is for most people.

(2) Representative agent. Another attribute of the AK model is that within an age cohort there is no income inequality. This stems from the generally democratic flavor of the life cycle model, in which the retirement saving of the common man is the source of the country's capital stock. Again, whether this is a problematic assumption depends on how democratic saving is in the real world. But a key fact is that the distribution of wealth is incredibly skewed — for example, 10 per cent of U.S. households own 85 per cent of net financial assets[1] — and that other than social security, pensions, and a house, most Americans have no assets.

---

[1] Cf. Avery *et al.* (1984).

(3) Particular specification of the bequest motive. AK model parents as receiving utility from giving bequests; they predict that as the number of children per parent declines, bequests will fall. But if bequests are accidental, this result will not hold. Similarly, to the extent that bequests are composed of houses, which the elderly hold because they want to live in them, the size of bequests will be invariant to the number of children. Correct modelling of bequests is crucial to correctly forecasting the saving rate, given the evidence of Kotlikoff and Summers (1981) on the importance of intergenerational transfers to the aggregate capital stock.

Such problems, and others discussed in Weil (1991), may lead one to conclude that the life-cycle model (or indeed any far-forward looking model) is not a good explanation for saving in the real world — and thus inappropriate for forecasting purposes.

Given that they do not test the theory underlying their forecasting exercise, I was disappointed at the authors' limited evaluation of their model's ability to forecast. AK focus on the failure of the model to predict aggregate saving in the 1980s — which I am willing to believe is a special case. But I was sorry to see no effort to compare the fit of the model to the aggregate saving rate in other periods (earlier decades) or to the saving rates of other countries.

There is a second way of evaluating their model that I would like to see the authors pursue. That is to look at the changes it has predicted in the age/saving profile over time, and to see if they are reflected in the data. Recall that the whole reason we need a model is because we do not think these coefficients are constant over time.

Given the problems with the exercise as conducted, is there an alternative way of predicting changes in saving? One approach would be to try to capture relations between generations empirically rather than theoretically, i.e., to try to get better micro data. Using micro data, saving could be measured as a function of not only a person's age, but also the number and ages of his relatives. Then to forecast changes in savings, the number of people that will be alive, as well as their relations, could be plugged into these equations. The hope, in other words, would be that the coefficients in *these* equations would be more stable than the simple age/saving coefficients.

Of course, this is asking for micro data that does not yet exist. It also deals with only some potential sources of changes in the age/saving profile that would follow from demographic change (i.e., effects within one's own family such as bequests, inter vivos transfers, etc.) while ignoring others (i.e., changes in aggregate level variables such as interest rates or social security taxes). Is there an alternative way to go?

One alternative might be to look at data not at the micro level, but rather at the aggregate level. The problem with data at the micro level is that the saving of a person of a certain age is determined by the existence of persons of other ages. Each person has a twofold effect on total saving: his own saving, and his effect on other people's saving. This cannot be picked up in micro data. But under some assumptions, it *can* be picked up by looking at aggregate data.

In the remainder of this discussion, I propose a simple model which encompasses the effects that motivate AK, but in which looking at data at the aggregate level provides a way of accurately forecasting savings.

The population is divided into two age groups: parents aged two and children aged one. Let $w_{2,i}$ be the number of parents with i children,[2] and let $w_{i,j}$ be the number of children from families with j children. The saving of a young person, s_1 is taken to be a function of both the person's age and the person's relation to members of the older generation:

$$s_1 = \beta_1 + \pi_{2,1}\left(\frac{1}{1 + \#\text{ siblings}}\right) + \gamma_{2,1}\left(\frac{w_2}{w_1}\right) \tag{1}$$

where $\gamma_{2,1}$ is the effect of the aggregate ratio of old to young people on an individual young person's saving, $\pi_{2,1}$ is the effect of the saving of children on parents (note that this depends on the number of siblings a person has) and β_1 is the saving of a young person in the absence of any intergenerational relations.

Similarly, the saving of people in the older generation is:

$$s_2 = \beta_2 + \pi_{1,2}(\#\text{ children}) + \gamma_{1,2}\left(\frac{w_1}{w_2}\right). \tag{2}$$

The average saving of people in the younger generation will depend on the aggregate age structure of the population as well as the average size of their families:

$$\bar{s}_1 = \beta_1 + \gamma_{2,1}\left(\frac{w_2}{w_1}\right) + \pi_{2,1}\left(\sum_{i=1}^{\infty}\frac{1}{i}\,w_{1,i}\right)\Big/ w_1$$

$$= \beta_1 + (\pi_{2,1} + \gamma_{2,1})\frac{w_2}{w_1}. \tag{3}$$

---

[2] For convenience, I assume that each child has one parent and that every member of the older generation has at least one child.

Similarly, the average saving of people in the older generation will depend on their average number of children as well as the aggregate age structure of the population:

$$\bar{s}_2 = \beta_2 + \gamma_{1.2}\left(\frac{w_1}{w_2}\right) + \pi_{1.2}\left(\sum_{j=1}^{\infty} jw_{2.j}\right)\bigg/ w_2$$

$$= \beta_2 + (\pi_{1.2} + \gamma_{1.2})\frac{w_1}{w_2}. \tag{4}$$

Looking at the expression for the average saving of each group, it is clear that the average saving measures will change as demographics change. Thus, armed only with measures of the average saving of people in each age group, one would not be able to forecast how saving would change in response to demographic change. In essence, AK attempt to use a model to determine the π and γ coefficients.

Average saving of all individuals in the economy is just a weighted average of the saving of individuals in each group:

$$\bar{s} = \frac{w_1\bar{s}_1 + w_2\bar{s}_2}{w_1 + w_2} = \left(\frac{w_1}{w_1 + w_2}\right)(\beta_1 + \pi_{1.2}) + \left(\frac{w_2}{w_1 + w_2}\right)(\beta_2 + \pi_{2.1})$$

$$= \alpha_1\left(\frac{w_1}{w_1 + w_2}\right) + \alpha_2\left(\frac{w_2}{w_1 + w_2}\right). \tag{5}$$

Note that in this (admittedly stylized) example, there is a stable relation between average saving and the aggregate age structure of the population. Thus, even if the β, γ, and π coefficient were not known, aggregate data could be used to estimate the α coefficients, and thus forecast how saving would change in response to changes in demographics.

References

Avery, R. B. *et al.*: Survey of consumer finances, 1983: A second report. *Federal Reserve Bulletin*, Dec. 1984.

Kotlikoff, L. & Summers, L.: The role of intergenerational transfers in aggregate capital accumulation. *Journal of Political Economy 89*(4), 1981.

Carroll, C. & Summers, L.: Consumption growth parallels income growth: Some new evidence. In B. D. Bernheim & J. B. Shoven (eds.), *National Saving and Economic Performance*, University of Chicago Press, Chicago, 1991.

Weil, D. N.: What determines saving? A review essay. *Journal of Monetary Economics*, 1991.

Generational Accounting: A New Approach to Understanding the Effects of Fiscal Policy on Saving

Alan J. Auerbach

University of Pennsylvania, Philadelphia, PA and NBER, Cambridge, MA, USA

Jagadeesh Gokhale

Federal Reserve Bank, Cleveland, OH, USA

Laurence J. Kotlikoff

Boston University and NBER, Cambridge, MA, USA

Abstract

An alternative to deficit accounting is proposed for understanding the government's treatment of current and future generations. The alternative, called generational accounting, is based on the government's intertemporal budget constraint. Generational accounting is used to describe the redistributive and saving impacts of four alternative policies. The findings indicate that the fiscal deficit is thoroughly unreliable as a measure of either generational policy or the policy-induced stimulus to aggregate demand. The findings also suggest that fiscal policies that redistribute across generations can have important effects on national saving rates.

I. Introduction

Recent years have witnessed a growing unease with use of the fiscal deficit to gauge the stance of economic policy. Many economists as well as non-economists are questioning whether a single number, that relates primarily to a government's current cash flow, is the kind of measure needed to understand longer-term effects of fiscal policy on saving, investment and growth. They also ask whether the deficit can tell us how we are treating different generations, both those currently alive and those yet to come. Economists and policymakers have long criticized the deficit for failing to account for inflation, economic growth and government assets. They have also pointed out the complete failure of the deficit to record the enormous integenerational redistribution arising from unfunded social security programs, "revenue-neutral" changes in the tax structure, and government-induced changes in the market values of real and financial assets.

Doubts about the deficit have been accentuated by the demographic transition occurring in most OECD countries. The aging of populations, with its attendant increase in the number of retirees dependent on workers, raises major concerns about the viability of a short-run, pay-as-you-go approach to fiscal budgeting. In recognition of these concerns about the demographic transition, the U.S. federal government decided in 1983 to accumulate a very large social security trust fund to help finance the "baby boom" generation's social security benefits. This decision represented a remarkable and highly praiseworthy break with short-term budgeting. But it also raised new questions about using the unified federal deficit, which includes social security, as a measure of fiscal policy. In particular, it has opened to question the goal of balancing the federal budget inclusive of social security. If funds for future needs are to be accumulated, should the U.S. not be running a unified federal budget surplus? But if so, how large should the surplus be? And will such surpluses reduce aggregate demand and depress the economy?[1]

This study focuses on an alternative to the deficit — generational accounting — and its use in assessing fiscal policy, particularly the impact of fiscal policy on saving. Generational accounting indicates how changes in policies alter different generations' present expected values of remaining lifetime net payments to the government. According to the standard life cycle theory, one's lifetime present value net payment, rather than one's immediate cash-flow payment to the government, is the critical determinant of one's consumption response to government policy. From the perspective of the life cycle and other neoclassical consumption theories, the government's deficit does not properly measure policy-induced stimuli to consumption. Indeed, from a theoretical perspective, the measured deficit need bear no relationship to the underlying intergenerational stance of fiscal policy since it simply reflects the economically arbitrary labelling of government receipts and payments; see Kotlikoff (1984, 1989) and Auerbach and Kotlikoff (1987).

The paper proceeds in Section II by discussing the use of generational accounting to measure directly generational burdens. Section III reports baseline U.S. generational accounts for 1989. It also examines four

---

[1] The U.S. government's response to the problem of using the short-term budget deficit as an instrument for long-term planning is to exclude social security from the federal deficit. While this redefinition has occurred formally, it has not precluded the continued calculation of and attention paid to the unified budget deficit. Indeed, in its January 1991 report on the FY91 deficit, the U.S. Congressional Budget Office not only discussed the deficit inclusive of social security, but three other deficits as well. The $166 billion difference between the largest and smallest of these numbers is roughly 3 per cent of predicted 1991 U.S. GNP!

hypothetical policies to illustrate the ability of the new approach to keep track of changes in generational burdens. While all four of the hypothetical policies affect major redistribution across generations, in the case of three of the four policies the deficit is completely unaffected. Section IV discusses the potential use of generational accounting for assessing the saving impact of fiscal policy. Section V concludes the paper.

II. Generational Accounting

How Should We Measure Generational Policy?

How does economic theory suggest we measure the government's generational policies? The answer is generational accounts. Generational accounts indicate in present value what the typical member of each generation can expect, on net, to pay to the government now and in the future. A generational account is thus a set of numbers, one for each existing generation, indicating the average remaining lifetime burden imposed by the government on members of the generation. The proper use of these accounts leads to an assessment of generational policy that is independent of the words the government uses to label its receipts and payments.

Generational accounts indicate not only what existing generations will pay, but also the likely payments required of future generations. The burden on future generations is determined by working through the government's intertemporal budget constraint. This constraint says that the present value of the government's spending on goods and services cannot exceed the sum of three terms: (1) the government's net wealth, (2) the present value of net payments by current generations (the sum of the generational accounts multiplied by the number of people in each generation), and (3) the present value of net payments of future generations. In other words, the government must ultimately pay for its spending with its current assets or with resources obtained from current and future generations. At any point in time we can project the present value of the government's spending and also estimate terms (1) and (2). By subtracting (1) and (2) from the present value of government spending, we can determine the aggregate present value burden on future generations.

How will the total burden on all future generations be spread over the different generations that show up in the future? No one knows for sure. But let's assume the burden is spread smoothly across all future generations, such that each new generation's burden keeps pace with the economy's rate of productivity growth. Then knowing the total amount future generations will pay and projecting the number of people who show up in the future, we can determine the growth-adjusted burden (generational account) on those who will be born in the future.

The Simple Mathematics of Generational Accounting[2]

To make the above description of generational accounting more precise, we write the government's intertemporal budget constraint for year t as

$$\sum_{s=0}^{D} N_{t,t-s} + \sum_{s=1}^{\infty} N_{t,t+s} = W_t^g + \sum_{s+t}^{\infty} G_s \prod_{j=t+1}^{s} \frac{1}{(1+r_j)}. \tag{1}$$

The first term on the l.h.s. of (1) adds together the present value of the net payments of all generations alive at time t. Net payments refers here to all taxes paid to the government less all transfers received from the government. Government refers here to federal, state and local government. The expression $N_{t,k}$ stands for the time t present value of remaining lifetime net payments of the generation born in year k. The index s in this summation runs from age 0 to age D, the maximum age of life. The first element of this summation is $N_{t,t}$ which is the present value of net payments of the generation born in year t; the last term is $N_{t,t-D}$, the present value of remaining net payments of the oldest generation alive in year t, i.e., those born in year $t - D$. The second term on the l.h.s. of (1) adds together the present value of remaining net payments of future generations. The r.h.s. consists of W_t^g, the government's (federal, state and local) net wealth in year t, plus the present value of government consumption. In the latter expression, G_s stands for government consumption expenditure in year s, and r_j stands for the pretax rate of return in year j.

Equation (1) indicates the zero-sum nature of intergenerational fiscal policy. Holding the r.h.s. of equation (1) fixed, increased (decreased) government payments to (receipts taken from) existing generations means a decrease in the first term of the l.h.s. of (1) and requires an offsetting increase in the second term on the l.h.s. of (1); i.e., it requires reduced payments to or increased payments from future generations.

The term $N_{t,k}$ is defined as

$$N_{t,k} = \sum_{s=\max(t,k)}^{k+D} \overline{T}_{s,k} P_{s,k} \prod_{j=t+1}^{s} \frac{1}{1+r_j}. \tag{2}$$

In expression (2) $\overline{T}_{s,k}$ stands for the projected average net payment to the government made in year s by a member of the generation born in year k. A generation's average net payment in year s refers to the average across all members of the generation alive in year s of payments made, such as income, payroll and consumption taxes, less all transfers received, such as social security, welfare and unemployment insurance. The term $P_{s,k}$ stands

---

[2] The remainder of this section draws heavily on Auerbach, Gokhale and Kotlikoff (1991).

for the number of surviving members of the cohort in year s who were born in year k. For generations who are born prior to year t, the summation begins in year t. For generations who are born in year k, where $k > t$, the summation begins in year k. Regardless of the generation's year of birth, the discounting is always back to year t.

A set of generational accounts is simply a set of values of $N_{t,k}$ divided by $P_{t,k}$ (the generations's current population size in the case of existing generations or initial population size in the case of future generations), with the property that the combined total value of the $N_{t,k}$ s adds up to the r.h.s. of equation (1). In our calculation of the $N_{t,k}$'s for existing generations (those whose $k \leq 1989$) we distinguish male from female cohorts, but, to ease notation, we did not append sex subscripts to the terms in (1) and (2).

Assessing the Intergenerational Stance of Fiscal Policy

Given the r.h.s. of equation (1) and the first term on the l.h.s. of equation (1), the value of the second term on the r.h.s. of equation (1), which is the present value of payments required of future generations, can be determined as a residual. The amount that needs to be taken from each successive generation to balance the government's intertemporal budget can also be determined, assuming that each successive generation's payment is the same up to an adjustment for growth.

Understanding the size of the $N_{t,k}$'s for current generations and their likely magnitude for future generations certainly does not fully reveal the intergenerational incidence of fiscal policy. As studied in Auerbach and Kotlikoff (1987), intergenerational redistribution (changes in generational accounts) will alter the time path of factor prices, which has additional effects on the intergenerational distribution of welfare. Such changes in factor prices result from changes in the supply of capital relative to labor. But the policy-induced changes in the supplies of capital and labor can, in turn, be traced back to changes in consumption and labor supply decisions which reflect changes in generational accounts. Hence, knowing how generational accounts change in response to policy is essential to understanding not only the direct generational welfare effects of government policy, but also the indirect (though not necessarily smaller) effects associated with factor price changes.

Advantages of Generational Accounting

Generational accounting automatically deals with each of the major concerns raised by those who think the deficit is conceptually sound, but simply needs to be adjusted. It deals with inflation by measuring all payments and receipts in inflation-adjusted (constant) dollars. It nets all the government's real assets against all its real liabilities (including liabilities such as the S&L bailout) to form the value of government net worth which is ultimately used to help determine the burden on future generations. It directly considers the government's implicit obligations to future transfer payments and future consumption spending and the public's implicit obligations to pay future taxes. It accounts for state and local as well as federal government fiscal policy. In using replacement cost valuation of assets, it accounts for government redistribution through asset markets. Finally, in projecting transfers, spending and taxes through time and the implied burden on future generations, generational accounting deals with the question of economic growth, including growth associated with demographic change.

III. Illustrating Generational Accounting

U.S. Generational Accounts as of 1989

Tables 1 and 2 illustrate generational accounting for the U.S. based on policy as of 1989 (prior to the 1990 budget agreement). These tables are reproduced from Auerbach, Gokhale and Kotlikoff (1991), which, incidentally, contains all the details on the data used to form these tables. The tables include three aspects. First, they report each age–sex group's generational account. Second, they provide a decomposition of each age–sex group's generational account into the different present value taxes and transfers that are netted against each other to form the generational account. Second, they provide a decomposition of each age–sex group's generational account. Third, at the bottom of each table, they indicate the implied burden on future generations based on our illustrative assumptions that policy toward current generations remains unchanged and that the lifetime bill facing each new future generation is identical except for an adjustment for growth. As discussed below, there are other ways to use generational accounting to document the imbalance in generational policy. What we do here is assess the burden on typical members of future generations if current generations are treated, in the future, no better or worse than can be predicted on the basis of current policy.

In looking at the accounts, it should be kept in mind that they are forward looking. They do not consider net payments particular generations made in the past. The generational accounts are not total lifetime bills, but rather remaining lifetime bills. This explains why the accounts are positive for young and middle-age generations, but negative for older generations. Through the rest of their lives, young and middle-age Americans can expect, on balance, to pay money to the government, whereas older Americans can expect, on balance, to receive money from the government.

Table 1. *The composition of male generational accounts (r = 0.06, g = 0.0075). Present values of receipts and payments (thousands of dollars)*

| | Payments | | | | | | | Receipts | | Welfare | | | |
Generation's Age in 1989	Net Payment	Labor Income Taxes	FICA Taxes	Excise Taxes	Capital Income Taxes	Seigno-rage	Property Taxes	OASDI	HI	AFDC	General	UI	Food Stamps
0	73.7	24.8	26.5	22.9	9.5	0.0	1.6	4.5	1.1	0.3	4.4	1.0	0.3
5	93.2	31.8	34.0	26.3	12.2	0.1	2.0	5.5	1.5	0.4	4.3	1.2	0.4
10	116.8	40.8	43.6	29.8	15.6	0.1	2.6	6.7	1.9	0.5	4.6	1.6	0.5
15	145.3	52.2	55.8	32.8	20.0	0.1	3.3	8.1	2.4	0.6	5.1	2.0	0.7
20	169.1	61.9	66.2	33.9	24.8	0.1	4.1	9.5	2.9	0.7	5.3	2.4	0.8
25	193.0	70.3	75.1	35.8	32.4	0.1	5.3	12.0	3.8	0.9	5.6	2.6	0.9
30	194.5	69.6	74.4	34.2	38.4	0.1	6.1	14.3	4.6	0.8	5.4	2.3	0.9
35	186.0	65.2	69.7	32.0	43.8	0.0	6.9	17.2	5.7	0.6	5.2	2.0	0.8
40	176.2	60.9	65.1	30.5	49.8	0.0	7.6	21.9	7.4	0.5	5.3	1.8	0.7
45	155.4	54.4	58.1	28.7	54.2	0.0	7.8	29.8	10.0	0.4	5.5	1.5	0.6
50	114.1	42.1	45.0	24.4	52.1	0.0	7.1	37.1	12.4	0.3	5.4	1.1	0.5
55	69.7	31.0	33.2	20.8	48.7	0.0	6.6	47.9	16.0	0.2	5.4	0.7	0.4
60	18.9	20.2	21.5	17.9	44.1	0.0	6.1	62.6	22.0	0.1	5.6	0.3	0.3
65	-31.8	9.1	9.7	14.7	37.0	0.0	5.4	71.2	30.7	0.0	5.6	0.0	0.2
70	-42.7	4.0	4.3	11.9	29.3	0.0	4.5	61.9	29.6	0.0	4.9	0.0	0.2
75	-41.5	1.8	2.0	9.5	22.5	0.0	3.7	48.9	27.9	0.0	4.1	0.0	0.1
80	-35.6	0.6	0.6	7.5	17.2	0.0	3.0	36.9	24.4	0.0	3.0	0.0	0.1
85	-28.2	0.0	0.0	6.1	14.3	0.0	2.4	28.2	20.9	0.0	1.8	0.0	0.1
90	-1.5	0.0	0.0	1.2	6.7	0.0	0.5	5.4	4.2	0.0	0.2	0.0	0.0
Future Generations	89.5												

Table 2. The composition of female generational accounts (r = 0.06, g = 0.0075). Present values of receipts and payments (thousands of dollars)

Generation's Age in 1989	Net Payment	Payments						Receipts						
		Labor Income Taxes	FICA Taxes	Excise Taxes	Capital Income Taxes	Seigno-rage	Property Taxes	OASDI	HI	Welfare		UI	Food Stamps	
										AFDC	General			
0	36.4	14.0	14.9	20.2	3.5	0.0	2.1	5.0	1.5	2.3	7.8	0.4	1.3	
5	46.5	17.7	18.9	23.0	4.5	0.0	2.6	6.1	1.9	2.9	7.2	0.6	1.7	
10	60.4	23.3	24.9	27.2	5.9	0.1	3.5	7.5	2.5	3.8	7.8	0.7	2.2	
15	70.7	28.1	30.1	29.0	7.2	0.1	4.2	8.6	3.0	4.6	8.2	0.9	2.6	
20	85.5	34.8	37.2	32.2	9.3	0.0	5.4	10.9	3.9	5.2	9.2	1.1	3.3	
25	91.0	36.3	38.8	33.2	11.7	0.0	6.5	13.1	4.8	4.5	9.0	1.1	3.0	
30	90.9	35.1	37.5	33.1	14.9	0.0	7.4	15.7	6.1	3.5	8.5	1.0	2.4	
35	86.9	32.9	35.2	32.1	18.3	0.0	8.1	18.6	7.7	2.5	8.2	0.9	1.9	
40	78.2	29.7	31.7	30.1	21.4	0.0	8.6	21.9	9.8	1.7	7.8	0.7	1.4	
45	62.9	25.4	27.2	27.4	23.8	0.0	8.9	27.0	12.6	1.0	7.6	0.6	1.0	
50	41.0	20.4	21.8	24.2	25.0	0.0	8.9	34.0	16.3	0.6	7.3	0.4	0.7	
55	11.7	14.9	15.9	20.8	24.9	0.0	8.7	43.9	21.3	0.2	7.2	0.3	0.5	
60	−22.5	9.3	9.9	17.4	23.4	0.0	8.2	55.1	27.8	0.0	7.2	0.2	0.4	
65	−53.7	4.8	5.1	14.2	20.8	0.0	7.6	61.2	37.4	0.0	7.2	0.1	0.4	
70	−60.2	2.0	2.2	11.5	17.3	0.0	6.9	56.5	36.8	0.0	6.5	0.0	0.3	
75	−57.9	0.7	0.7	9.1	13.2	0.0	6.0	47.4	34.5	0.0	5.5	0.0	0.3	
80	−50.8	0.0	0.0	7.2	8.8	0.0	5.1	37.4	29.9	0.0	4.5	0.0	0.2	
85	−42.7	0.0	0.0	5.8	4.5	0.0	4.2	28.7	24.7	0.0	3.6	0.0	0.2	
90	−7.4	0.0	0.0	1.0	0.4	0.0	0.7	4.7	4.2	0.0	0.6	0.0	0.0	
Future Generations	44.2													

Compare, for example, the $176,200 average bill of 40 year old males with negative $42,700 average bill of 70 year old males. Males aged 40 can anticipate spending many more years working and paying income and payroll taxes on their labor earnings. While these males will receive some welfare and unemployment benefits in the short run, most of their transfers will come much later from social security (including Medicare). The substantial taxes 40 year-olds will pay over the next 20 or so years have a larger present value than do the substantial transfers they will receive in the following 20 or so years.[3] For 70 year old males, the story is quite different. These males are generally retired and are already receiving substantial social security retirement and Medicare benefits. On average, the present value of the ongoing benefits of these males exceeds the present value of their remaining tax payments. For 70 year old males, social security and Medicare benefits combined have a present value of $91,500, while the present value of capital income taxes, which is the tax with the largest present value, is only $29, 300.

The usefulness of generational accounts is in (1) comparing their values before and after a particular policy change and (2) comparing the burden on future generations (the last row in the tables) with the burden on the youngest members of current generations, i.e., newborns. These comparisons, rather than the initial level of the accounts, should be the focus of the reader's attention.[4]

The Relative Burden on Future Generations

Tables 1 and 2 indicate that as of 1989, U.S. fiscal policy was out of generational balance in the sense that the burden on both future male and

---

[3] Take the case of 40 year old males. The present value of their social security retirement and disability benefits, which is the transfer component with the largest present value, is $21,900. But this figure is less than a third of 40 year old males' $65,100 projected average present value payroll tax payment.

[4] The reason to focus on policy-induced changes in the accounts and on comparisons of future generations with current newborns is that such analyses are not sensitive to the choice of labels attached to government receipts and payments. In contrast, the initial levels of the accounts (with the exception of the accounts for newborns and future generations) are sensitive to the choice of accounting labels. To understand this point, consider again the negative $42,700 account of 70 year old males. Now think how much larger (less negative) that number would be had the government historically called social security contributions "loans" rather than "taxes" and social security benefits "repayment of principal plus interest on the loans" plus an "old-age tax", where the old-age tax adjusts for the fact that benefits may not precisely equal principal plus interest on contributions. With this alternative language, today's 70 year-old's generational account would be a lot larger (a lot less negative); it would exclude the $61,900 in present value of social security (OASDI) benefits indicated in Table 1, and it would include the present value of the "old-age tax".

female generations was 20 per cent larger than that on 1989 male and female newborns. The equal size of the male and female differentials is no accident; rather, this equivalent percentage treatment of future males and females was assumed for purposes of describing the imbalance in generational policy. What exactly does it mean that future American newborns will be handed bills that are larger, even after adjusting for growth, than the bills being handed today's American newborns? It means that Americans alive today, including today's newborns, not slated to pay enough to keep the fiscal burden on future generations from rising.

If we spread the burden in a proportionate manner across everybody who comes along in the future it means that, even after taking growth into account, future generations will all pay 20 per cent more than current newborns in net tax payments over their lifetimes. What does "adjusted for growth" mean? Well, suppose the economy's growth rate of output per worker is 1 per cent per year. Then the payment scenario under discussion means that next year's newborn will pay 1 per cent more than this year's newborn because of growth and 20 per cent more because of the imbalance of fiscal policy. The following year's newborn will pay 2 per cent more because of growth and 20 per cent more because of the imbalance of policy. And on and on…

What if the U.S. government does not immediately start requiring successive new generations to pay more — indeed, 20 per cent more than the additional amount they will pay due to growth? What if instead it waits say, 10 years, to start raising the lifetime net payments of new generations? Then when we do generational accounting 10 years from now, we will learn that the 20 per cent figure has grown to 35 per cent (not shown in the table). And if the U.S. government waits 20 years to start extracting more from future generations, those born in 2010 and thereafter will face a 57 per cent growth-adjusted larger burden than today's newborns. This is the zero-sum nature of generational accounting. If Americans now alive are not going to pay more, and if the U.S. government is not going to make those coming along in the short term pay more, it will have to extract a much more substantial sum from those coming along in the long term.

What would it cost Americans now alive to keep future Americans from paying a bigger share of their lifetime incomes to the government than the share current newborns are scheduled to pay? One way to answer this question is to calculate the size of the immediate and permanent increase in income or other tax rates that would equalize the burden on current and future newborns. If the U.S. chose to raise income tax rates, immediately and permanently, the required increase in the average rate would be 5.3 per cent, which would raise the average rate from 14.5 per cent to 15.3 per cent.

Using Generational Accounting to Detect Generational Policy

Table 3 considers four hypothetical policies, each of which has a significant impact on the U.S. generational distribution of fiscal burdens. The first, but only the first, of these policies, alters the U.S. federal deficit. This policy (reported in Column 1) is a five-year, 20 per cent reduction in the average federal income tax rate. At the end of the tax cut, the tax rate is increased above its initial value in order to maintain constant the ratio of the U.S. debt (including the newly accumulated government debt) to GNP; i.e., the tax rate increase is sufficient to cover the product of the interest rate less the growth rate, times the additional accumulated stock of government debt.

The second policy, reported in Column 2, is an immediate and permanent 20 per cent increase in social security retirement and disability

Table 3.* *Changes in generational accounts arising from four hypothetical policies (thousands of dollars)*

	5 Year Tax Cut	20 Per cent Social Security Benefit Increase	Shifting from Payroll to Sales and Excise Taxes	Eliminating Investment Incentives
Males Ages				
0	1.9	2.7	1.0	0.9
10	3.2	3.9	− 1.3	1.5
20	2.2	5.5	− 6.5	2.3
30	− 0.3	5.2	− 8.8	2.1
40	− 2.7	2.4	− 7.5	0.2
50	− 4.4	− 2.7	− 3.8	− 2.5
60	− 5.0	− 10.2	0.7	− 4.7
70	− 2.6	− 11.9	3.4	− 5.0
80	− 1.6	− 7.3	2.8	− 4.0
Future Generations	1.9	3.1	0.4	0.2
Females Ages				
0	1.0	1.0	3.5	0.4
10	1.7	1.5	3.2	0.6
20	0.7	1.9	1.5	0.8
30	− 0.2	0.9	1.8	1.2
40	− 1.0	− 1.0	2.4	0.6
50	− 1.9	− 4.5	3.1	− 0.5
60	− 2.1	− 10.0	3.9	− 1.8
70	− 1.5	− 11.0	3.9	− 2.4
80	− 0.9	− 7.5	2.8	− 2.4
Future Generations	1.0	1.1	3.8	0.1

*Reprinted from Kotlikoff (1992).

benefits financed on a pay-as-you-go basis by increases in payroll taxes. The third policy, reported in Column 3, involves an equal revenue switch in the tax structure. Specifically, payroll taxes are reduced immediately and permanently by 30 per cent, and the reduced revenue is made up by increases in consumption taxes, which, in the U.S. context, mean increases in sales and excise taxes.

The fourth policy, reported in Column 4, involves the elimination of U.S. investment incentives. Elimination of investment incentives refers to a present value revenue neutral equalization of effective tax rates of assets of different vintages. To understand how this policy alters the generational accounts, we need to clarify our treatment of investment incentives in our generational accounting. Specifically, the reduction in the market value of existing capital, arising from the availability of investment incentives for new capital, is treated as a one-time tax paid by the current owners of this existing capital; i.e., rather than value this capital at market prices, we valued it at replacement cost less a tax discount. The elimination of investment incentives is then treated as (a) the elimination of this one-time tax discount (as opposed to treating it/labelling it as a capital gain) and (b) an increase in the effective capital income tax rate necessary to offset, in present value, this one-time windfall; in the first year, this requires an increase in aggregate capital income taxes equal to the product of the interest rate less the growth rate times the initial tax discount on existing capital. Subsequent year increases in capital income taxes equal the first year increase times the appropriate growth factor.

There are several points to make about the results of these policy experiments. First, the magnitude and pattern of integenerational redistribution bears no necessary relation to the reported deficit. The tax cut policy of Column 1 generates over three quarters of a trillion dollars of official debt, but does substantially less damage to young and future generations than the pay-as-you-go social security benefit increase in Column 2, which leads to zero increase in official I.O.U.s. For instance, under the tax cut policy, males aged 20 lose, on average, $2,200 in present value. Under the social security benefit increase policy, they lose $5,500, which is over two and a half times as much.

Second, some policies that redistribute to current older generations do so primarily to the detriment of current young generations, rather than future generations. Column 4, involving the elimination of investment incentives, illustrates this point. This policy does most of its damage to generations that are now young; the increased payment required of future males is only $200, while 20 year old males lose $2,300. Of course, policies that just redistribute from the current young to the current old could end up hurting future generations as well if these policies are reactivated during the years such generations are young.

Third, by using generational policies that do not show up in the official deficit, it is easy to offset the generational impact of policies that do. For example, the generational impacts of the tax cut of Column 1 could be overcome by running the reverse of the policy in Column 4, i.e., by increasing, rather than decreasing investment incentives and, thereby, reversing the sign of all the numbers in Column 4.

Fourth, since changes in consumption decisions depend, according to the life cycle model, on changes in each generation's total projected lifetime payments, generational accounting, such as that in Table 3, indicates the true stimulus to national consumption of policy changes. In contrast, as the examples in Table 3 show, the deficit need bear no relationship to the underlying stimulus to consumption. Thus, generational accounting, rather than the deficit, provides the proper guide to stabilizing the economy and assessing the impact of policy on saving.

IV. Using Generational Accounting to Assess Policy-Induced Changes in Saving

Changes in national saving can be traced to changes in national income and changes in national consumption. While additional work is needed to connnect changes in generational accounts to changes in national income, we are able here to assess the income effects of policy changes on national consumption by multiplying changes in the generational accounts by generation-specific propensities to consume. This analysis abstracts from the incentive effects arising from policy changes. Certainly, incentive effects can be quite important for labor supply decisions as well as inter-temporal consumption choice. Such incentive effects would, in our framework, be captured as changes in the propensities to work and consume out of lifetime resources. Unfortunately, at the present time there are available only initial estimates of propensities to consume by age and sex, but no indication of how these propensities respond to changes in the structure of incentives. Another caveat involves the issue of uncertainty. The appropriate propensities to consume in the case of policies which accentuate economic uncertainy will, presumably, be smaller than those in the case of policies that reduce uncertainty. In this analysis we ignore both incentive issues and uncertainty.

The age and sex-specific consumption propensities used here were calculated using data from the U.S. Bureau of Labor Statistics Consumer Expenditure Survey for the years 1981 through 1986 to determine households' propensities to consume out of household lifetime income by the age of the household head. In this calculation, human wealth, nonhuman

Table 4. *Consumption propensities by age and sex*

Age	Males	Females
18	0.029	0.065
20	0.032	0.066
25	0.038	0.070
30	0.044	0.073
35	0.050	0.077
40	0.055	0.080
45	0.061	0.084
50	0.067	0.087
55	0.073	0.091
60	0.079	0.094
65	0.085	0.097
70	0.091	0.101
75	0.097	0.104
80 +	0.108	0.111

wealth, social security wealth and pension wealth of survey adults were estimated.[5]

For purposes of this study, we formed the average ratio of consumption to lifetime income (the sum of human wealth, nonhuman wealth, social security wealth and pension wealth) by age and sex for adult generations. In these calculations we ascribe the consumption expenditure on children living at home to their parents. In the case of married parents, we ascribed half of the children's consumption to the husband and half to the wife. For purposes of this calculation, we excluded observations on households in which individuals other than children co-reside with the household head. The consumption expenditures that were identifiably those of the husband (wife) were ascribed to the husband (wife). The remaining household consumption expenditures were divided evenly between the husband and wife.

Table 4 reports the weighted average ratios of consumption to the present value of lifetime income by age and sex arising between the fifth and sixth deciles of the distribution of lifetime income. We used these consumption propensities to determine the first year impact on U.S. consumption and saving of the four hypothetical policies of Table 3.[6] We

---

[5] This calculation is part of ongoing research of Andrew Abel, Douglas Bernheim and Laurence J. Kotlikoff.
[6] Specifically, for each policy, we multiply the changes in generational accounts for each age–sex group by the number of individuals in that group times the group's consumption propensity. The sum of these numbers across all age–sex groups give the policy's first-year impact on U.S. consumption.

then recalculated the U.S. net national saving rate for 1989 based on each of the four policies. The actual 1989 U.S. net national saving rate was 3.67 per cent. Under the tax cut policy the saving rate falls to 3.32 per cent. It is 2.76 per cent for the pay-as-you-go social security policy, 3.73 per cent for the shift from payroll to consumption taxation, and 3.44 per cent for the elimination of investment incentives.

Of the four hypopthetical policies, the 20 per cent increase in unfunded social security benefits has the largest first year impact on national saving, reducing the saving rate by almost one quarter. The 0.91 per cent point initial year drop in the saving rate is of the same order of magnitude as the saving rate decline reported in Auerbach and Kotlikoff's (1987) simulation analysis of unfunded social security.

In comparison with the saving decline from the social security experiment, the decline in national saving arising from the five-year income tax cut is less than half as large. Part of the explanation for the smaller impact is, as indicated above, that the generational impact of this policy is substantially smaller than that of the change in social security. The second part of the explanation is that we consider here only the income effects of these policies on saving; i.e., we ignore substitution effects. Finally, the results here ignore general equilibrium changes in factor prices which, when anticipated, could influence even the initial year impact of policy changes on saving.

As predicted by Summers (1981), a partial shift from wage to explicit consumption taxation does increase the national saving rate, but the increase reported here is modest. The elimination of implicit consumption taxation arising from the removal of investment incentives has a somewhat larger effect on national saving.

V. Conclusion

We have explored the use of generational accounting in understanding the intergenerational redistribution arising from alternative fiscal policies. It has also been demonstrated how policy-induced changes in generational accounting can be used to consider the impact of policy changes on national saving. The findings confirm what many economists have long suspected: that the fiscal deficit is thoroughly unreliable as a measure of either generational policy or the policy-induced stimulus to aggregate demand. The findings also suggest that fiscal policies of the type actually conducted by OECD countries in the postwar period could have important effects on OECD national saving rates.

The results discussed here should, however, be viewed as preliminary. There are many refinements of generational accounting that need to be implemented. In addition, the analysis of average consumption propensities needs to be improved and extended to the consideration of marginal consumption propensities. Finally, the sensitivity of the findings to alternative growth and interest rate assumptions deserves careful exploration.

References

Auerbach, A. J., Gokhale, J. & Kotlikoff, L. J.: Generational accounts — A meaningful alternative to deficit accounting. In D. Bradford (ed.), *Tax Policy and the Economy*, NBER volume, MIT Press, Cambridge, MA, 1991.

Auerbach, A. J. & Kotlikoff, L. J.: *Dynamic Fiscal Policy.* Cambridge University Press, 1987.

Feldstein, M. S.: Social security, induced retirement, and aggregate capital accumulation. *Journal of Political Economy 82*, 1974.

Kotlikoff, L. J.: Taxation and savings — A neoclassical perspective. *Journal of Economic Literature*, Dec. 1984.

Kotlikoff, L. J.: From deficit delusion to the fiscal balance rule — Looking for a sensible way to measure fiscal policy. NBER WP, Mar. 1989; forthcoming, *Journal of Economics*, 1992.

Kotlikoff, L. J.: *Generational Accounting: Knowing Who Pays — and When — for What We Spend.* The Free Press, New York, 1992.

Summers, L. H.: Capital taxation and accumulation in a life cycle growth model. *American Economic Review 71* (4), Sept. 1981.

Comment on A. J. Auerbach, J. Gokhale and L. J. Kotlikoff, "Generational Accounting: A New Approach to Understanding the Effects of Fiscal Policy on Saving"

John Muellbauer

Nuffield College, Oxford, England

This is a very thought provoking paper. It suggests that U.S. generations born after 1989 will contribute a significantly higher (20 per cent higher) share of their lifetime incomes in net payments to U.S. governments (federal, state and local) than the 1989 generation. A-G-K compute that a 5.3 per cent permanent increase in the average rate of income tax enacted in 1990 would have "equalized the generational burden". But if 1989 policies remain in place, by 1999 the deficit built up raises the permanent tax increase to close on 10 per cent.[1]

Should we worry? Let me begin with some general issues.

Intergenerational Justice and Observed Inequality

Should we impoverish ourselves in order to make our children, already rich because of productivity growth, even richer? Or does justice entail equality between generations? If the latter, did the U.S. government of 1989 go far enough?

Why do people object to such outrageous reasoning? Why do we not observe greater equality in consumption between generations (observed at the same age)? A partial answer to the last question could lie in habits or consumption standards positional on the previous generation. Suppose utility depends not on c_i but on

$$\frac{1}{1-a}(c_t - ac_{t-1}), 0 < a < 1.$$

---

[1] It would be nice to examine the sensitivity of these results to different assumptions on the growth rate and the real rate of interest.

Given diminishing marginal utility, a fall in consumption is more painful, the higher the level of consumption I got used to when I grew up in my parents' house. Equality between generations then requires not $c_{t+1} = c_t$ but

$$c_{t+1} - ac_t = c_t - ac_{t-1} \text{ so that}$$

$$c_{t+1} = c_t + a\Delta c_t.$$

So, if consumption grows between $t-1$ and t because, for example, the economy hits a good patch, integenerational justice suggests that some of this growth be carried over into $t+1$.

But the chief reasons for the generational inequality in consumption we observe surely lie in individual behaviour, given the constraints individuals actually face. There are four groups of factors:

(i) credit or liquidity imperfections: borrowing constraints, transactions costs, resale restrictions, different interest rates on different debts or assets. Hence, for example, there is forced saving by the young to build up down payments for housing, and reduced dissaving by the old who cannot access their housing wealth;

(ii) uncertainty[2] about income, length of life and its interaction with (i). Adverse selection arguments suggest failures in private insurance markets in consequence;

(iii) myopia;

(iv) habits at the individual level.

One implication, incidentally, of these features is that the intertemporal budget constraints of the goverment and of individuals cannot be easily combined. This is a limitation on the A-G-K analysis.

It most respects, these motives for individual saving suggest that there is a social inefficiency for such excess saving. From this point of view, the U.S., the U.K. and the Nordic countries look notably efficient, having liberalized credit and, at least for the latter, instituted far-reaching social insurance which ameliorates private uncertainty.

However, there are at least four important qualifications of these arguments:

(i) There are tradeoffs between incentives and insurance.

(ii) There are deadweight losses from taxation and can be crowding out effects via credit markets that have consequences for real capital accumulation in the private sector.

---

[2] By the way, despite the authors' disclaimer that they ignore uncertainty, the empirical propensities to consume by age and sex may well take some of the uncertainty into account.

(iii) There are *national* precautionary reasons for saving: the macro environment could turn sour e.g. because of an oil shock. Perceptions of growth may be illusory because of environmental degradation that becomes obvious only later. For example, it would be quite untenable for the global environment if all countries had the U.S. standard of living.
(iv) There can be problems of transition: adjustment costs, overheating, the persistence of inflation — see U.K., Finland (and Italy to come?).

Does the A-K-G Approach Capture the Most Important Intergenerational Tradeoffs?

They treat government consumption as "pure waste". But human and physical capital formation is part of it. They could go further in imputing this to individuals.

Surpluses or deficits in international trade are another way in which intergenerational transfers can be made — just another aspect of the accumulation of relevant capital stock. *International* financial liberalization can expand the intertemporal opportunity set; see the pictures in Muellbauer and Murphy (1990, p. 351).

I understand that A-G-K or others are thinking of applying this framework to the U.K. Would it capture the biggest intergenerational stories of the last 20 years? Let me examine some aspects of the U.K. experience. In the inflationary 1970s the real mortgage interest rate for standard rate taxpayers averaged minus 5 per cent. Of course, credit controls were in force. Many older people, especially those without housing wealth, were impoverished. Many young people — mortgage borrowers, especially those in the financial sector who received *both* a mortgage subsidy *and* a bigger credit ration — were enriched.

How much of this would be picked up in their framework? Some of it would be, e.g. the tax system being biased towards borrowers and against savers. But how, within their framework, does one handle the low level of interest rates balanced by credit controls?

Financial liberalization further enriched the beneficiaries of the 1970s through the asset price boom that it helped engender, leaving house price/ income ratios perhaps 10 per cent higher permanently. This would not be captured in the A-G-K framework.

On the other hand, the abolition of property taxes (though this has proved only temporary) would be captured. So, of course, would the reforms to the state pension system. These include the encouragement of private pensions to replace state pensions and indexing state pensions to the retail price index instead of to earnings. The government's policy of selling the "family silver" and running down the public capital stock could also be incorporated within their framework.

Overall, I conclude that their framework would require substantial changes to incorporate the key intergenerational transfers in the U.K. of the last 20 years. However, their approach is an illuminating and stimulating beginning to the analysis of these issues.

Reference

Muellbauer, J. & Murphy, A.: Is the UK balance of payments sustainable? *Economic Policy*, 347–395, Oct. 1990.

World Interest Rates and Investment

Robert J. Barro

Harvard University, Cambridge, MA, USA

Abstract

In a world of integrated capital markets, the price of credit — which is measured by short-term expected real interest rates — is determined to equate the world aggregate of investment demand to the world aggregate of desired national saving. This approach is implemented empirically by approximately the world by aggregates for ten major developed countries. For the period since 1959, the common component of expected real interest rates for these countries relates especially to developments on world stock and oil markets and secondarily, to world monetary and fiscal policies.

I. Introduction

In a world of integrated capital markets, the price of credit — which I measure by short-term expected real interest rates — is determined to equate the world aggregate of investment demand to the world aggregate of desired national saving. In this framework, shifts to the perceived profitability of investment, which are reflected as movements in world stock-market prices, change investment and real interest rates in the same direction. Shifts to the willingness to save, which I relate to changes in oil prices and to fiscal and monetary policies, move investment and real interest rates in opposite directions.

I implement this approach empirically by approximating the world by aggregates for ten major developed countries. For the period since 1959, the common component of expected real interest rates for these countries relates especially to developments on world stock and oil markets and secondarily, to world monetary and fiscal policies. Although real interest rates for individual countries differ significantly from world averages, the country-specific components of interest rates do not relate significantly to variables that I have examined. In particular, these components do not depend on country-specific stock-market returns or monetary and fiscal policies.

II. Framework of the Analysis

As in Barro and Sala-i-Martin (1990) — henceforth B/X — the aggregate of ten industrialized economies — Belgium, Canada, France, Germany, Italy, Japan, Netherlands, Sweden, United Kingdom, and United States — is treated as a closed economy with a single capital market. The expected real interest rate is determined to equate total investment demand to total desired saving.

I use a version of investment demand and desired saving that makes small modifications to the framework in B/X. The ratio of real gross domestic investment demand to real GDP for country i at time t depends on a q variable:

$$(I/Y)_{it} = \alpha_{0i} + \alpha_1 \cdot \log(q_{i,t-1}) + \text{error term} \tag{1}$$

where I_{it} is investment during period t, q_{it-1} is market valuation per unit of capital at the start of period t, the constant term α_{0i} can vary by country, and $\alpha_1 > 0$. The first difference of the investment ratio depends on the growth rate of q, which can be measured by the growth rate of real stock prices in country i, denoted STOCK. (Adjustments for retained earnings would have a minor effect here.)

Distinctions between average and marginal q, generated for example by oil shocks, can shift the relation between changes in the investment ratio and stock returns. I therefore include the ratio of expenditures on crude-oil consumption to GDP, denoted OILCY, as an additional proxy for marginal q. This oil variable is driven mainly by changes in the relative price of crude oil. For 1959–89, the correlation of OILCY_t (aggregated over the ten industrialized countries in the sample) with the relative price of crude oil (based on the U.S. PPI) is 0.87 in levels and 0.77 in first differences. The specific functional form used for the investment ratio is

$$(I/Y)_{it} = a_0 + (I/Y)_{i,t-1} + a_1 \cdot \text{STOCK}_{i,t-1} + a_2 \cdot D(\text{OILCY}_{i,t-1}) + u_{it} \tag{2}$$

where D is the first-difference operator. I treat the error term, u_{it}, as white noise, which means that shocks to the investment–demand ratio are permanent in character.

The desired national saving rate is given, following B/X, as

$$(S/Y)_{it} = b_{0i} + b_1 r_t^e + b_2(\text{OILCY}_{i,t-1}) + b_3 \text{DM}_{i,t-1}$$
$$+ b_4 F_{i,t-1} + b_5(S/Y)_{i,t-1} + \varepsilon_{it} \tag{3}$$

where the constant term b_{0i} can vary by country, r_t^e is the world expected real interest rate, DM is monetary growth, F is a fiscal variable, and ε_{it} is treated as a white-noise error. If the variables other than r_t^e hold constnat income effects, then $b_1 > 0$ from the usual substitution effect. If high oil consumption, OILCY, signifies temporarily low income, then $b_2 < 0$.[1] Monetary growth generates temporarily high income in some models; hence, $b_3 > 0$ in these models. If F represents a temporarily high ratio of government purchases to GDP, then $b_4 < 0$. In some models, a high ratio of the public debt to GDP or a high prospective ratio of real government deficits (changes in the real debt) to real GDP motivate low current national saving. Therefore, $b_4 < 0$ holds for these fiscal variables in these models. The term, $b_5(S/Y)_{i, t-1}$, picks up slow adjustment in the saving rate. Alternatively, this term can proxy for serial correlation in the error term, ε_{it}.

Note that the interest rate, r_t^c, does not enter directly into equations (1) and (2). Changes in the interest rate affect investment demand indirectly by first influencing the market valuation of capital. I assume also that the stock-return variable, STOCK, does not enter into the saving equation. This assumption allows identification of the coefficient b_1, the interest-sensitivity of the saving rate. The important condition is not that stock returns have a zero effect on desired saving, but rather that the effect on investment demand is much greater than that on desired saving.

The "world" expected real interest rate, r_t^c, is determined by equating the sum of the I_{it} from equation (2) to the sum of the S_{it} from equation (3). Therefore, r_t^c is determined as

$$r_t^c = (1/b_1) \cdot [a_0 - b_0 + a_1 \text{STOCK}_{t-1} + a_2 D(\text{OILCY}_{t-1}) - b_2 \text{OILCY}_{t-1}$$
$$- b_3 \text{DM}_{t-1} - b_4 F_{t-1} + (1 - b_5)(I/Y)_{t-1} + u_t - \varepsilon_t]. \tag{4}$$

The variables written without i subscripts on the right side of the equation are GDP-weighted averages of the variables that appear in equations (2) and (3). For example, STOCK_{t-1} is a GDP-weighted average over the countries i of $\text{STOCK}_{i, t-1}$, and so on. I refer henceforth to these GDP-weighted averages as world variables.

I assume that the observed real interest rate for country i, r_{it}^c, differs from r_t^c by a country-specific constant and an error term:

$$r_{it}^c = r_t^c + \text{constant}_i + (\text{error term})_{it} \tag{5}$$

where the error term can be serially correlated. Substitution from equation (4) into equation (5) implies

$$r_{it}^c = \beta_{0i} + (1/b_1) \cdot [a_1 \text{STOCK}_{t-1} + a_2 D(\text{OILCY}_{t-1}) - b_2 \text{OILCY}_{t-1}$$
$$- b_3 \text{DM}_{t-1} - b_4 F_{t-1} + (1 - b_5)(I/Y)_{t-1}] + v_{it}. \tag{6}$$

---

[1] An ARMA (1, 1) regression for OILCY$_t$ (the GDP-weighted average of OILCY$_{it}$ for the ten countries in the sample) over the period 1959–89 yields the AR(1) coefficient, 0.86 (s.e. = 0.09), and the MA(1) coefficient, 0.17 (0.20).

Thus, r_{it}^c depends on a set of world variables: $STOCK_{t-1}$, $D(OILCY)_{t-1}$, $OILCY_{t-1}$, DM_{t-1}, F_{t-1}, and $(I/Y)_{t-1}$. The only own-country variables that appear are the constant, β_{0i}, and the serially-correlated error term, v_{it}, which I model as an AR(1) process. In contrast, equation (2) implies that $(I/Y)_{it}$ depends only on the own-country variables, $(I/Y)_{i,t-1}$, $STOCK_{i,t-1}$, and $D(OILCY)_{i,t-1}$. I check below for effects of own-country variables on r_{it}^c and for effects of world variables on $(I/Y)_{it}$.

III. Data

I use annual observations of variables for the ten countries, usually from 1957 to 1990. World measures (GDP-weighted averages) of the investment ratio, $(I/Y)_t$, the ratio of expenditures on crude-oil consumption to GDP, $OILCY_t$, the growth rate of real stock prices, $STOCK_t$, and the growth rate of M1, DM_t, appear in Figure 1. Figure 2 shows various concepts of world fiscal variables: the ratio of real government consumption to real GDP, (G/Y_t), the ratio of government revenue (for consolidated general government) to GDP, $GREVY_t$, the ratio of real central government debt to real GDP, $RDEBTY_t$, and the cyclically-adjusted ratio of the central government's real deficit to real GDP, $RDEFYA_t$.[2]

Short-term nominal interest rates (3-month Treasury Bill rates or comparable money-market rates), denoted R_{it}, are available over the sample period for all of the countries except Italy. I construct expected inflation, π_{it}^c, using forecasts generated from an ARMA (1, 1) specification for CPI inflation on quarterly data with deterministic seasonals (see B/X). The inflation process is estimated from 1950.2 until the quarter preceding the date to which π_{it}^c applies. The variable r_{it}^c is then constructed as $R_{it} - \pi_{it}^c$. (The 3-month nominal interest rates for January, April, July, and October match up with inflation anticipated between January and April, and so on.) The annual data, r_{it}^c, are averages of the four quarterly values for the year.

Figure 3 shows world values (GDP-weighted averages for nine countries with Italy excluded) for the nominal interest rate, R_t, expected inflation, π_t^c, and the expected real interest rate, r_t^c. Note that I use these averages of interest and inflation rates only for illustrative purposes. The estimation uses the expected real interest rate, r_{it}^c, observed separately for each country in the form of equation (6). Figure 4 plots the series for r_{it}^c for the

---

[2] The real deficit is the change in the real debt over the year. The ratio of the real deficit to real GDP, $RDEFY_{it}$, for each country was regressed on the current and four annual lags of the growth rate of real GDP. The residual from this regression is the cyclically-adjusted variable, $RDEFYA_{it}$.

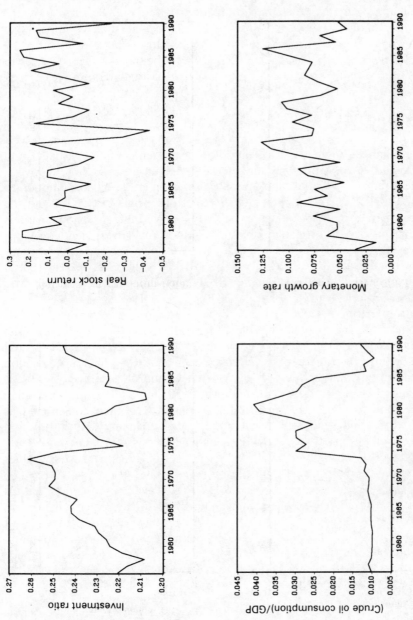

Fig. 1. World variables for investment ratio, stock returns, oil consumption and monetary growth.

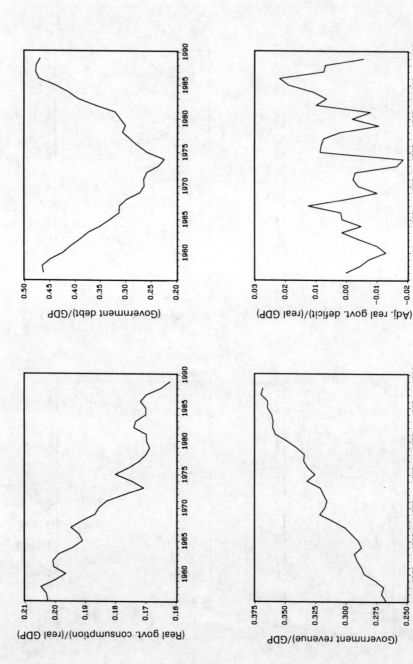

Fig. 2. World fiscal variables.

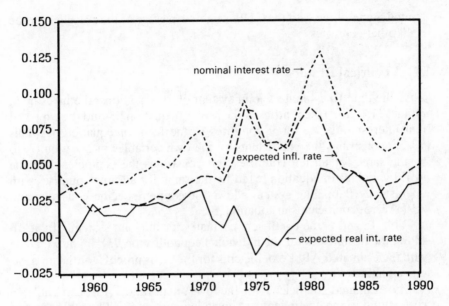

Fig. 3. World nominal and real interest rates and expected inflation.

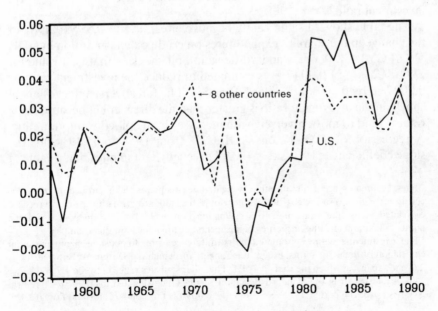

Fig. 4. Expected real interest rates in the U.S. and 8 other countries.

United States along with the GDP-weighted average of the r_{it}^c values for the eight other countries.

IV. Empirical Results

I use the data to estimate a joint system of 19 equations: the investment ratio, $(I/Y)_{it}$, for 10 countries in the form of equation (2) and the expected real interest rate, r_{it}^c, for 9 countries in the form of equation (6). This system constrains the coefficients on the own variables in equation (2) to be the same for all ten countries and constrains the coefficients on the world variables in equation (6) to be the same for all nine countries with interest-rate data. The system allows for country-specific constants and AR(1) error coefficients in equation (6).

Table 1a shows the coefficient estimates for the joint system.[3] Table 1b shows the fit statistics for the individual equations for $(I/Y)_{it}$ and r_{it}^c, along with the estimated AR(1) coefficients for the error process for the interest-rate equations.[4]

The estimated coefficients for the investment ratio, $(I/Y)_{it}$, in Table 1a correspond to the coefficients a_i shown in equation (2). The table shows a significantly positive effect, $\hat{a}_1 = 0.0231$ (s.e. = 0.0028), of the lagged own-country stock return, $STOCK_{i,t-1}$. A stock return that is one standard deviation (0.156) above normal is estimated to raise the investment ratio by 0.0036 or by 0.40 of a standard deviation for the change in the world investment ratio.[5]

The table shows a significantly negative effect, $\hat{a}_2 = -0.585$ (0.098), of the change in the share of expenditures on crude oil consumption in GDP, $D(OILCY)_{i,t-1}$. A one standard-deviation oil shock — that is, a value for $D(OILCY)_{t-1}$ of 0.0047 — is estimated to reduce the investment ratio by 0.0027 or by 0.30 of a standard deviation. The full adverse effect of an oil shock on the investment ratio is greater than the direct effect because stock returns tend to move inversely with increases in the oil-consumption ratio. A regression of $STOCK_t$ on $D(OILCY)_t$ from 1959 to 1989 yields the slope coefficient -19.7 (s.e. = 4.7).[6] This coefficient implies that a value of

---

[3] These estimates are from iterative, weighted least-squares. This procedure provides consistent estimates of the coefficients, but not of the standard errors if the error terms are correlated across the equations. GLS estimation is feasible, but introduces a very large number of parameters; the properties of this technique are unclear in small samples.

[4] The investment equations, estimated in first-difference form, do not show significant serial correlation of the error terms, except for Canada, for which the Durbin-Watson statistic is 2.6, and Japan, for which the statistic is 1.1. The other statistics range between 1.7 and 2.2.

[5] The value 0.156 is the standard deviation of the GDP-weighted average stock return, $STOCK_t$, over the period 1958–89. Similarly, 0.0090 is the standard deviation of $(I/Y)_t - (I/Y)_{t-1}$.

[6] The R^2 of this regression is 0.38.

Table 1a. *Regression estimates for investment and saving*

Variable	$(I/Y)_{it}$	$(S/Y)_t$
$(I/Y)_{i,t-1}$	1	—
$STOCK_{i,t-1}$	0.0231 (0.0028)	—
$DOILCY_{i,t-1}$	−0.585 (0.098)	—
r_t^e	—	0.557 (0.092)
$OILCY_{t-1}$	—	−0.715 (0.140)
DM_{t-1}	—	0.131 (0.025)
$(G/Y)_{t-1}$	—	0.038 (0.125)
$RDEBTY_{t-1}$	—	−0.067 (0.019)
$RDEFYA_{t-1}$	—	0.120 (0.070)
$(I/Y)_{t-1}$	—	0.592 (0.091)

Notes: Estimates are from iterative, weighted least squares on a system of 10 countries for the investment ratio and 9 countries for the expected real interest rate. Sample period is 1959–90, except 1959–89 for investment for Belgium, Italy, and Sweden. I/Y is the ratio of real domestic investment to real GDP, STOCK is the real return on the stock market (exclusive of dividends), OILCY is the ratio of crude oil consumption to GDP, DOILCY is the first difference of OILCY, DM is the growth rate of M1, G/Y is the ratio of real government consumption to real GDP, RDEBTY is the ratio of real central government debt to real GDP, RDEFYA is the cyclically-adjusted ratio of the real government deficit (the change in the central government's real debt) to real GDP. Variables without i subscripts are GDP-weighted averages over the countries. r^e is the expected real interest rate. Constant terms are not shown. Standard errors are in parentheses.

Table 1b. *Statistics for individual countries*

Country	$(I/Y)_{it}$	r_{it}^e	
	$R^2(\hat{\sigma})$	$R^2(\hat{\sigma})$	AR(1)
Belgium	0.81 (0.0130)	0.73 (0.0090)	0.80 (0.11)
Canada	0.12 (0.0148)	0.70 (0.0157)	0.44 (0.16)
France	0.83 (0.0104)	0.78 (0.0129)	0.66 (0.10)
Germany	0.85 (0.0119)	0.38 (0.0183)	0.58 (0.14)
Italy	0.84 (0.0152)	—	—
Japan	0.86 (0.0153)	0.07 (0.0219)	0.64 (0.13)
Netherlands	0.87 (0.0125)	0.66 (0.0147)	0.61 (0.14)
Sweden	0.74 (0.0148)	0.71 (0.0165)	0.64 (0.13)
U.K.	0.58 (0.0122)	0.51 (0.0301)	0.53 (0.15)
U.S.	0.21 (0.0115)	0.65 (0.0136)	0.60 (0.14)

Notes: The column for $(I/Y)_{it}$ indicates the values of R^2 and the standard-error-of-estimate $(\hat{\sigma})$ for the regressions reported in the first part of the table. The statistics for the regressions for r_{it}^e appear in the next column. The estimated coefficient and standard error for the AR(1) error process for the r_{it}^e equations are in the final column.

$D(OILCY)_{t-1}$ equal to 0.0047 induces $STOCK_{t-1}$ to fall 0.093 below normal, a change that leads to a decline in $(I/Y)_t$ by 0.0021. Hence, the full effect of a one-standard-deviation oil shock is a reduction in next year's investment ratio by 0.0048 or by 0.54 of a standard deviation for the change in the world investment ratio.

The estimated coefficients for the aggregate saving rate, $(S/Y)_t$, in Table 1 correspond to the coefficients b_i in equation (3). The estimated effect, b_1, of r_t^e on the desired saving rate is 0.56 (0.09). Thus, for given values of the other influences on saving, a higher expected real interest rate induces an increase in the saving rate. Recall that the identification of this coefficient depends on the exclusion of the stock-return variable, $STOCK_t$, from the saving equation.[7]

The oil variable, $OILCY_{t-1}$, has an estimated coefficient $\hat{b}_2 = -0.72$ (0.14). I interpret this effect as the negative response of the desired saving rate to a shortfall of current from permanent income. This interpretation follows if people view shifts in the ratio of expenditures on crude-oil consumption to GDP (and the underlying movements in the relative price of crude oil) as partly transitory. Although this perspective is consistent with the time-series behavior of $OILCY_t$ (n. 1), the time-series evidence is, as usual, not definitive.

The growth rate of M1 (presumably representing unanticipated movements in money) has a positive estimated coefficient, $b_3 = 0.131$ (0.025), on the desired saving rate. This result corresponds to the negative estimated relation between r_{it}^e and DM_{t-1} in the form of equation (6). Quantitatively, a one-standard-deviation movement (0.0225) in monetary growth shifts the desired saving rate by 0.0029 or by 0.33 of the standard deviation of the first difference of the world investment ratio. The interpretation of this monetary effect is unclear, but it is worth noting that the relation is between world monetary growth and the real interest rate in the typical country, and not between an individual country's monetary growth and its own real interest rate (see below).

The fiscal variable for government purchases, $(G/Y)_{t-1}$, has an insignificant effect on the desired saving rate. Theoretically, a temporary increase in the government–purchases ratio would lower the desired saving rate, whereas a permanent increase would have little or no effect. Therefore, the insignificant coefficient may reflect the permanent nature of much of the movements in government purchases.[8] Typically, the main temporary

---

[7] The system as written is overidentified because the lagged first difference of the oil variable appears in the investment equation, whereas the lagged level appears in the saving equation. This restriction is tenuous, however, because it depends on the exclusion of the second lag of the oil variable from the saving equation. A test of the overidentifying restriction leads to the value for $-2 \cdot \log$ (likelihood ratio) of 0.9, which corresponds to a p-value of 0.35 (using the χ^2 distribution with one d.f.). Therefore, the restriction accords with the data.

[8] An ARMA (1, 1) equation for $(G/Y)_t$ over the period 1959–89 yields the AR(1) coefficient 0.914 (s.e. = 0.042) and the MA(1) coefficient 0.725 (0.118). The MA(1) coefficient likely picks up business-cycle effects related to fluctuations in GDP for given levels of government purchases.

action in government purchases reflects changes in military spending due to war and peace, but little of this behavior arises (even for the Vietnam or Persian Gulf Wars) over the sample period for the ten countries under study.

The debt-GDP ratio, $RDEBTY_{t-1}$, has a significantly negative coefficient on the saving rate, $-0.067\,(0.019)$. This coefficient implies that a one-standard-deviation movement in the debt ratio (0.019) shifts the desired saving rate by 0.0012 or by 0.14 of the standard deviation of the first difference of the world investment ratio. In contrast, the cyclically-adjusted deficit-GDP ratio, $RDEFYA_{t-1}$, has an insignificant coefficient of the "wrong" sign, $0.120\,(0.070)$. Of course, in respectable models in which the public debt influences desired national saving — such as Blanchard (1985) — the current budget deficit matters only to the extent that it predicts a weighted sum of future deficits. Thus, the deficit variable may be insignificant in the saving-rate equation because the current deficit–GDP ratio (even cyclically adjusted) is a poor predictor of future deficits.[9]

The estimated coefficient on $(I/Y)_{t-1} - b_5 = 0.59\,(0.09)$ — suggests that shocks to the desired saving rate are persistent but not permanent. (Note, however, from the second part of the table that the estimated AR(1) error coefficients for the interest-rate equations are all significantly positive.)

The values of R^2 and $\hat{\sigma}$, the standard-error-of-estimate, for the individual equations for $(I/Y)_{it}$ and r_{it}^e are in the second part of Table 1. With respect to investment, the low R^2 values for Canada and the United States are notable, although the values of $\hat{\sigma}$ for these countries are not especially high. For the interest-rate equations, the low R^2 for Japan indicates that virtually none of the movements in Japanese real interest rates are explained by the model. The high $\hat{\sigma}$ value for the United Kingdom reflects some very large negative values in the mid 1970s that the model cannot explain. This result likely indicates overestimation of expected inflation (in the face of high actual inflation) and hence, measurement error in r_{it}^e, rather than a problem with the rest of the model.

V. Simulated Effects of a Stock-Market Boom and an Oil Shock

I simulate the effects of some disturbances by using the results from Table 1 for investment demand and desired saving, and hence for the expected real interest rate. I assume in these simulations that the fiscal variables do

---

[9] Empirically, over the period 1959–89, the variable $RDEFYA_t$ is virtually uncorrelated with $RDEFY_{t+i}$ for $i > 1$. The correlation of $RDEFY_t$ with $RDEFY_{t+i}$ is around 0.3 for i between 3 and 5. This correlation reflects mainly the persistence of the business cycle and hence, the real budget deficit.

not change. The processes for OILCY$_t$, STOCK$_t$, and DM$_t$ come from estimated relations over the period 1959–89:

$$OILCY_t = 0.0020 + 0.89 \cdot OILCY_{t-1}$$

$$STOCK_t = 0.0243 - 19.7 \cdot D(OILCY)_t$$

$$DM_t = 0.0513 + 0.37 \cdot DM_{t-1} - 2.30 \cdot D(OILCY)_t - 0.078 \cdot STOCK_{t-1}. \quad (7)$$

Hence, the simulations incorporate a negative contemporaneous response of the stock market to an increase in the oil variable, as well as responses of monetary growth to its own lag (positive), to an increase in the oil variable (negative), and to lagged stock returns (negative). The simulations begin with a history of values for DM, STOCK, and OILCY equal to their respective steady-state values (0.078, 0.024, and 0.019). The variables r_t^c and $(I/Y)_t$ begin with a history of values equal to the respective sample means (0.0215 and 0.234). As the model is written, these variables are not stationary.

The first simulation pertains to a one-standard-deviation (0.156) stock to stock returns. Figure 5 shows the path of $(I/Y)_t$ and Figure 6 shows the path of r_t^c. The shock in year 3 leads in year 4 to an increase in $(I/Y)_t$. The effect on the investment ratio is permanent because nothing in the model generates mean reversion in the stock market; that is, no force tends to bring q back to unity. In fact, the increase in r_t^c in year 4 would depress the shock market and lead thereby to a reduction in $(I/Y)_t$ in year 5. The model should be modified to allow for this feedback effect from r_t^c to stock

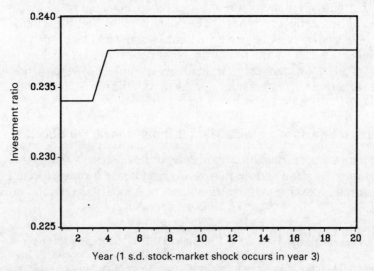

Fig. 5. Simulated effect of stock-market boom on investment ratio.

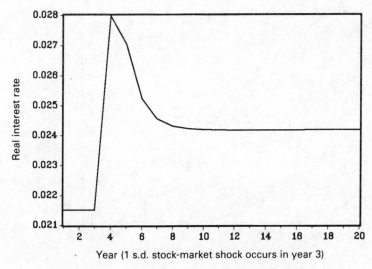

Fig. 6. Simulated effect of stock-market boom on real interest rate.

returns. In Figure 6, r_t^c spikes upward in year 4 and then comes down gradually toward a permanently higher plateau, which corresponds to the permanently higher investment ratio. The real interest rate overshoots mostly because the desired saving rate adjusts only gradually to changes in r_t^c and its other determinants. (The temporary reduction in monetary growth in year 4 tends also to keep r_t^c high in year 5.)

The second simulation considers an oil shock in the form of a one-standard-deviation (0.0047) increase in $OILCY_t$. (In the data, the largest changes in $OILCY_t$ are the rises by 0.017 from 1973 to 1974 and by 0.014 from 1979 to 1981, and the fall by 0.013 from 1985 to 1986.) Recall that the simulation assumes that the rise in OILCY causes a low stock return ($STOCK_t = -0.069$ in the year of the oil shock). The shock in year 3 leads in Figure 7 to a decline in $(I/Y)_t$ in year 4. As OILCY returns gradually to its steady-state value, $(I/Y)_t$ returns gradually toward its initial position. Figure 8 shows that r_t^c declines by a small amount in year 4 because the decline in investment demand is initially greater than the fall in desired saving. Subsequently, the fall in the desired saving rate dominates (according to the estimates) and r_t^c rises to a peak in year 6 (3 years after the shock). After year 6, r_t^c declines gradually back to its initial value.

VI. World and Own-Country Variables

Table 2 adds various world and own-country variables to the systems shown in Table 1. The first case introduces the world stock return,

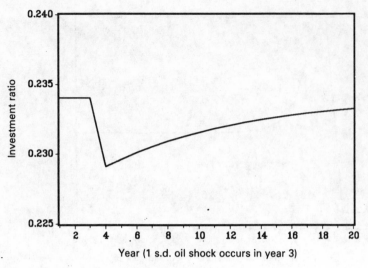

Fig. 7. Simulated effect of oil shock on investment.

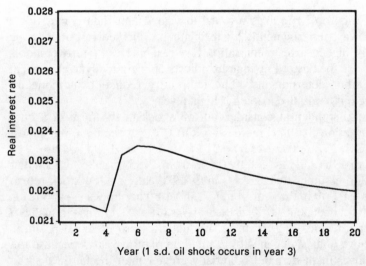

Fig. 8. Simulated effect of oil shock on real interest rate.

$STOCK_t$, as a determinant of country i's investment ratio, $(I/Y)_{it}$, in the form of equation (2). The coefficient of $STOCK_t$ is constrained to be the same in all ten investment equations. The estimated coefficient of $STOCK_{t-1}$ is positive, 0.0096 (0.0058), but insignificant at the 5 per cent level (t-value = 1.7). In contrast, the estimated coefficient of the own stock return, $STOCK_{i,t-1}$, remains significantly positive, 0.0175 (0.0044).

Table 2. *World and own-country variables*

Variable	$(I/Y)_{it}$	$(S/Y)_t (r_{it}^c)$
$STOCK_{i,t-1}$	0.0175 (0.0044)	—
$STOCK_{t-1}$	0.0096 (0.0058)	—
$DOILCY_{i,t-1}$	−0.262 (0.244)	—
$DOILCY_{t-1}$	−0.402 (0.279)	—
$DOILCY_{i,t-1}$	−0.639 (0.132)	—
$DOILPY_{i,t-1}$	0.125 (0.197)	—
DM_{t-1}	—	0.135 (0.026)
$DM_{i,t-1}$	—	−0.005 (0.009)
$(G/Y)_{t-1}$	—	0.034 (0.097)
$(G/Y)_{i,t-1}$	—	−0.266 (0.074)
$RDEBTY_{t-1}$	—	−0.089 (0.023)
$RDEBTY_{i,t-1}$	—	0.024 (0.010)
$RDEFYA_{t-1}$	—	0.127 (0.072)
$RDEFYA_{i,t-1}$	—	−0.011 (0.026)
DM_{t-1} [a]	−0.058 (0.036)	—
$(G/Y)_{t-1}$	0.021 (0.030)	—
$RDEBTY_{t-1}$	0.003 (0.011)	—
$RDEFYA_{t-1}$	0.044 (0.099)	—

Notes: The estimated coefficients and standard errors refer to variables added (one set at a time) to the regressions for the system shown in Table 1. DOILPY is the first difference of the ratio of oil production to GDP.
[a] The likelihood-ratio statistic for the test that all four of these coefficients are zero is 3.7, p-value = 0.45.

The next case in the table adds the world measure of the change in the oil consumption ratio, $D(OILCY)_{t-1}$, to the investment equations. The estimated coefficients of this variable and the own-country counterpart are each negative but insignificant. Thus, the analysis cannot distinguish between the world and own-country effects in this case. One consideration is that the paths of the oil-consumption ratios are similar across the countries. Moreover, measurement error in the data for expenditures on crude-oil consumption for individual countries could enhance the explanatory power of the world average variable for an individual country's investment ratio.

For three of the countries in the sample — Canada, United Kingdom, and United States — the presence of crude-oil production creates a distinction between oil imports and expenditure on crude-oil consumption. (Canada and the Netherlands are also large exporters of natural gas, which should be brought into the analysis.) The next case shown in Table 2 adds the lagged change in the ratio of the value of crude-oil production to

GDP, $D(OILPY)_{i,t-1}$, to the investment equations for these countries. The coefficient of this variable is restricted to be the same across the countries. The estimated coefficient is positive but insignificant, 0.125 (0.197), and the estimated coefficient of $D(OILCY)_{i,t-1}$ remains significantly negative. Thus, although an increase in expenditures for oil consumption is bad for investment, there is not much evidence here of an offsetting positive effect associated with higher receipts from oil production.[10]

I have also added own-country variables to the equations for r_{it}^c in the form of equation (6). In each case, the coefficient of the new variable is constrained to be the same in all nine interest-rate equations. Table 2 shows that an individual country's monetary growth rate, $DM_{i,t-1}$, has an insignificant effect. The estimated coefficient, -0.005 (0.009), refers to the effect on the saving rate in the form of equation (3). The estimated coefficient of DM_{t-1} remains significantly positive, 0.135 (0.026), corresponding to a significantly negative effect on r_{it}^c. Thus, the results suggest a role for world monetary growth in the determination of the world real interest rate, but not for an individual country's monetary growth in the determination of its own real interest rate.

For the government-purchases ratio, the estimated coefficient of $(G/Y)_{t-1}$ remains insignificant, but the estimated coefficient of $(G/Y)_{i,t-1}$ is significantly negative for the saving rate: -0.0266 (0.074). (This result corresponds to a significantly positive effect of $(G/Y)_{i,t-1}$ on r_{it}^c.) As mentioned before, theoretical reasoning suggests a negative effect of temporary government purchases on desired saving, but a global capital market implies that r_{it}^c would respond to world government purchases rather than own-country purchases. One possibility is that $(G/Y)_{it}$ is a proxy for country i's tax rate on interest income: even with a global capital market, r_{it}^c would react to the local tax rate to the extent that interest earnings are taxable at that rate. It turns out, however, that ratios of real government purchases to real GDP have behaved very differently from ratios of government revenues (for consolidated general government) to GDP for the countries and sample period considered. Figure 2 shows, for the world aggregates, that the purchases ratio has trended downward over the sample, whereas the revenue ratio has trended upward. (The correlation between the two variable is -0.91 in levels and -0.05 in first differences.) The divergence between purchases and revenues corresponds to the substantial increases in transfer payments as a ratio to GDP. If I include the government revenue ratios, $GREVY_{i,t-1}$ and $GREVY_{t-1}$,

---

[10] The effects should all be interpreted for given stock returns. For the United Kingdom, stock returns, $STOCK_{it}$, are significantly positively related to the contemporaneous change in the oil-production variable, $D(OILPY)_{it}$, and significantly negatively related to $D(OILCY)_{it}$. The variable $D(OILPY)_{it}$ is, however, insignificant for $STOCK_{it}$ for Canada and the United States.

as determinants of r_{it}^c, then the estimated coefficients of these variables are insignificant, whereas the estimated coefficient of $(G/Y)_{i,t-1}$ remains significantly negative for the saving rate (hence, significantly positive for r_{it}^c). Since GREVY$_{it}$ would seem to be a better proxy than $(G/Y)_{it}$ for country i's tax rate on interest income, the significantly negative effect of $(G/Y)_{i,t-1}$ on the saving rate likely does not involve a tax-rate effect.

Table 2 shows that the public-debt variable, RDEBTY$_{t-1}$, has a significantly negative effect, -0.089 (0.023), on the saving rate, whereas the own-country variable, RDEBTY$_{i,t-1}$, has a significantly positive effect, 0.024 (0.010). These results correspond to effects on r_{it}^c that are significantly positive for RDEBTY$_{t-1}$ and significantly negative for RDEBTY$_{i,t-1}$. Quantitatively, the results indicate that the main link between public debt and expected real interest rates is from world debt to world real interest rates. There is no evidence that an increase in a country's debt — GDP ratio — for a given world debt — GDP ratio — raises the real interest rate in that country.

With respect to the deficit variables, Table 2 shows that RDEFYA$_{t-1}$ and RDEFYA$_{i,t-1}$ are each insignificantly related to the saving rate. That is, neither world nor own-country budget deficits (cyclically adjusted) are significantly related to r_{it}^c.

A number of world variables — DM$_{t-1}$, $(G/Y)_{t-1}$, RDEBTY$_{t-1}$ and RDEFYA$_{t-1}$ — were included as possible determinants of the saving rate but were excluded from the equations for the investment ratio. In particular, with the change in marginal q held constant (by the stock-return and oil variables), the theory says that variables that influence desired saving would not matter for changes in the investment ratio. Table 2 shows that the four world variables from the saving equation are jointly insignificant if added to the ten equations for the investment ratio. (The coefficient for each variable is constrained to be the same in all ten equations.) The likelihood–ratio statistic that corresponds to the exclusion of the four variables from the investment equations is 3.7 and the p-value (corresponding to a χ^2 distribution with 4 d.f.) is 0.45.

The last finding does not mean that determinants of the saving rate, including the significant effects from DM$_{t-1}$ and RDEBTY$_{t-1}$, have no effect on investment. The effects on investment work through changes in r_t^c that are transmitted to shifts in the market valuation of capital; that is, to movements in the stock-return variables, STOCK$_{i,t-1}$. Unfortunately, the present empirical results provide no direct evidence about the strength of this channel. The effects depend on the responses of STOCK$_{it}$ to DM$_t$ and RDEBTY$_t$ (working through changes in r_t^c), but the endogeneity of the monetary and fiscal variables makes it difficult to sort out the contemporaneous interactions among these variables. (The response of STOCK$_{it}$ to DM$_{t-1}$ and RDEBTY$_{t-1}$ is, not surprising, essentially zero.)

Table 3. *Forecasts of real interest rates and investment ratios*

Var.	Date	BE	CA	FR	GE	IT	JA	NE	SW	UK	US	WD
Actual Values[a]												
r^e	1989	0.043	0.072	0.051	0.037	0.061	0.001	0.042	0.052	0.060	0.036	0.035
	1990	0.056	0.084	0.061	0.053	0.058	0.024	0.052	0.051	0.052	0.025	0.037
	1991	0.058	0.035	0.066	0.072	—	0.033	0.053	0.063	0.043	0.002	0.027
I/Y	1989	0.216	0.264	0.226	0.230	0.261	0.374	0.222	0.221	0.206	0.206	0.244
	1990	—	0.252	0.228	0.245	0.261	0.388	0.234	—	0.192	0.199	0.245
Forecasts from data through 1989, using average values of STOCK and OILCY for 1990												
r^e	1990	0.058	0.070	0.058	0.053	—	0.024	0.050	0.058	0.058	0.048	0.047
	1991	0.056	0.059	0.051	0.051	—	0.026	0.042	0.051	0.047	0.044	0.043
I/Y	1990	0.216	0.266	0.229	0.235	0.260	0.377	0.225	0.224	0.209	0.209	0.247
	1991	0.217	0.266	0.230	0.235	0.261	0.378	0.226	0.225	0.210	0.210	0.248
Forecasts from data through 1990												
r^e	1991	0.043	0.054	0.041	0.040	—	0.015	0.032	0.034	0.032	0.018	0.025
I/Y	1991	—	0.245	0.221	0.241	—	0.375	0.228	—	0.187	0.195	0.240
Forecasts based on update of STOCK and OILCY to 1991.1												
r^e	1991	0.048	0.059	0.047	0.045	—	0.020	0.038	0.040	0.037	0.024	0.031
I/Y	1991	—	0.248	0.224	0.242	—	0.378	0.233	—	0.191	0.199	0.243

[a] 1991 data for r^e based on interest rates for January and April 1991 and on inflation through March 1991. 1990 data for I/Y estimated from first three quarters, except for U.S.

VII. Behavior in 1990–91

Table 3 shows actual values of r_t^e and $(I/Y)_t$ for 1989–90 and values of r_t^e for the first parts of 1991. Forecasts of r_t^e and $(I/Y)_t$ for 1990–91 are shown conditioned on first, information through 1989, second, information through 1990, and third data through 1990 plus updated information on stock returns and oil prices for 1991.1.

Using information through 1989, the model (estimated with data through 1990) "predicts" the values $r_t^e = 0.047$ for 1990 and 0.043 for 1991, compared to the value for 1989 of 0.035 and the sample mean of 0.021. (See Figure 3 for the time series of r_t^e.) In particular, the forecast for 1990 matches the high point for r_t^e (over the period since 1959) reached in 1981. As a related matter, the model forecasts an expansion of $(I/Y)_t$ from 0.244 in 1989 to 0.247 in 1990 and 0.248 in 1991.

The actual values for 1990 were $r_t^e = 0.037$ and $(I/Y)_t = 0.246$, thus the real interest rate was substantially overpredicted. The stock return for 1990 was -0.23, the third worst of the sample period (after 1973 and 1974). The bulk of the low return reflects the decline in real stock prices by 19 per cent with the start of the Persian Gulf crisis in the third quarter. Taking account of the information on stock returns for 1990 (along with an estimate for $D(OILCY)$, of 0.0017 and the value $DM_t = 0.052$) leads to substantially revised forecasts for 1991: $r_t^e = 0.025$ and $(I/Y)_t = 0.240$. If data for the first quarter of 1991 on stock returns and the oil variable are also incorporated (averaged with a one-quarter weight with the annual data for 1990), then the forecast for 1991 becomes $r_t^e = 0.031$ and $(I/Y)_t = 0.243$. The key element here is the increase in real stock prices by about 11 per cent with the resolution of the Gulf War.

The shifts in the forecasts with the changes in the conditioning information involve primarily the volatility of the stock returns, which in this case reflect primarily the developments in the Persian Gulf. For example, the shift of $STOCK_t$ from 0.16 in 1989 to -0.23 in 1990 means, by itself, that the projected value of r_t^e for 1991 (conditioned on 1990 information) is 0.016 less than the projected value for 1990 (conditioned on 1989 information). Similarly, the projected value of $(I/Y)_t$ for 1991 is lower on this count by 0.009 relative to the value for 1990. The inclusion of the favorable stock return for 1991.1 accounts for the upward revision in the 1991 forecast of r_t^e from 0.025 to 0.031 and for $(I/Y)_t$ from 0.240 to 0.243.

VIII. Conclusions

The world perspective explains a good deal of the common experience of real interest rates for the developed countries and this common experience comprises a large part of the variations of real interest rates for each country individually over the last three decades. The framework of a single world credit market leaves unexplained the divergence of each country's real interest rate from the average of rates across the countries. Although these individual-country components are substantial and often persistent over time, these components do not relate systematically to observable variables, such as stock returns, investment ratios, or monetary and fiscal policies, for the various countries.

As an example, my estimate from Table 3 of the U.S. expected real interest rate in early 1991 is only 0.2 per cent, whereas that for the six European countries averages 5.9 per cent. It is tempting to explain this unusually large gap between real interest rates in the United States and Europe by appealing to differences in monetary policies and investment opportunities in the two regions. Unfortunately, the historical analysis does not support this kind of interpretation, at least if monetary policies can be measured by M1 growth and if investment opportunities can be gauged by stock returns and investment-GDP ratios. The analysis does predict that the spread in real interest rates between the United States and Europe will vanish over time.

For the common world component of real interest rates, developments in stock and oil markets play a major role and the patterns in world monetary growth and public debt exert a secondary influence. Thus, although traditional governmental macro policies seem to matter somewhat — when expressed as world aggregates — the policy instruments have not been the central driving forces for world real interest rates over the last thirty years. A more appropriate perspective is that governments operate as relatively minor actors in the overall arena of world credit markets. Governments have a substantial impact on real interest rates through political events such as the Persian Gulf war and the oil crises. These exercises in political instability, rather than conventional monetary and fiscal policies, are the major channel by which governments have influenced world financial markets and hence, the behavior of real interest rates and investment in the developed countries.

References

Barro, R. J. & Sala-i-Martin, X.: World real interest rates. In O. J. Blanchard & S. Fischer (eds.), *NBER Macroeconomics Annual 1990*, MIT Press, Cambridge MA, 1990.

Blanchard, O. J.: Debt, deficits, and finite horizons. *Journal of Political Economy 93*, 223–247, April 1985.

Comment on R. Barro, "World Interest Rates and Investment"

Nicola Rossi

University of Modena, Italy

This paper represents an important attempt to offer an explanation for the evolution of world real interest rates over the last three decades. Needless to say, the paper is skillfully written, candid about some disappointing results and stimulating for the overall picture of international capital markets which it manages to provide. As it turns out, much of the increase in real rates between the second half of the 1970s and the first half of the 1980s can be attributed to developments on world stock and oil markets, with individual governments playing a relatively minor role in the worldwide credit market.

The paper draws heavily on the work by Barro and Sala-i-Martin (1990) and, in discussing it, I will avoid repeating Brainard and Lucas' illuminating comments on this work. Nevertheless, this paper is still very much worth discussing, in the light of other contributions to this conference.

In fact, a perusal of the empirical evidence reveals some peculiarities in the behavior of young consumers and the same could be said, in some cases, of the elderly. Consumers' time horizons, far from being infinite, turn out, in some cases, to be shorter than a lifetime and could even span a single period. Moreover, it is increasingly apparent that credit and insurance market imperfections need to be accounted for when interpreting consumer behavior and assessing differences in behavior across countries. In short, the evidence at hand forcefully suggests that no model can possibly account for the vast complexity of the world around us. Notwithstanding this commonsense remark, Barro pushes us to see things differently and forces us to face the following important question: how it happens that an exceedingly simple model[1] (someone, somewhat unfairly, might even say a simplistic model) apparently does a wonderful job in

---

[1] The term "simple" is used here not as synonymous with "rule of thumb" behavior but, quite the contrary, as indicating a set of otherwise standard assumptions on the functioning of specific markets and/or on agents' homogeneity.

tracking and explaining an inherently difficult and complex phenomenon such as the evolution of world real interest rates? Quite clearly, answering this question in one sense or the other could substantially contribute to redirecting current research efforts.

To answer this question one has to suggest, first, that in the case under consideration the model is, in fact, exceedingly simple. Here I will briefly mention some of the simplifying assumptions underlying the model. Others may be found in the above-mentioned comments by Brainard and Lucas.

Let me start with the investment equation. This is cast in terms of a fixed gross investment to income ratio. Usually, q-type investment models tend, instead, to be formulated in terms of investment capital ratios. I suppose that some simplifying assumptions on the evolution of the capital to output ratio turn out to be badly needed at this stage. Furthermore, gross fixed investment includes residential investment as well as public investment. Needless to say, for both items, a q-type investment model is not necessarily an obvious choice. Furthermore, the use of the variable crude oil consumption to income ratio instead of the relative oil price again entails a number of rather simplifying assumptions. Reverting to the saving equation, a number of simplifying assumptions are needed to derive the estimated equation. Among them is the zero restriction on the coefficients of some variables otherwise usually regarded as belonging to the saving ratio equation: the growth rate of income and/or demographics. Moreover, if we still believe that what matters for private consumption decisions is some measure of disposable income, then, under certain conditions, the difference between gross domestic product and some measure of government dissipation is an obvious candidate. In this respect a strong simplifying assumption is the one that allows the coefficient of gross domestic product in the saving equation (that is, the constant term in the saving rate equation) to be different across countries, while forcing the coefficient of government expenditure to be the same across countries.

By equating the sum of investments and savings across countries, the paper determines the "world" real interest rate. Since real interest rates are quite different among countries, this rate turns out to be a quantity which is actually not paid by anybody in any actual market. It is defined instead as a GDP weighted average of national rates. In this respect a further set of simplifying assumptions refers to the conditions which allow the aggregation process across countries to go through. (We want to keep this in mind for further reference.) In the light of the above comments it seems fair to conclude that, among the many virtues of the model underlying the paper is its simplicity.

To answer the second part of my original question, let us now turn to the model's performance. In this respect it should be noted that the paper presents a number of interesting tests on various zero restrictions, but no systematic attempt is made to evaluate the model performance through misspecification tests.

Admittedly, the model turns out not to reject the tenuous overidentifying restrictions given by the exclusion of the second lag of the energy input/output ratio in the saving equation, but this is more or less all we are told about.

Looking in between the figures, one can, however, recover some additional information. For example, by looking at the forecast errors implicit in Table 3[2] and comparing them to the regression standard errors reported in Table 1, simple one-period ahead forecast tests can be computed for the real rates equations. As it turns out, four out of nine cases (Canada, France, Germany and the U.S.) could be regarded as borderline cases, and economists ready to be rather skeptical about the truth of the null hypothesis would consider them as indication of misspecification. As a second example, the variable addition exercise undertaken in Section VI of the paper could, rather informally, be taken as a misspecification test procedure. As it turns out, some own-country variables, when added to the real rate equation, happen to be quite significant. In the light of my previous comment this should definitely come as no surprise, since the own-country effect appears to concern the government expenditure to income ratio as well as the public debt to income ratio. Last, but not least, one should recall the autocorrelated error term reported in Table 1. In the absence of a convincing story, some economists would take that result as an indication of misspecification.

Fortunately, a discussant is not supposed to provide a full set of regressions supporting his case, although I hope to have been able to suggest that something somewhere may be going wrong. But I will not escape the duty of pointing out where things may actually be going wrong. In particular, it looks like the fatal simplifying assumption is that of behavioral homogeneity across countries. This is clearly shown by the outcome of the variable addition exercise referred to above, which is as should have been expected were the coefficients of the behavioral equations different across countries. In other words, it is the aggregation process which seems to be somewhat shaky and it is not by chance that, in Barro and Sala-i-Martin (1990), the hypothesis of coefficient homogeneity turned out to be decisively rejected. Quite clearly, the implication of this finding could (in principle) be quite damaging for the ideas underlying the whole paper in that, as the author himself states, "a global capital market

---

[2] Reference is made here to the forecast of real rates for 1991 based on updated information on stock returns and prices.

implies that national real rates would respond to world variables rather than own-country variables".

To sum up, it may happen that a simple model sometimes turns out to explain a complex and difficult phenomenon, but I personally would not easily take that for granted.

Reference

Barro, R. J. & Sala-i-Martin, X.: World real interest rates; with comments by W. Brainard & R. Lucas. In O. J. Blanchard & S. Fischer (eds.), *NBER Macroeconomics Annual,* MIT Press, Cambridge, MA, 1990.

Saving, Investment and the Current Account

Hans Genberg and Alexander K. Swoboda *

Graduate Institute of International Studies, Geneva, Switzerland

Abstract

In this review of recent work on the relationship between saving, investment and the current account, it is shown that focusing on national saving and investment behavior and modeling these in a modern intertemporal optimization framework will modify some conventional results regarding the relationship between the current account and the terms of trade, the exchange rate and fiscal policy. It is also shown that such a framework can explain the close empirical correlation between national saving and investment rates without relying on limited international capital mobility. It is conjectured that a better empirical understanding of current account developments could be gained if modern theories of investment and saving behavior were used more systematically in applied studies.

I. Introduction

The title of this paper, and the fact that it is presented at a conference on savings behavior, suggest that there is something more to the relationship between saving, investment and the current account than the well-known accounting relationship which states that the current account must be equal, *ex post*, to the difference between national saving and investment. Indeed, recent theoretical work on the determinants of the current account balance has tended to emphasize the intertemporal aspects highlighted by the "saving-investment approach". In contrast, many of the existing empirical studies as well as popular policy discussions stress competitiveness and trade policy measures as being the driving forces behind the current account.

The first objective of this paper, dealt with in Section II, is to clarify the relationship between alternative, seemingly competing, approaches to the analysis of current account movements, and to discuss conditions under which one approach or the other may be the most appropriate. It is concluded that each partial approach may give a correct answer in

---

*We are grateful to T. Gylfason and two anonymous referees for comments which have encouraged us to clarify some of the analysis.

particular circumstances, but that a general equilibrium approach is necessary as a rule. In addition, intertemporal aspects emphasized by a focus on the determinants of saving and investment should be a central feature of any analysis of current account developments. This basic idea has important and interesting implications for a number of issues relating to our topic. In the remainder of the paper we provide a selective survey of some of the major developments in the literature that have altered the way in which current-account issues are analyzed. In Section III we look briefly at the question of whether the current account balance should be a target of policy. Perhaps not surprisingly, the answer in the recent literature is that the current account is at best an imperfect intermediate target. It seems, however, that voters and policymakers in many countries do pay some attention to the current account. This is used to motivate the discussion in Section IV of the determinants of current account movements. Recent theoretical studies have examined the impact of terms-of-trade and exchange-rate changes as well as of monetary and fiscal policies from the intertemporal perspective. New insights have appeared from these studies that in some cases challenge conventional wisdom. The empirical literature based on the intertemporal perspective is just emerging, but here as well some unexpected and interesting results have been obtained.

Section V takes up the issues raised by the empirical finding that domestic saving and investment rates are highly correlated in most countries. It has been asserted that this is an indication of the lack of international capital mobility. We review both the empirical and theoretical literature that has addressed this issue and conclude that on both grounds there are good reasons to question this assertion. In fact, the literature shows that it is possible to account for the high correlation between saving and investment even if capital mobility is perfect. In the final section of the paper we summarize the main themes and conclusion, and discuss their implications for empirical modeling of the links between saving, investment and the current account.

II. Saving, Investment and the Current Account: Accounting Relationships and Analytical Issues

It is well known that the current account balance can be expressed in a number of alternative ways by manipulating *ex post* national income accounting relationships. An "approach" to current account analysis has become associated with each of them. The three most common accounting measures of the current account are expressed in equations (1)–(3):[1]

---

[1] The notation in these equations is conventional so that X = exports of goods and services, IM = imports, F = the domestic currency value of net foreign assets, i^* = the interest rate

$$CA = EX - IM + i^* \cdot F \tag{1}$$

$$CA = Y - A \tag{2}$$

$$CA = S - I + BuS. \tag{3}$$

Equation (1) corresponds to the elasticity approach, equation (2) to the income-absorption approach, and equation (3) to the saving-investment approach if one looks mainly at the first two terms on the r.h.s., and to the fiscal approach if one emphasizes the third term. A fourth representation is sometimes also used to make the link between the current account and the accumulation of foreign assets. This is given by:[2]

$$CA = \dot{F}. \tag{4}$$

This relationship has been emphasized by those who see capital flows as a driving force behind the current account.[3] Expressed slightly differently in the context of explaining the overall balance of payments in a fixed exchange rate situation, this last way of looking at the current account has also become known as the monetary approach.

These four "approaches" can easily be doubled by recognizing that our current account surplus is the current account deficit of the rest of the world, measurement errors apart. When we analyze "small" countries, this may not be of great importance, but it certainly should be in the context of entities like the U.S., Japan and the EEC.

Accounting identities are useful because they provide consistency checks on reasoning based on partial and simplified models. For instance, an analysis of changes in the current account which is carried out in terms of the determinants and evolution of exports and imports should be required to explain by what mechanisms the required changes in domestic saving and/or investment will come about. Vice versa, an analysis which is couched in terms of the determinants of saving and investment must demonstrate how changes in exports and imports will come about to justify the resulting current account position.

Partial approaches may provide the whole story in particular circumstances. For instance, an exogenous increase in the demand for exports will improve the current account position if there are no (or only limited) feed-

---

received on F, Y = Gross National Product (GNP), A = domestic aggregate absorption, S = private sector savings, I = private sector investment, BuS = the public sector budget surplus. In equation (1) the only factor payment included is net interest earnings on foreign asset holdings. In practice items such as workers remittances should, of course, be included.
[2] In this equation, $\dot{F}$ stands for the rate of change in F and it should (with apologies for abuse of notation) be interpreted as excluding valuation adjustments of the existing net foreign asset position due to exchange-rate and/or interest-rate changes.
[3] See, for instance, Makin (1990).

back effects through other variables. In an unemployment context, increased export demand could lead to an expansion of output without domestic wage and price increases and hence without feedback to exports through reduced competitiveness. The required increase in saving would be assured by the increase in income together with a Keynesian style saving function. But alternative scenarios could equally well be imagined. One would involve a situation of full employment where the increased demand for exports would result in improved terms of trade rather than a current account surplus. In another plausible scenario, increased exports would generate a higher rate of domestic investment in order to meet the additional demand, and increased consumption in response to higher permanent income. In this case the current account may actually deteriorate.

Similar examples can, of course, also be given for the other partial approaches. For example, a reduction in the government's fiscal deficit will not necessarily improve the current account if the budget improvement is obtained by a tax increase which reduces incentives to save.

Is it correct to contend that one approach to current account determination is superior to the others? Certainly not as a general rule. As the examples above should have made clear, in some circumstances one partial approach may give the correct answer, in others not. At a minimum, any analysis should pass a consistency test whereby the conclusions can be rationalized in each of the approaches. Better still, saving, investment and current account developments should be studied in a general equilibrium framework in which the consistency between different partial methods is automatically ensured. This being said, one of the main points of emphasis of the saving-investment approach, the focus on the intertemporal nature of the current account, should be an integral part of any analysis of current account behavior.[4]

III. Should the Current Account be a Target of Policy?

The "old view" of the current account maintains that external imbalances should be a concern of policymakers and that policy instruments should be actively used to correct them.[5] To the extent that current account deficits

---

[4] That intertemporal considerations really belong in the elasticity approach as well, first impressions to the contrary, follows from the fact that import demand is likely to depend on total consumption (rather than income) on one hand and investment spending on the other. Both consumption and investment are likely to be determined in part by intertemporal considerations.

[5] The qualifier "old" to characterize this view is coined in an excellent and exhaustive paper by Corden (1991); our discussion borrows heavily from that paper.

have to be financed by official reserves which are limited in supply, one justification for this view is that imbalances need to be watched and reduced lest a crisis situation develops in the future when reserves are depleted.

If capital is at least somewhat mobile internationally, private agents can borrow or lend to finance current account imbalances. In this situation, Corden's, *op.cit.,* "new" view of current account determination (which we refer to as the saving-investment approach) holds that the current account per se need not be of concern to policymakers. If private sector saving and investment decisions are made in an optimal (private and social) fashion, the outcome for the current account is also optimal, whether it is in deficit, surplus or balance. Therefore there is no need to make it a target of policy. To the extent that private saving and investment decisions are made suboptimally, the current account is also likely to be suboptimal, and the policymaker should consider intervening. But the appropriate reason for intervention is the saving and investment decisions of private agents and not the imbalance in the current account.

Having made the case against viewing the current account as a target, Corden discusses a number of qualifications, among them the possibility that the current account can serve as a signal of nonoptimality and therefore be watched, that there may be a difference between the private and social cost of external borrowing due to country-risk considerations, and the fear that current account imbalances lead to protectionist pressures. He shows, however, that even in these cases the basic source of the problem need not be the current account itself.[6] It remains a fact never-theless that many policymakers and private pressure groups do focus on current account imbalances and require that something be done about them. This, in addition to intellectual curiosity, justifies the focus of the next section on the determinants of the current account balance.

IV. Determinants of the Current Account

The inclusion of intertemporal considerations in open-economy macro-economic models has modified many traditional conclusions regarding the effects of exogenous disturbances on current account movements. This is

---

[6] Frenkel and Goldstein (1991) come to the same conclusion. They emphasize that one has to look at the underlying sources of current account imbalances in order to decide whether or not policy intervention is needed. In some cases imbalances are the result of optimal responses to particular shocks and as such they are "good". In other instances they may be the outcome of miscalculations, misguided decisions, or distortions elsewhere in the economy. It is only in this latter situation that policy intervention is appropriate and it should in principle be focused directly on the source of the problem

particularly the case for terms-of-trade shocks, for changes in fiscal policy, and for the relationship between exchange-rate changes and the current account. We illustrate the main developments in each of these areas.

The Terms-of-Trade

In order to illustrate the importance of intertemporal considerations, we start by recalling the standard analysis of the effect of changes in the terms of trade. To this end, we define the current account in terms of the export good and write the quantity of exports and imports as functions of the terms of trade and foreign and domestic output, respectively. Ignoring factor payments we then get:[7]

$$ca = \mathrm{ex}(\tau, y^*) - \tau \cdot \mathrm{im}(\tau, y). \tag{5}$$

Holding the outputs in the two countries constant and assuming trade to be initially balanced, it is seen that an increase in the terms of trade, i.e., a fall in τ, will deteriorate the current account if the Marshall–Lerner condition is satisfied.[8]

In order to depart from the obviously partial-equilibrium nature of this result, the current account equation can be incorporated into the usual income-determination model such that

$$y = c(y) + i(r) + g + \mathrm{ex}(\tau, y^*) - \tau \cdot \mathrm{im}(\tau, y). \tag{6}$$

If the interest rate r is held constant by the appropriate use of monetary policy or by international interest rate arbitrage, then the effect of a change in the terms of trade on the current account will be determined by the Marshall–Lern elasticity formula multiplied by the ratio $s/(s+m)$ where s and m are the marginal propensities to save and import, respectively.

The current account improves with a terms-of-trade deterioration because of the induced increase in saving brought about by the increase in output. In their classic contributions, Harberger (1959) and Laursen and Metzler (1950) pointed to the importance of this assumption concerning saving behavior. They argued that saving depends (positively) on real income rather than domestic output. Consequently, a terms-of-trade deterioration must reduce saving for a given level of output, and it is no

---

[7] This equation can be obtained from equation (1) by dividing by the price of the export good and denoted the resulting real magnitudes by lower-case letters. The symbol τ represents the inverse of the terms of trade.

[8] This is the trade-theory version of the Marshall–Lerner condition where the elasticities are those of the reciprocal offer curves. The partial equilibrium, so-called Bickerdike–Metzler–Robinson condition assumes in addition fixed domestic prices and refers to elasticities of import demand curves. The latter version is associated with equation (6).

longer certain that the current account will improve even in the context of the type of model represented by equation (6) above.[9]

While consistency between the elasticity approach and the saving-investment approach is ensured in the above illustrations by the use of a "complete" model of the economy, the simplicity of the savings and investment functions employed is striking in relation to what is considered appropriate in modern macroeconomic analysis. Indeed, as Gylfason correctly points out in his comments, if it is assumed, contrary to Harberger, Laursen and Metzler, that savings as a share of output *falls* instead of rises with the terms of trade, then the Marshall–Lerner elasticity condition is more than enough to ensure that a terms-of-trade deterioration improves the balance of trade. The form of the savings function is thus seen to be of considerable importance for the outcome, and greater attention to its specification is called for. Prompted in part by a desire to base such a specification on sounder microeconomic foundations and in part by the experience in the mid- to late 1970s with large changes in terms of trade, the consequences of which were more complicated than suggested in the standard analysis, a number of economists re-examined the effect of the terms of trade on saving and hence on the current account.[10] A distinguishing feature of the models that were used for this purpose was that consumption decisions were based on optimization of an intertemporal utility function defined over both current and expected future levels of consumption. Typically the implication then is that the path of consumption will be smooth relative to the path of income since it will depend not only on the current level of income but also on expected future levels as in the permanent-income or life-cycle theories. As a consequence it becomes crucial to distinguish between permanent and temporary shocks, on one hand, and between anticipated and unanticipated shocks, on the other, since they generally have very different implications for the time path of real income. To illustrate the effects involved, consider the case where output is constant and the country suffers a *temporary* terms-of-trade deterioration and thus a temporary fall in real income. Assume further that the country can borrow or lend internationally at a fixed real rate of interest and that investment is constant.[11] Because consumption decisions

---

[9] A deterioration of the trade balance would occur if the marginal propensity to import times the marginal effect of τ on consumption is larger than the marginal propensity to save times the Marshall–Lerner elasticity formula.

[10] See e.g. Obstfeld (1982), Persson and Svensson (1985), Sachs (1981) and Svensson and Razin (1983).

[11] The models most frequently used to study the effects of terms-of-trade changes in an intertemporal optimization framework assume outputs to be given at the full-employment level, and that the real rate of interest and the terms of trade are determined abroad and given for the home country, which is assumed to be "small". In this framework it is clearly

take into account future as well as current income, current spending will fall by only a fraction of the fall in real income, so that the current account will deteriorate. Contrast this with the effects of a *permanent* fall in the terms of trade. In this case both current and future real income will fall. The consumption level will hence be reduced by the full amount of the fall in income, leaving the current account unchanged. Consider next a deterioration in the terms of trade that is expected to happen sometime in the near future but which has not yet occurred. As a result of the consumption smoothing implied by the life-cycle hypothesis, current saving will increase and the current account will improve.

Although the previous description seems to imply that the effects of terms-of-trade on saving and the current account are determined exclusively by the nature of the time path of the terms of trade, a formal analysis, as provided by e.g. Svensson and Razin *op.cit.*, reveals that this is not always the case. Additional effects due to changes in the real rate of interest[12] and to the dependence of the rate of time preference on real income may overturn the initial intuition. In other words, the inter-temporal approach implies a rather complex relationship between changes in the terms of trade and saving that depends not only on the stochastic properties of the exogenous shock but also on the structure of the economy and the nature of preferences.

While the literature surrounding the Harberger–Laursen–Metzler controversy focused on saving behavior as the link between terms-of-trade changes and the current account, it is presumably true that effects operating on investment spending are equally important. Analytical treatment of this case is also more complicated, however, since the production structure of the economy is likely to be important for the outcomes. The case which has motivated most analysis is where the economy produces one output using an imported good (oil) as one of the factors of production. In this case a change in the terms of trade can be thought of as a productivity disturbance. Using this analogy, Sachs (1981), Bruno and Sachs (1985) and Blanchard and Fischer (1989, Ch. 2), among others, show that a permanent deterioration in the terms of trade will reduce domestic investment under reasonable assumptions concerning the complementarity/substitutability relationship between factors of production. Although investment falls, the current account may improve or deteriorate, even abstracting from the reaction of saving, because output is

---

not possible to specify *independently* an import demand function and an export supply function. The balance of trade is determined residually by the given output levels and the optimally chosen consumption path.

[12] Note that the real interest rate relevant for consumption decisions may change when the terms of trade change temporarily, even if the foreign real interest rate is constant and capital is perfectly mobile.

also affected by the change in the terms of trade in this setup. A temporary change in the terms of trade would have a smaller impact on the rate of investment and would therefore be more likely to deteriorate the current account, again abstracting from changes in saving, since output of the final good would still fall. The importance of distinguishing between permanent and temporary changes is also stressed by Persson and Svensson (1985), who in addition show that the contrast between unanticipated and anticipated changes is crucial for understanding the medium-term dynamics of investment.

Once the simplifying assumption of a one-sector production structure is relaxed, the number of possible results multiplies rapidly. The reason is that changes in the terms of trade lead to both a reallocation of production between sectors of the economy and to a change in the overall level of production. Whether the process of reallocation entails an increase or decrease in the overall level of investment in the economy depends on differences in the adjustment costs assumed in the different sectors. In addition, the long-run impact on the economy's capital stock will depend on the factor intensity of production in the exportable sector versus the importable sector.[13]

The upshot of this discussion is that the impact of changes in the terms of trade on both saving and investment as well as on their difference depends on a number of factors including the expected time path of the terms of trade, the production structure of the economy, and the nature of consumers' time preference. Estimated regression coefficients linking the current account to the terms of trade should therefore be interpreted with care. Application of the arguments of Lucas (1976) suggests that such coefficients may well be unstable over time and that the equation should not be assumed to be invariant to the nature of the shocks that characterize a given data sample.

Fiscal Policy

The simultaneous emergence of large fiscal imbalances and external imbalances in the early 1980s, notably in the U.S., has led to suggestions that fiscal policy actions constitute the major source of current account fluctuations. The most rudimentary form of the argument simply makes use of the accounting identity expressed in equation (3) to assert that changes in the budget deficit of the government must automatically translate into a corresponding current account deficit, the "twin-deficit hypothesis". A slightly more sophisticated formulation of the same

---

[13] Mussa (1978) discusses the intersectoral adjustment of capital. Fischer and Frenkel (1972) investigate the dynamics of investment and growth in a two-sector model.

proposition employs a version of the Mundell–Fleming model to show that even in a context where private saving and investment are determined endogenously, the twin-deficit result obtains. In order to illustrate how specific even this result is, consider equations $(7)-(10)$ which represent that model under conditions of a flexible exchange rate, perfect capital mobility and fixed domestic prices:[14]

$$y = c(y^d, r) + i(r) + g + ex(\tau, y^*) - \tau \cdot im(\tau, y) \tag{7}$$

$$m = L(y, r) \tag{8}$$

$$r = r^* \tag{9}$$

$$y^d = y - t. \tag{10}$$

The combination of perfect capital mobility and static exchange-rate expectations implies that the domestic rate of interest is determined by the exogenous foreign rate. This in turn implies that money-market equilibrium determines the equilibrium level of output independently of aggregate demand conditions. The given interest rate implies a given level of investment; combined with the level of income given by the money stock, it also determines a unique level of private saving. Consequently, changes in government spending financed by borrowing will lead to one-for-one changes in the current account balance.

It does not take much to break the tight link between the fiscal deficit and the external deficit, even maintaining essentially the same analytical framework.[15] For instance, financing government expenditures with taxes rather than borrowing, breaking the tight link between the domestic and foreign interest rate by allowing for exchange-rate expectations other than of the static variety, and letting the exchange rate influence money demand directly by deflating the nominal money supply by a price index including import prices would be sufficient. Once the straight-jacket of the formulation in equations $(7)-(10)$ is removed by even such relatively minor modifications, a number of additional considerations become important, for instance, the structure of government expenditures (domestic goods versus imports) and the structure of taxes (do they influence incentives to save and invest) to mention only the two most obvious.

With the conventional analysis as a background, let us return to our main theme, i.e., that the intertemporal decisions underlying private saving and investment behavior should be taken into account explicitly. The

---

[14] The assumption of fixed domestic prices implies that the nominal and real exchange rate can be used interchangeably, and that there is no need to distinguish between the nominal and the real money supply, m. Disposable income, y^d, is obtained by subtracting lump-sum taxes, t, from output.

[15] See Genberg (1988).

analysis of the impact of fiscal policy on the current account must then be broadened significantly in at least three directions: being explicit about the time path of changes in taxes and government spending, considering that the private sector may anticipate future tax implications of current policies, and considering how the evolution of domestic and foreign debt influences private sector behavior. The consequences of each of these factors will be discussed briefly in turn.[16]

The simplest way to illustrate the importance of the time path of government spending is to consider a model in which output in each period is given and to observe that the net supply available to the private sector is obtained simply by subtracting government purchases from this total.[17] A temporary increase in government spending financed by lump-sum taxes will thus decrease the *current* net supply *relative* to the supply in the *future*, requiring a rise in the relative price of the former, i.e., a rise in the current interest rate. The resulting increase in private sector saving will partially offset the increase in government spending, thereby lessening the impact on the current account. An expected *future* increase in spending will have exactly the opposite effects; the reduction in the future net supply of goods to the private sector requires a reduction in the current rate of interest, which brings about an increase in current foreign spending and a domestic current account surplus. A *permanent* increase in government spending will require a rise or fall in the entire structure of interest rates depending on the initial current account position.[18] If the home country has a deficit, i.e., is a current net borrower, the rate of interest must fall and the current account will improve. If the current account is initially in surplus, the opposite occurs.

While the consequences of a temporary fiscal expansion in this analysis are the same as the outcome of the static Mundell–Fleming model, the intertemporal approach brings out the critical importance of the assumed time path of fiscal policy. Forward-looking asset markets incorporate this time path in the structure of interest rates and exchange rates, thereby altering current spending patterns and current accounts.[19]

---

[16] Many authors have contributed to the analysis of the effects of fiscal policies in an open economy from an intertemporal perspective. The most comprehensive treatment is without doubt Frenkel and Razin (1987) which also includes an extensive list of references to additional contributions.

[17] The discussion in this paragraph is closely related to Frenkel and Razin (*op. cit.*, Section 7.3).

[18] It is assumed here that the growth rate of output at home and abroad is similar.

[19] Empirical tests of the importance of the time profile of fiscal policy are, of course, difficult since expectations of future fiscal changes are unobserved by the econometrician. Attempts such as those presented in Feldstein (1986) seem to show that expected fiscal deficits did play a role in the behavior of the external value of the dollar in the 1970s and 1980s. In a

One of the ways in which models that emphasize intertemporal aspects differ from the more common static ones is that they take into account not only the government's current-period budget constraint but also its intertemporal constraint. This intertemporal constraint states that a current budget deficit must be matched by future surpluses with the same present value. If private economic agents incorporate this in their own decisions, and provided certain other conditions hold,[20] the Ricardian equivalence proposition implies that the mode of financing a given path of government spending is of no consequence for the saving behavior of the private sector. It then follows that the evolution of the current account in relation to government budget deficits will depend crucially on whether the deficits are caused by changes in taxes or changes in expenditures.

The last implication of a dynamic framework for analyzing the link between the current account and fiscal policy we wish to highlight relates to the evolution of domestic government debt and the net foreign asset position over time. To the extent that the Ricardian equivalence proposition does *not* hold, and that domestic debt and foreign debt are not perfect substitutes, a current bond-financed fiscal expansion will bring about changes in wealth, and hence changes in private saving, over time that eliminate any simple contemporaneous association between fiscal deficits and the current account. Morris (1988) contends that the persistence of the current account deficit of the U.S. in the second half of the 1980s, despite some fiscal consolidation and the dollar's depreciation, can be explained in part by the consequences of internal and external debt dynamics induced by fiscal policies in the earlier part of the decade.

The Exchange Rate

The vast majority of empirical models of current account determination place a large burden of explanation on exchange rate movements in line with the partial-equilibrium elasticity approach represented by equation (5).[21] In analyses of the emergence and persistence of the current account deficit of the U.S. in the early 1980s, the appreciation and the subsequent depreciation of the dollar played and continues to play an important role. A "puzzle" has even been associated with this episode, i.e., the failure of

---

related literature, modern time-series econometrics has been used to study certain implications of imposing the government's intertemporal budget constraint, notably for issues of sustainability of the public sector's expenditure and revenue plans; see e.g. Hamilton and Flavin (1986), Trehan and Walsh (1988) and Wilcox (1989).

[20] Notably that the private sector's and the government's discount rates are the same.

[21] See e.g. Krugman and Baldwin (1987). Hooper (1988) refers to the models based on the elasticity approach as the "industry standard" in empirical modeling of the trade balance.

the external deficit to improve substantially as the dollar started to depreciate after March 1985.

There are two key problems with the "industry standard" model, one associated with the endogeneity of the exchange rate, and the other with whether it is consistent with the intertemporal considerations emphasized by the saving-investment approach.

Certainly in a floating-exchange rate environment, but also in fixed-rate periods, both the trade balance and the real exchange rate are endogenous variables reacting to exogenous shocks. It is therefore inappropriate to treat any observed association between them as a causal relationship. It is quite easy to show that both the sign and the size of the correlation between them will depend on the nature of the underlying disturbance. The implications of this for the interpretation of distributed lag regression of the current account or the trade balance on the exchange rate will be taken up shortly.

Even if it were possible to find situations where the exchange rate is determined independently from the current account,[22] it is not in general possible to ascertain its influence on the current account, as our discussion of the effects of the terms of trade made clear.[23] We showed in particular that the expected time path of the terms of trade is of crucial importance for the current-account outcome. The same is likely to be true with respect to changes in the real exchange rate. Indeed empirical evidence presented in Burda and Gerlach (1990) suggests that trade-balance adjustments in the U.S. depend significantly on "intertemporal prices" which in our context can be related to the expected time path of the real exchange rate.

In view of this discussion, how should one interpret distributed lag regressions of the current account (or the trade balance) on the real exchange rate and the level of output? In view of equation (2), holding output constant by including it in the regression implies that the distributed lag on the exchange rate captures the influence on domestic absorption, which in turn reflects saving and investment decisions. The estimated coefficients thus measure the impact of past changes in real exchanges on such variables as expected future income, wealth and interest rates which

---

[22] Perhaps as a result of shifts in portfolio preferences that have no *direct* influence on savings and investment decisions.

[23] There exist many definitions of the "real exchange rate" in the literature. The most common is perhaps the ratio EP^*/P where E is the nominal exchange rate, P is a general price index in the home country, and P^* is a similarly constructed index in the rest of the world. It can be shown that this measure of the real exchange rate is related inversely to the terms of trade; see, for instance, Saïdi and Swoboda (1983). This justifies applying the analysis in Section II to the present case. Edwards (1989) contains an extensive analysis of alternative definitions of the real exchange rate.

are important in saving and investment functions. In view of this very indirect link, it should not come as a surprise that it is difficult to find *any* stable statistical relationship between past changes in the exchange rate and the current account.[24]

V. Saving-Investment Correlations and the Capital Mobility Issue

A working hypothesis of most economists analyzing the relationships between industrial countries has for some time been the notion of perfect capital mobility, or more precisely that financial markets are so highly integrated that the relevant interest rates are everywhere the same. Tests showing that the covered interest parity condition is fulfilled on Euro-markets have often been used to justify this modeling strategy. This widespread analytical approach was jolted somewhat by the Feldstein and Horioka (1980) study which concluded, on the contrary, that the degree of capital mobility is very low. They found that in a regression of domestic saving on domestic investment, both measured relative to GNP, the slope coefficient was significantly different from zero and often not significantly different from unity, and interpreted this result as an indication of low capital mobility.

The motivation for the form of the Feldstein–Horioka regression equation and the meaning they gave to the estimated coefficient can be explained as follows. If capital is completely immobile in the sense that international borrowing and lending is either not possible or determined by completely exogenous forces, then the current account of the balance of payments is either zero or determined independently of domestic saving and investment rates. Equation (3) then tells us that a decrease in domestic saving must be accompanied by an equivalent decrease in domestic investment. In other words, absence of capital mobility implies a unit slope coefficient in the Feldstein–Horioka regression. As we shall see, the converse, however, is not true; a unit regression coefficient does not imply capital immobility.

Another justification for the analysis carried out by Feldstein and Horioka was that if capital is freely mobile, then an increase in domestic investment *need* not cause any change in saving because it can be financed

---

[24] From a survey of the empirical evidence, Blackhurst (1983) concludes that there was an "...absence of credible empirical support for the popular view that an exchange-rate change has an independent and predictable effect on the current account". (p. 88) Rose and Yellen (1989) studied the U.S. evidence for the period 1960 to 1985 and found "...that the aggregate data does not provide reliable evidence of either the negative short-run effect or the positive long-run effect..." of the real exchange rate on the trade balance. See also Rose (1991).

by a capital inflow. The regression coefficient in this case would be zero. However, that *certain* specific shocks to investment have no effect on saving does not mean that *all* shocks to investment will. The problem, of course, is that saving and investment are jointly determined by the whole variety of disturbances that influence an economy. Many of these disturbances will lead to a positive correlation between observed saving and investment rates. This is particularly true in more sophisticated approaches to saving and investment than those implicit in equation (7) above. For instance, in a framework that emphasizes intertemporal effects, Obstfeld (1986) shows that a domestic permanent productivity shock will increase both saving and investment even if capital is perfectly mobile.[25]

In view of the difficulty in interpreting the results of Feldstein–Horioka style regressions, it does not serve much purpose to dwell on the extensive empirical literature that has used the same basic methodology, but has applied it to different countries and different time periods. These studies may simply say more about the nature of the shocks that are most prevalent in these countries or time periods than about the degree of capital mobility.[26]

The main problem with most studies that use regressions of saving on investment as a test of the hypothesis of perfect capital mobility is that theory is not used to determine what size the regression coefficient should have under the null hypothesis. To our knowledge, so far only one study, Ghosh (1988), derives a test based on an explicit intertemporal model of saving and investment behavior and, applied to time-series data on five countries, it does not permit rejection of the hypothesis of perfect capital mobility.[27]

While the procedure adopted by Ghosh is not immune to criticism, it does, as already emphasized, have the advantage of relying on an explicit theoretical paradigm in which saving and investment behavior is modeled in line with modern intertemporal analysis. In our view, such an approach is necessary in order to make progress in testing for capital mobility within

---

[25] Other studies which show that a positive correlation between savings and investment can be consistent with perfect capital mobility include Bayoumi (1990), Tesar (1988) and Baxter and Crucini (1990), to mention only three examples of a large and growing literature.

[26] Attempts to apply more sophisticated estimation techniques than OLS to the basic equation do not necessarily clear up the problem of interpretation either; see Obstfeld (1991).

[27] The reasoning of Ghosh is based on the fact that capital mobility allows for consumption smoothing in the face of variations over time in output, investment and government spending. Given the stochastic properties of these variables, the current account will show a certain variance under the null hypothesis of perfect capital mobility. If the measured variance of the current account is lower than the theoretical value, the null hypothesis must be rejected.

the general framework of studying the interrelationships between saving, investment and the current account.[28]

It may also be of interest to draw attention to one alternative method of looking at the capital mobility issue. One of the reasons for attempting to test the hypothesis of perfect capital mobility in the first place is that the effects of a number of policy interventions differ significantly depending on the degree of capital mobility. By studying these effects directly, it may be possible to make inferences about the mobility of capital. For instance, with perfect mobility, the real interest rate in a small country would depend less on the local variables such as the government's budget deficit than on world variables. Morris (1988, Chapter 5) tests this implication and finds support for the hypothesis of internationally integrated capital markets.[29]

VI. Concluding Remarks

One of the themes of this paper has been that an analysis of current account developments in terms of the determinants of national saving and investment force us to reconsider a certain number of results that fit the label "conventional wisdom". This is particularly true for the analysis of the effects of exchange rate movements and changes in fiscal policy. One important reason why the emphasis on saving and investment behavior alters traditional results may be that it focuses attention on the macro-economic nature of the current account. Another reason is that it naturally leads to the adoption of analytical models that emphasize intertemporal aspects.

The majority of recent *theoretical* discussions of current acount determination have incorporated the intertemporal approach fully. The same cannot be said for empirical models.[30] The "industry standard" in this respect is still closely linked to the partial-equilibrium elasticities approach, resulting in misplaced emphasis on current and past exchange-rate movements as explanatory factors. The emphasis on current relative prices also naturally leads to suggestions that tariffs and other trade policy measures are the most efficient tools of current-account adjustment or, conversely that current-account imbalances are a sign of unfair trade practices on the part of the surplus country. Analysis carried out using

---

[28] For further developments based on explicit intertemporal models to test for international capital mobility, see Obstfeld (1989) and Uctum and Wickens (1990).

[29] See also Barro (1991) and Tanzi and Lutz (1991) for an approach based on the same reasoning as Morris'.

[30] Knight and Masson (1986), Andersen (1990) and Sheffrin and Woo (1991) are notable exceptions. These studies estimate models of current account determination based on the saving-investment approach.

models and variables appropriate for saving and investment decisions is likely to put another light on these questions.[31]

A general-equilibrium macroeconomic approach also refocuses the analysis of the impact of monetary and fiscal policy away from transmission mechanisms involving primarily the current exchange rate towards those that operate through intertemporal prices such as rates of interest. This also obliges those who offer policy advice about the need for exchange-rate adjustments as a way of dealing with current-account imbalances to be specific about how these adjustments should be engineered; by monetary policy or by fiscal policy, and in the latter case, by changes in taxes or by changes in expenditures. In a macroeconomic analysis where saving and investment decisions of the private sector are modeled seriously, the consequences for the current-account of each of these policies is likely to be quite different for a given impact on the exchange rate.[32]

The implication of these arguments for empirical modeling of the current (or trade) account is that a focus on the estimation of saving and investment equations is preferred to the conventional estimation of aggregate export and import equations or of their difference, the trade balance. The reason is twofold. First of all, a trade balance equation is not a structural equation but rather a reduced form reflecting the behavior of a number of different economic agents. For this reason, it is hazardous to impose the exclusion restrictions typically associated with trade equations and difficult to interpret estimated coefficients in terms of economic theory.

A second reason for preferring direct estimation of saving and investment equations is that exports and imports in a country in any case depend on both income and expenditures, so that all factors that determine saving and investment also belong in a properly specified aggregate trade equation. Hence it may be more efficient to estimate the former directly.[33]

---

[31] For instance, it would emphasize the expected *time profile* of tariffs and other trade policy measures in addition to the current levels. According to this view, expectations of future restrictions on a country's exports by its trading partners may well induce this country to accumulate foreign assets to finance future imports, i.e., to generate a surplus in its current account.

[32] Simulation results presented in McKibbin and Sachs (1991, Chapter 6) strongly support this argument.

[33] It can also be argued that aggregate import and export equations are not structural in the same sense as savings and investment equations. The former can be thought of as the residual outcome of decisions of domestic suppliers of exportables and importables and consumers of these goods. No individual economic agent has a demand for imports (as opposed to importables) per se. This argument should clearly not be pushed too far since aggregation problems also exist in savings and investment equations. But it is at least conceivable to think of representative agents making decisions on these variables.

While we think that an empirical analysis of the current account based on the estimation of saving and investment equations has a number of advantages, it is true, of course, that such an approach is not to be recommended in all circumstances. For instance, the current account of a highly indebted country which faces a credit constraint in the international capital market is determined by the decisions of the lenders and not in any reasonable sense by domestic saving and investment decisions, even though the *ex post* accounting relationship between these variables still holds. Other aspects of the structure and constraints facing a country may also influence the choice of a particular empirical model. This choice also presumably depends on the purpose of the empirical analysis. If we are interested only in the forecasting performance of a model, then the link between theory and econometric specification is not necessarily important and an atheoretical time-series approach may well win the horse-race. However, if the goal is to understand how policy interventions influence the current account balance, then a model that has a strong foundation in theory and that is based as closely as possible on structural equations seems preferable. It is the contention of this paper that an approach that pays careful attention to the determinants of national saving and investment decisions, in particular their intertemporal nature, contains many advantages in this respect. But the ultimate proof of the pudding is as usual in the eating.

References

Andersen, P.A.: Developments in external and internal balances, A selective and eclectic review. BIS Economic Paper No. 29, Bank for International Settlements, Basle, Oct. 1990.

Barro, R.: World interest rates and investment. Conference on Saving Behavior: Theory, International Evidence and Policy Implications, Espoo/Helsinki, 1991.

Baxter, M. & Crucini, M.: Explaining saving/investment correlations. WP 224, University of Rochester, Mar. 1990.

Bayoumi, T.: Saving-investment correlations: Immobile capital, government policy, or endogenous behavior? *International Monetary Fund Staff Papers 37*, (2), 360–87, June 1990.

Blackhurst, R.: The relation between the current account and the exchange rate: A survey of the recent literature. In P. DeGrauwe & T. Peeters (eds.), *Exchange Rates in Multicountry Econometric Models,* Macmillan, London, 58–99, 1983

Blanchard, O. & Fischer, S.: *Lectures on Macroeconomics,* MIT Press, Cambridge, MA, 1989.

Bruno, M. & Sachs, J.: *Economics of Worldwide Stagflation,* Harvard University Press, Cambridge, MA, 1985.

Burda, M. & Gerlach, S.: Intertemporal prices and the U.S. trade balance. WP No. 90/55, INSEAD, Fontainebleau, July 1990.

Corden, W. M.: Does the current account matter? The old view and the new. Conference in Honor of J. J. Polak, Washington, D.C., Jan. 1991.

Edwards, S.: *Real Exchange Rates, Devaluation and Adjustment,* MIT Press, Cambridge, MA, 1989.

Feldstein, M.: The budget deficit and the dollar. NBER WP No. 1898, April 1986.

Feldstein, M. & Horioka, C.: Domestic saving and international capital flows. *Economic Journal,* 314–29, 1980.

Fischer, S. & Frenkel, J.: Investment, the two-sector model, and trade in debt and capital goods. *Journal of International Economics 2,* 211–33, Aug. 1972.

Frenkel, J. & Goldstein, M.: Monetary policy in an emerging European economic and monetary union. *International Monetary Fund Staff Papers 38,* (2), 356–73, June 1991.

Frenkel, J. & Razin, A.: *Fiscal Policies in the World Economy,* MIT Press, Cambridge, MA, 1987.

Genberg, H.: The fiscal deficit and the current account: Twins or distant relatives? Research DP No. 8813, Research Department, Reserve Bank of Australia, Dec. 1988.

Genberg, H. & Swoboda, A.: The "stages in the balance of payments hypothesis" revisited. Mimeo, Graduate Institute of International Studies, Geneva, Nov. 1984.

Ghosh, A. R.: How mobile is capital? Some simple tests. Mimeo, Harvard University, Cambridge, MA, Nov. 1988; also as DP50, Princeton University, 1990.

Hamilton, J. & Flavin, M.: On the limitations of government borrowing: A framework for empirical testing. *American Economic Review 76,* (4), 808–19, 1986.

Harberger, A. C.: Currency depreciation, income and the balance of trade. *Journal of Political Economy 58,* (1), 389–98, Feb. 1959.

Hooper, P.: Exchange rates and the U.S. external adjustment in the short run and the long run. Brookings DP No. 65, Oct. 1988.

Knight, M. & Masson, P.: International transmission of fiscal policies in major industrial countries. *International Monetary Fund Staff Papers 33,* 387–438, Sept. 1986.

Krugman, P. & Baldwin, R.: The persistence of the U.S. trade deficit. *Brookings Papers on Economic Activity,* No. 1, 1987.

Laursen, S. & Metzler, L.A.: Flexible exchange rates and the theory of employment. *Review of Economics and Statistics 32,* 281–99, Nov. 1950.

Lucas, R.: Econometric policy evaluation: A critique. In K. Brunner & A. H. Meltzer (eds.), *The Phillips Curve and Labor Markets,* Carnegie–Rochester Conference Series on Public Policy, Vol. 1, North Holland, Amsterdam, 1976.

Makin, J.: International "imbalances": The role of exchange rates. In R. O'Brien & I. Iversen (eds.), *Finance and the International Economy,* Oxford University Press, Oxford, 1990.

McKibbin, W. & Sachs, J.: *Global Linkages: Macroeconomic Interdependence and Cooperation in the World Economy,* Draft, Jan. 1991.

Morris, D.: *Government Debt in International Financial Markets.* Pinter Publishers, London, 1988.

Mussa, M.: Dynamic adjustment to relative price changes in the Heckscher–Ohlin–Samuelson model. *Journal of Political Economy 86,* 775–91, 1978.

Obstfeld, M.: Aggregate spending and the terms of trade: Is there a Laursen–Metzler effect? *Quarterly Journal of Economics 97,* 251–70, May 1982.

Obstfeld, M.: Capital mobility in the world economy: theory and measurement. In K. Brunner & A. Meltzer (eds.), *National Bureau Method, International Capital Mobility and Other Essays,* Carnegie–Rochester Conference Series on Public Policy, Vol. 24, North-Holland, Amsterdam, 55–104, Spring 1986.

Obstfeld, M.: How integrated are world capital markets? Some new tests. In G. Calvo, R. Findlay, P. Kouri & J. Braga de Macedo (eds.), *Debt Stabilization and Growth,* Basil Blackwell, Oxford, 134–55, 1989.

Obstfeld, M.: Comment. In D. Bernheim & J. Shoven (eds.), *National Saving and Economic Performance,* University of Chicago Press, Chicago, 261–70, 1991.

Persson, T. & Svensson, L.: Current account dynamics and the terms of trade: Harberger–Laursen–Metzler two generations later. *Journal of Political Economy 93,* 43–65, Feb. 1985.

Rose, A.: The role of exchange rates in a popular model of international trade. *Journal of International Economics 30,* 301–16, 1991.

Rose, A. & Yellen, J.: Is there a J-curve? *Journal of Monetary Economics 24,* (1), 53–68, July 1989.

Sachs, J.: The current account and macroeconomic adjustment in the 1970s. *Brookings Papers on Economic Activity,* No. 1, 201–68, 1981.

Saïdi, N. & Swoboda, A.: Nominal and real exchange rates: Issues and some evidence. In E.-M. Claassen & P. Salin (eds.), *Recent Issues in the Theory of Flexible Exchange Rates,* North-Holland, Amsterdam, 3–27, 1983.

Sheffrin, S. & Woo, W. T.: Present value tests of an intertemporal model of the current account. *Journal of International Economics 29,* (3/4), 237–53, Nov. 1990.

Svensson, L. & Razin, A.: The terms of trade and the current account: The Harberger–Laursen–Metzler effect. *Journal of Political Economy 91,* 97–125, Feb. 1983.

Tanzi, V. & Lutz, M.: Interest rates and government debt: Are the linkages global rather than national? IMF WP/91/6, International Monetary Fund, Washington, D.C., Jan. 1991.

Tesar, L.: Saving, investment, and international capital flows. WP 154, University of Rochester, Aug. 1988.

Trehan, B. & Walsh, C. E.: Common tends, the government budget constraint, and revenue smoothing. *Journal of Economic Dynamics and Control 12,* 1988.

Uctum, M. & Wickens, M. R.: National insolvency: A test of the U.S. intertemporal budget constraint. CEPR DP No. 437, 1990.

Wilcox, D. W.: The sustainability of government deficits: Implications of the present-value constraint. *Journal of Money Credit and Banking 21,* 1989.

Comment on H. Genberg and A. Swoboda, "Saving, Investment and the Current Account"

Thorvaldur Gylfason

University of Iceland, Reykjavik, Iceland

This paper provides a useful exposition and overview of the saving–investment approach to modeling the current account of the balance of payments and its relationship to exchange rates, fiscal policy, and capital mobility in particular. The authors compare and contrast different partial approaches to current account analysis: (1) the elasticity approach, (2) the absorption approach, (3) the saving–investment approach, and (4) the monetary approach. They emphasize the advantages of the saving–investment approach in theoretical and, especially, empirical work, in consideration of the valuable insights that can be gained into the inherently intertemporal nature of the current account by viewing it as the difference between saving and investment. This is the main thrust of their selective survey.

One of the points that the authors make most clearly and forcefully is that the partial approaches are complements, not substitutes, in current account analysis. For the analysis of some problems, one partial approach may be more useful than others. In other cases, the situation may be reversed. For example, the simple Marshall–Lerner condition under which devaluation improves the current account is easier to derive from the absorption approach than from the elasticities approach when prices and output are allowed to vary, while the elasticities approach is more straightforward when prices and output are held fixed. At the same time, Genberg and Swoboda (GS) stress the fundamental equivalance of the partial approaches to the current account. They write "…saving, investment and current account developments should be studied in a general equilibrium framework in which the consistency between the different partial methods is automatically ensured" (cf. the concluding paragraph of Section II). I agree.

It may be worthwhile to recall that this important point has not always been very well understood. For instance, an important tenet of the monetary approach to the balance of payments in the 1970s was that output and the balance of payments were positively related through money demand, in contrast to the allegedly negative relation between output and the balance of payments through the demand for imports postulated by the Keynesian approach. Some economists attempted to discriminate empirically between the two approaches by regressing the balance of payments on output, apparently not realizing or believing that *both* the balance of payments *and* output are simultaneously determined endogenous variables. Like virtually all such pairs of (stationary) macroeconomic variables, however, output and the balance of payments can move in the same direction or in opposite directions, depending on the exogenous forces that move both of them. As I see it, one might as well have regressed quantity on price in an attempt to discriminate empirically between the theory of demand and the theory of supply as if the two were substitutes, not complements.[1] Stressing the partial approaches as two sides of the same coin, Hahn (1977, p. 241) once made essentially the same point by commenting that the exchange of cheese for money did not make cheese a monetary phenomenon any more than it made money a dairy product.

The fundamental equivalence of the partial approaches to current account analysis implies that virtually any proposition about the current account that can be derived by using one of the approaches within an appropriate general equilibrium framework can also be derived by using the others. For example, one does not need to define the current account as the difference between saving and investment to appreciate the intertemporal aspects of the phenomenon. After all, the current account, defined as the difference between the flow of exports and of imports, equals the accumulation of the stock of net foreign (monetary and financial) assets.

Flows and stocks are related by definition. Assume for simplicity that only the government borrows at home and abroad. The difference between saving and investment equals the difference between the accumulation of total assets and of real capital: $S - I = \Delta A - \Delta K$, where Δ denotes the first-difference operator. The government budget deficit equals the accumulation of bonds in the hands of the public and of domestic and foreign credit to the government $G - T = \Delta B + \Delta D + \Delta F$. Net exports equal the accumulation of net foreign reserves less the accumulation of external debt $X - Z = \Delta R - \Delta F$. Therefore, the flow identity from the national income-expenditure accounts $S = I + (G - T) + (X - Z)$ implies the stock identity $\Delta A = \Delta K + \Delta B + \Delta M$, where the change in money supply $\Delta M = \Delta D + \Delta R$ by definition. This, in turn, is consistent with the balance-sheet definition of A as the sum of K, B, and M at

---

[1] See Frenkel, Gylfason and Helliwell (1980) and Gylfason and Helliwell (1983).

constant prices. The main point here, however, is that a nonzero current account inescapably entails changes in stocks of assets over time even if $S = I = 0$.

A related point concerns GS's refutation of the popular interpretation of the Feldstein–Horioka finding of a close empirical relationship between saving and investment within countries as evidence of limited international capital mobility. This can be seen clearly by noting that a close relationship between saving and investment, say, $S = I$, implies that $X - Z = T - G$, so that $\Delta M = -\Delta B$. Given that the government controls M through domestic credit D and also B, it is free to set $\Delta M = -\Delta B$ so that $S = I$. Therefore, the equality between saving and investment domestically does not, *per se*, have any bearing on the degree of capital mobility, or on any other structural parameters of the economic system for that matter.

Despite the authors' clear and unequivocal exposition of the fundamental equivalence of the partial approaches, some of their statements based on the saving–investment approach are not fully consistent with my view of the general equilibrium framework in which the partial approaches are imbedded in their discussion. In one place, for example, they discuss 'the case where output is constant and the country suffers a *temporary* terms-of-trade deterioration and thus a temporary fall in real income… Because consumption decisions take into account future as well as current income, current spending will fall by only a fraction of the fall in real income so that the current account will deteriorate." This statement is potentially misleading in my view because it does not take into account all aspects of the macroeconomic adjustment mechanism. To see this, ignore the distinction between output and real income and hence the Harberger–Laursen–Metzler effect for a moment, and consider a rock-bottom model where net exports NX depend on the real exchange rate e and on real output Y which is fixed by assumption:

$$NX = X(e) - eZ(Y, e). \tag{1}$$

Because Y is held fixed we have $dNX/de > 0$, provided that the Marshall–Lerner condition is satisfied. We also know that net saving NS depends on output and the interest rate r as follows:

$$NS = S(Y, r) - I(r). \tag{2}$$

Because $NS = NX$ by definition if $G = T$, we know that dNS/de must be greater than 0. Therefore, devaluation must increase the interest rate, because that is the only way in which NS can rise for given output. Output and the rate of interest cannot both be held fixed in this model, implying that NS is fixed by equation (2), unless (a) the export and import functions in equation (1) are discarded from the analysis, a common practice in the literature (cf. footnote 11 in GS), or (b) the real exchange rate is also held constant throughout by equation (1), an implication which is contrary to the analysis of GS who are, after all, discussing the effects of a terms-of-trade deterioration.

Now we can see why the statement quoted above can be misleading. Assuming a negative link between the terms of trade and saving, defined implicitly by GS as the difference between real income and consumption, net saving becomes

$$NS = Ye^{-a} - C(Ye^{-a}, r) - I(r) = S(Ye^{-a}, r) - I(r), \tag{3}$$

where Ye^{-a} is the purchasing power of output, a is the share of imports in domestic consumption, and the domestic price level is set equal to 1 for simplicity. A terms-of-trade deterioration or devaluation (i.e., an increase in e) raises the price of imports, and thus reduces the purchasing power of domestic output (which is held fixed by assumption). Net exports are

$$NX = X(e) - eZ(Ye^{-a}, r, e), \tag{4}$$

assuming now that imports depend on expenditure rather than income as well as the real interest rate and the real exchange rate.

In this case a terms-of-trade deterioration or a real devaluation has a stronger effect on net exports than before. It improves the current account through the Marshall–Lerner effect as before and, in addition, it reduces real income and hence expenditure and imports for given output through the Harberger–Laursen–Metzler effect. Therefore, the increase in e must also increase NS. And this is possible in the present model only if the interest rate increases for given output. If both output and the interest rate are to be held constant, then some other variable must be introduced into the story to equilibrate the model. Focusing on the negative partial effect of e on S in equation (3), as GS do in effect, without taking the adjustment of the interest rate or some other appropriate variable into account, thus leads to a conclusion different from the one that would be reached otherwise. A similar discrepancy would arise even if saving was defined as the difference between output and consumption as in Laursen and Metzler (1950), implying a positive relationship between saving and the real exchange rate. In my view, this problem has marred virtually the entire literature on the Harberger–Laursen–Metzler effect.

I have a similar difficulty with part of GS's discussion of the simple Mundell–Fleming model presented in equations (7) to (10). As it stands, and on the assumptions stated, the model implies that the current account is completely insensitive to changes in the exchange rate. The domestic interest rate is equal to the exogenously given foreign interest rate, so that output is determined solely by the real money supply which is held fixed.

Thus, with the interest rate and output and hence also saving and investment held fixed, and in the absence of a Harberger–Laursen–Metzler effect, the current account is also fixed. This setup implies either that the exchange rate must be afloat or else — and this is the missing link in their story — that either government spending or taxes must be endogenous in the model under a fixed exchange rate (figuratively, to ensure that their *IS* curve passes through the intersection of the LM curve and the horizontal $r = r^*$ line). With real money supply and output held fixed, it would not be advisable anyway to attempt a devaluation without lowering government spending or raising taxes. Suppose taxes adjust. Then there is no reason why the current account cannot be affected by changes in the real exchange rate. On the contrary, a depreciation combined with a tax increase will stimulate the current account and reduce consumption and thus increase saving, so as to keep aggregate demand unchanged. In this example, taking the adjustment of taxes into account, as one should, restores the standard link between the exchange rate and the current account. At the same time, GS point out, correctly, that if the real exchange rate is an endogenous variable in this model, its reduced-form correlation with the current account can be either positive or negative, depending on the source of the exogenous shock that moves both. For example, an exogenous export boom would strengthen both the currency and the current account under a floating exchange rate, whereas an exogenous fiscal expansion would strengthen the currency (given perfect capital mobility), but weaken the current account.

The upshot of all this is that the structural or quasi-reduced-form relationship between relative prices, exchange rates and the current account that has been thoroughly documented in a host of econometric studies[2] over many years remains in full force. In my view, it would be a mistake to discard this relationship. No amount of emphasis on saving and investment will relieve us of the need to estimate price elasticities in world trade and to incorporate these estimates into general equilibrium models of current account determination in which all partial approaches have useful insights to offer. This is not to say that it cannot be useful to study current account developments in view of saving and investment behavior, *inter alia,* far from it. But we should not lose sight of the important interaction of saving and investment with the several other relevant variables, all of which jointly influence the current account of the balance of payments and macroeconomic performance and policy effectiveness in general.

---

[2] See, for example, the survey by Goldstein and Khan (1985).

References

Frenkel, J. A., Gylfason, T. & Helliwell, J. F.: A synthesis of monetary and Keynesian approaches to short-run balance-of-payments theory. *Economic Journal 90*, 582–592, 1980.

Goldstein, M. & Khan, M. S.: Income and price effects in foreign trade. In R. W. Jones & P. B. Kenen, (eds.), *Handbook of International Economics*, North-Holland, Amsterdam, 1041–1105, 1985.

Gylfason, T. & Helliwell, J. F.: A synthesis of Keynesian, monetary, and portfolio approaches to flexible exchange rates. *Economic Journal 93*, 820–831, 1983.

Hahn, F. H.: The monetary approach to the balance of payments. *Journal of International Economics 7*, 231–249, 1977.

Laursen, S. & Metzler, L. A.: Flexible exchange rates and the theory of employment. *Review of Economics and Statistics 32*, 281–299, 1950.

Index